Infants
and
Mothers

T. BERRY BRAZELTON, M.D.

Infants
and
Mothers

DIFFERENCES IN DEVELOPMENT

Revised Edition

FOREWORD BY Jerome S. Bruner

A Merloyd Lawrence Book
DELTA/SEYMOUR LAWRENCE

A MERLOYD LAWRENCE BOOK

Delta/Seymour Lawrence

Published by
Dell Publishing Co., Inc.
1 Dag Hammarskjold Plaza
New York, New York 10017

Delta ® TM 755118, Dell Publishing Co., Inc.

Printed in the United States of America

9 8   7   6 5

Library of Congress Cataloging in Publication Data

Brazleton, T. Berry, 1918–
Infants and mothers.

Bibliography: p.
Includes index.
1. Mother and child.   2. Infant psychology.
I. Title. [DNLM: 1. Child development.   2. Mother-Child
relations. WS 105 B827i]
BF720.M68B73   1983b   649'.122   83-5142
ISBN 0-385-29231-7
ISBN 0-385-29209-0 (pbk.)

A hardcover edition of this book is available from
Delacorte Press/Seymour Lawrence,
1 Dag Hammarskjold Plaza, New York, New York 10017.

To my wife, Christina,
whose belief in this project from the beginning
has provided opportunities to write;
and to my daughter Christina II,
whose perceptions in the revision process
have been exciting to share

Contents

CHAPTER XII. *THE TENTH MONTH*

CHAPTER XIII. *THE ELEVENTH MONTH*

CHAPTER XIV. *THE TWELFTH MONTH*

Acknowledgments
TO FIRST EDITION

An attempt to record the names of all of the people who contributed to the concept of this book takes me back many years. I first became aware of the importance of literature as an influence on childrearing practices after reading and relying on Benjamin Spock's remarkable book *Baby and Child Care.* Medical school and internships in hospital pediatrics had in no way prepared me for coping with the real mothers of normal, healthy children and their problems. Dr. Spock's book made practice seem possible and even exciting. His wisdom has continued to support me and my patients' mothers for nearly twenty years.

My colleagues in the practice of pediatrics, Ralph A. Ross, M.D., and John S. Robey, M.D., have helped me keep my feet on the ground and have been a constant source of rewarding suggestions. Teachers such as Allan M. Butler, M.D., Charles A. Janeway, M.D., Milton Senn, M.D., and Stewart Clifford, M.D., opened doors with their substantial knowledge of pediatrics and its role in a larger picture. To such colleagues as Gertrude Reyersbach, M.D., William Cochran, M.D., Katherine Kiehl, M.D., and Elizabeth Gregory, M.D., I owe many of the wiser statements in this book.

An immersion in child psychiatry opened my eyes to the role of the mother in shaping her child, to the child's important strength in shaping his environment, and to the father's role in maintaining a safe anchorage for them both. At the James Jackson Putnam Children's Center, Marian C. Putnam, M.D. and Beata Rank provided a unique climate for learning about child development and for observing the effects of early intervention in the disturbed homes of small children. In this remarkable center, such mentors as Gregory Rochlin, M.D., Dorothy MacNaughton, M.D., Eveoleen Rexford, M.D., Eleanor Pavenstedt, M.D., Samuel Kaplan, M.D., Harriet S. Robey, Marta Abramowicz, and Irene Anderson taught me how to see the underlying mechanisms that produced behavior in mothers, fathers, and their children. Grace A. Young taught me how to look at behavior and see the rich language that it represented. Without her imagination and her ability to see the importance of each bit of behavior, I could never have learned how to recognize the many ways in which infants and their parents communicate long before speech takes its symbolic role.

In the area of research, Lucie Jessner, M.D., John Benjamin, M.D., Louis Sander, M.D., Bettye Caldwell, Ph.D., Sally Provence, M.D., Mary Louise Scholl, M.D., Sanford Gifford, M.D., and Margaret Bullowa, M.D. have provided opportunities for developing ideas central to this book. More recently, Professor Jerome S. Bruner in cognitive development and Professor Evon S. Vogt and George Collier in anthropology have opened for me new and exciting areas in infant research.

Deirdre Carr, editor of *Baby Talk* magazine, first urged me to conceptualize the three individual kinds of development that were possible in our culture. Stella Chess and Andrew Thomas had made it "de rigueur" to think of different styles of development in children after Margaret Fries's remarkable paper in the early 1950s, which recorded the observable differences in newborn babies. Esther S. Yntema first thought a book could be written along these lines and spurred me to a start. Marian Poverman and Elizabeth Hoffman supported me through periods of self-questioning about the importance of such a book. My wife has acted as critic and editor throughout the ordeal of recording and sorting out its ideas. Merloyd Lawrence has been a source of creative ideas in its editing. Lew Merrim and Gary Schweizer-Tong, as well as several parents, have furnished its important visual dimension, the descriptive photographs. Those taken by Mr. Merrim appeared first in *Baby Talk* magazine.

But, most important of all, I must pay just homage to the many hundreds of mothers of patients who taught me all I know about child rearing. Their wisdom, their rewarding insights brought in to me on routine visits, their patience in enduring my often too-personal questions and my temperamental outbursts of frustration and/or fatigue have made the practice of pediatrics a rewarding way of life and have made the recording of all the experiences depicted in this book the frosting of such a way of life. Without this rich communication between doctor and patient, I can see that medical practice could become sterile and unrewarding on each side of the relationship. I hope this book may help to keep alive that personal interdependence of doctor and patient that is such a vital element in the practice of medicine.

Acknowledgments
TO REVISED EDITION

In order to capture the important role of fathers in the families of these babies, a number of fine photographs taken by Steven Trefonides have been added to this revision.

My daughter, Christina, has been of enormous importance in helping me clarify my thoughts about the changing pressures on young families. She helped me shape a new introduction and meticulously scoured the text for opportunities to include changes in the roles of fathers and working mothers, and in family styles. We found, as she and I worked, that the changes were so important and that there were so many implications for childrearing that they deserved an entire volume. Hence, instead of changing the focus of this book from its present one—on the individuality of the infant—we intend to write a new book on childrearing. This will be for single parents and for working mothers and fathers. I hope this present revision will meet some of their needs, and the future volume will speak to the concerns that weigh upon over half of young families today.

Over the past thirteen years, several of my associates in research —Edward Tronick, Heideliese Als, Kevin Nugent, Kenneth Kaye, Frances Horowitz, Myrtle McGraw, Leila Beckwith, Elizabeth Maury Fox, Michael Yogman, Suzanne Dixon, Constance Keefer, Robert and Sarah LeVine, Barbara Koslowski, and Mary Main— have made lasting impressions on my thinking. I am deeply indebted to them all.

Foreword
TO FIRST EDITION

There is a zest and vitality in human infancy that shows itself at every turn. The infant looks with absorption, drinks in his environment well before he "knows how" to do anything about taking hold of it. He scouts his world for every sign of what is novel and monitors not only what goes on right before him but what is happening at the edges of his world. At the start, in the opening weeks of life, the baby is either alert, "turned on," and in a mood to explore, or he is "turned off" in the total way that young infants have of turning off. Gradually, alertness spreads over longer periods and the infant begins on new tasks—social life, manipulation of things, and the gradual lacing together of the world of the eyes with the world of the hands. A career of self-projected travel begins early—perhaps when the baby can turn from his back to his tummy—and the realm over which control extends expands as no empire ever has.

There are memorable landmarks. There is the first time the child sustains his look into his mother's eyes and begins on a career of social exchange of such complexity that no grammar has yet been devised to explicate it. There is the first smile, earlier than the books say, and a genuine expression of pleasure, in spite of early detractors who suspected gas pains. There is the first time that the infant is able to go on looking at the world around him while still feeding at breast or bottle—probably the opening achievement of the art of doing two things at once, which will burgeon later on. There is the first visually guided reach for an object, hand wide spread, attention long sustained, and a final capture with object delivered for inspection to the mouth—the mouth, that lighthouse in the midline, the all-purpose sense organ. And on it goes.

For those of us who study the growth of infant competence, the mysteries are no less deep than for any other observer. We are only beginning to appreciate how subtle the processes of growth are—

how natural endowment and environment interact to bring into being what exists potentially in the human genetic code. The infant needs his parents and their affection, needs a world of varied impressions, yet one with regularity, needs objects to manipulate and master, needs a chance to develop his own modes of controlling his excitements and hungers and of turning off to sleep or to disengagement. There is some deep biological principle that abhors the imposition of one person's will on another—even when one is mother and the other infant, or vice versa. The deepest principle is mutuality, and it begins early. But a baby is no clock and there is no timetable that can tell exactly when to expect a baby to reach a new landmark in his life.

And babies from the start go about the achievement of growth in such different ways. Dr. Brazelton has very wisely chosen to present the contrast between the very active, the moderately active, and the quiet baby. How right he is! Each baby has a style, and the management of energy is probably at the heart of that style. At our research center we have been doing studies of early sucking—both feeding and comfort sucking. By a rather elaborate device, we are able to record the form of the sucking on sensitive instruments that then print the pattern out on moving paper. Right from the start, each infant writes his own signature—one is a sturdy feeder with long trains of sucking and regular pauses, not readily disturbed from outside; another is more tentative, shorter trains and more pauses, more readily distractable. Their careers as individual people, indeed, start at the beginning. What delights me most in the pages of this book (more than any I've seen) is Dr. Brazelton's unflagging sense of human individuality. He invites us to be courteous to the infants who are our children (or our patients!). And he helps us to achieve this courtesy by sketching the range of individual expression that infancy can take. There is no "ideal baby," no "typical three-month-old." Those are statistical ideas, a bit like the average number of children of Radcliffe graduates being 2.3. There is *this* baby at *this* age in *this* setting at *this* time of day and with *this* history. Perish the confusion between real babies and statistical babies. The tooth that is pressing beneath the gum is a real one, not one of three incisors expected before a particular age.

Dr. Brazelton should not be permitted to remain anonymous behind these pages. He is a distinguished pediatrician, a physician who has made us better aware of the care of health in infancy and childhood, but also of the importance of opportunities for growing. Pediatric care is going through a revolution, with much greater emphasis placed on the "fitness of the environment" for growth— the environment not simply in the physical sense, but in the social and institutional sense as well. How to make a better environment in which to grow?

Dr. Brazelton has pursued his quest for an answer in the mountains of Mexico and the islands of Greece, seeking answers to the riddle of what helps children achieve competence and fullness. He has worked in the laboratory, and indeed is now deeply engaged in a study of the language of social interaction between mother and child during the first six months of life, using painstaking methods of computer analysis of films, frame by frame. But above all, Dr. Brazelton has worked with real children over real years of growth— in his practice in Cambridge, at the Children's Hospital in Boston, and in a variety of long-term studies of growth. I have often wondered how he manages such a load of work. I continue to marvel at the good-humored spirit in which he carries it off.

This book is still another one of his gifts—this time to his patients and their parents. His respect for them is one of the hallmarks of this volume.

JEROME S. BRUNER

Harvard University
Cambridge, Massachusetts
6 January 1969

Introduction
TO FIRST EDITION

Normal babies are not all alike. However obvious, this fact is invariably overlooked by the literature for new parents. It is therefore, together with its extensive implications for childrearing, the principal reason for this book. I have described the normal developmental paths of three very different infants, as well as the very different ways in which they affected their environments. These are not actual biographies of any one baby. Instead they are composites of many of each type—the active, the average, and the quiet babies—seen over fifteen years of pediatric practice. The active and quiet babies (Daniel and Laura) demonstrate how amazingly broad the spectrum of normal development can be. From the very moment of birth these differences become apparent and begin to determine the tone of the parents' reactions. Preconceived notions of childrearing crumble in the face of a Laura or a Daniel; but both a Laura or a Daniel can be infinitely rewarding to the mother and father who recognize the strengths of the individual with whom they have been presented.

The photographs running through the text show many different babies who correspond to each particular type. Though the descriptions of the parents are fictional, I am sure that mothers and fathers will find themselves in these pages, just as they will find their babies now in one, now in another of these three typical infants. I hope that they will feel identified with these parents as they react to the impact of their strong little individuals who have suddenly become a part of their lives. Above all, this book is intended to document my firm belief that the newborn affects his environment as much as it influences him. With this in mind, young parents need not feel quite so guilty when they find themselves in conflict with their new and precious, but not-so-helpless infant.

I am aware that too much is written for the new mother. Most of the literature, however, is aimed at giving her advice. Very little of it offers her support for her own individual reactions and intuition.

Baby books tell her how to become the perfect mother. Eminent authorities intellectualize the process of becoming a mother. They urge her to overwhelm her baby with love on the one hand and to give him independence from her on the other. The different advice she receives may conflict so thoroughly that she is left in a serious quandary. When she cannot follow all this advice, she becomes even more confused and guilty. She finds that many of her instinctual reactions to her baby are frowned upon by one authority or another. The literature that was designed to support her becomes an undermining influence.

In spite of this avalanche of advice, of "sure" ways to mother a child, a new mother must realize that no one of them is the only answer. *She must find her own way as a mother with her own special baby.* Each mother and baby is an individual. As such, each pair is stuck with its own ways of interacting. The idealized suggestions of an authority may be entirely wrong for a particular mother and her child. A young mother may be better advised to chart her own course via the markers set out by her own baby.

In order to help her do this, I have shown in the chapters that follow how widely divergent the courses set by perfectly normal babies can be. By means of a narrative style, I have tried to include as much of the activity appropriate to each month as I could. Thus parents can see how each step may be taken by different babies. I hope they will learn some of the reasons for the different paths each baby takes. My explanations are given in an attempt to reassure parents who see variations in their own infants. With this recognition of the wide swings in normal infant behavior, young parents may be shored up in their day-to-day understanding of their own babies. With an understanding of how and why they take each step in development, their role as parents may be clearer. I hope that this generation of young parents will not need to be "pals" with their children, but instead will realize and fill their children's need for a warm, understanding, and also strong figure of authority and respect. If this relationship can be established in the crucial first year, it will not be shaken when critical situations arise later in the children's lives.

I hope this book will help each parent to see each baby as an individual with strengths and weaknesses, with a special way of reacting to his world—and to foresee how all this goes to make up a unique, exciting person.

Introduction
TO REVISED EDITION

In the past twelve years, I have been teaching at the Harvard Medical School and conducting research at the Children's Hospital Medical Center in Boston. Our research unit has focused on the remarkable behavioral programs that are observable in the newborn infant. Not only is each baby unique, but he or she* is beautifully prepared for the role of learning about him or herself and the world all around. Human infants have the longest period of infancy of all the mammals. In this period of dependency, they must learn about their culture, about themselves, and how to live with the complex expectations of their parents. No small job! But we are identifying the many ways they are ready for all of this even at birth.

A second part of our research has been to study, via detailed analysis of videotaped interactions among mothers, fathers, and babies, how they learn about each other. We have come to respect and understand the reciprocity that develops between them and to see how each member of the triad interlocks with the other. Each one learns about him or herself as they learn how to relate to and live with the other. Parenting can be seen as a major opportunity for developmental progress for each parent as well as for the infant. In nurturing a small baby, adults learn as much about themselves as they do about the infant. This first year is an exciting time to write about. The intricate programming of human newborns' reactions to stimuli and their active use of quiet, alert states of consciousness in order to pay attention to interesting aspects of their environment demonstrate that they are "ready" to start learning from the very

---

*In the first edition I tended to call babies by the masculine pronoun and to speak mostly of mothers. This led the book into the posture of appearing to exclude fathers. That was furthest from my wishes. For I know how strong is the competition for a baby between two caring parents—from my own experience. Times have also changed and this revised edition attempts to reflect the more involved role of fathers and to acknowledge babies of both sexes.

first day of birth. Indeed, they probably have been "learning" in the uterus. The learning that they demonstrate as they perform a successful act, such as bringing a thumb up and into the mouth so that they can help themselves quiet in order to pay attention to the world around them, is evidence of this.

Many of these programmed acts of a new baby's behavior elicit immediate responses from his or her parents. For example, when a newborn searches for and looks at the speaking face, a parent is bound to feel rewarded. When an older infant smiles back at a parent's smiling face, he or she feels automatically that this baby "knows me!" The programming that is built into the baby's repertoire serves two purposes, that of rewarding the baby for his or her active attempt to perform the behavior and that of attaching the parent to the baby. The precision of the response makes it become even more rewarding to the parent who searches for confirmation of his or her own competence in parenting. In other words, the responses with which the newborn baby is so richly endowed not only create a feeling of "Wow! I've done it" in the baby, but also capture and reinforce adults' responses to him or her. The baby's behavior becomes a powerful confirmation of well-being and of competence in the development of the parents-infant relationship.

The strength of the baby's contribution should provide new, young parents with a feeling of reassurance. Babies are competent to withstand "mistakes" that their inexperienced parents might make and even to let the parents know when they are on the wrong track. By understanding their babies' responses better, parents can feel more and more sure of themselves. As they gain assurance, parenting can become more fun. One of the greatest gifts parents can hand on to their child is a sense of humor and a sense of the excitement of growing up!

With this strength of the baby in mind, young parents need not feel quite so guilty when they find themselves in conflict with their new and precious, but not-so-helpless infant. Conflict is at the base of caring. And learning about limits from these conflicts may be the most critical source of strength for the baby's own sense of him or herself.

The more each parent cares and wishes to be a care-giver for a baby, the stronger is the competition for that baby. At a time when fathers are becoming more and more important to both mothers and their babies, when the extended family as a source of support and excitement for the nuclear family is disappearing, my earnest desire is to reinforce fathers for more participation. In order to do this, I would like to unravel the reasons why fathers have tended to be remote from their infants and children in the past. Our culture has not reinforced men for nurturant behavior, and we have tended to think that taking care of a baby is "feminine" or a "woman's role." We have overlooked the strong desire of men to get to know their infants and the critical aspect of their role in infancy—not only enriching the infant's experience by providing at least two caring persons, but also enriching the father's own development.

When I studied the Mayan Indians in Southern Mexico for their early childrearing patterns, I longed for the revival in our society of at least two customs that we as a culture have given up. I longed for mothers to allow themselves more continual physical closeness with their infants and for the cushioning of the extended family for all young parents. A strong culture emphasizes the value of the extended family as a backup and a conveyor of customs and values to inexperienced parents. Rather than leaving them to learn about childrearing and about how to handle crises by floundering, other cultures emphasize the extended family as a source of strength and direction. We have lost the closeness of one generation to the other —both because of physical distance and because of the emphasis in our culture on the independence brought about by a generation gap. Although this independence may serve a purpose in other stages of emotional development, it seems to be counterproductive around a new baby. Young parents could profit by an easier method for learning their roles. Learning the roles of parenting by trial and error is a costly, frightening process. It leaves new, inexperienced parents anxious and even angry—angry that "no one" is there to back them up. Grandparents could give them a sounding board, even if their advice is refused in the end. I recommend their being included whenever possible in planning for and coping with a new baby. I don't include them in this book as much as they deserve, for I've figured that parents will want to use the book as a way of sorting out their own thinking—independent of, and even in reaction to their own parents' thinking. But I am sure that they will find their way to decisions more easily if they include their parents' opinions and experience among the options.

The percentage of families headed by a single parent has increased steadily over the past twenty years. Nineteen percent of the households in the United States where there are children under eighteen years of age are one-parent families. Seventeen percent are headed by females, two percent by the father alone. This is an enormous increase in the number of children who are being reared outside of the typical two-parent nuclear family model with which this book is mostly concerned. Raising a child alone is likely to be a lonely, demanding job. The extent of physical and emotional energy necessary to meet the demands of an infant is almost unforeseeable. To single parents, these demands can seem endless and insurmountable. They must seek supports and personal outlets wherever they can. Single parents need individualized, flexible sources of backup and help in day-to-day decision-making. The kind of cushioning that is inherent in a two-parent situation can be provided only with difficulty. I find that my role as a pediatrician with a single parent becomes critical. The most difficult jobs for a lone parent are 1) allowing for the child's autonomy or independence at each new stage of development and 2) providing necessary discipline and personal distance, which is critical to the child's learning his or her own limits. Being the sole disciplinarian, often about apparently unimportant issues, can be fraught with anxiety and frustration.

Divorce is on a rapid rise in our culture. New babies may cement stressed couples, but they may add more stress and may become the unwitting targets for the mixed emotions of their parents. Stress between parents is likely to affect infants in one way or another. The worst result for the child is to be used as a "football" between the parents. The baby becomes a way for each parent to act out his or her feelings, often unconsciously, about the other. The child's own development can be impaired as the parents struggle with each other, or as they recover from the anguish of a divorce. In such an instance, each parent needs to muster enough energy or to seek enough outside help to maintain the emotional freedom necessary to think of the child's needs. A healthy infancy is critical to every child's development. The separating parents can design ways of meeting their baby's needs that will cushion him or her for the future. I would always want each caring parent available—as long as each is capable of considering the baby's requirements for healthy emotional and physical development as foremost. This is a difficult assignment under the emotional stress of divorce.

Almost half the mothers of children under eighteen in the United States are employed outside the home. According to a report from the Department of Labor, 30 percent of these have at least one preschool child. The trend in the present generation has been toward an earlier return to work in the middle classes and toward more women working outside the home in lower-income families. Fortunately, coincident with this increase in numbers has been escalating attention to the plight of their children. As a nation we cannot afford to continue the tendency toward "latchkey children" who let themselves into an empty house at the end of their schoolday, or desperate working mothers who dump their small children on an inadequate neighbor. I feel that fathers must reconsider their roles in a family where the mother must work. The increasing tendency for men to take a role in childrearing is one of the most obvious and best trends of this generation. We as a nation must free fathers from their jobs at critical times, such as at the birth of a baby or during a child's sickness, so that they can and will consider the child their responsibility. If a father can free time to be the care-giver when a mother needs to be at work, both he and the child will certainly profit. Even when a father can fill in for just a few hours, the baby will have more sense of belonging and an opportunity to know him, and the mother will be less stretched. The father will gain immeasurably in his sense of himself as a nurturant person.

Day care and all-day preschool settings have come to be seen as an increasingly necessary solution for parents who must work—for either financial or emotional reasons. The necessity to improve the nurturant environment for the infant in day care must continue to be addressed. Without the advantage of a stimulating, individualized environment in infancy, a child's future development will be impaired. Working parents must realize that entrusting their small child to another's care is never an easy task. Mothers and fathers of infants will inevitably feel guilty, sad, and then competitive regarding whoever looks after the baby. These are feelings that are appropriate to the attachment that has been generated around the baby. The job for a working parent (mother *and* father) is to see to it that these inevitable, depressed feelings of separation do not interfere with their major, continuing job of being ready to parent the child when they return from work.

The women's movement has stressed the role of women in the workplace and has pushed women to find and satisfy that role. Indirectly, housewives have felt devalued in their jobs as nurturers, and many women feel deserted by this movement. They feel that no one values the role of mothers and that they would be more "valuable" in the workplace. When this book first appeared I hoped it would demonstrate the vital importance of nurturing a baby in the first year, and that intellectualizing the stages of the baby's development would make it more fun for mothers as they participated in each stage. Inadvertently, I may have added to mothers' feelings of guilt when they were not able to stay at home throughout the first year. This has not been my intent, for I have seen how critical it was to many young women to include a job in their daily lives. When they did, they could mother a baby with less ambivalence, and both flourished. But I have also seen that it is not easy. It takes a dedication to the double task: fulfilling the challenges of the job and saving emotional and physical energy for the baby at the end of the day.

Otherwise, the infant suffers and the mother knows it. She is bound to feel cheated, and her own development will be impaired. She will feel torn, angry, and stunted. Whereas, with proper investment in each role, she might grow in each.

Until recently, most men have never successfully faced the opportunity for the working out of two roles—their jobs and their nurturant role within the family. In this generation we have the opportunity to foster the development of two successful roles for each parent. Then the sense of guilt and sadness over leaving the baby will not interfere with the pleasure and excitement that can add to the reunion at the end of each working day. The roles of other members of the household must shift in order to accommodate a working mother. This presents the husband and older children with a real opportunity for playing a greater role in the baby's progress.

The challenges for new parents today are greater than before. The rewards of nurturing a small baby certainly seem to balance them. I hope this book will enhance those rewards. As an advocate for babies, I know that the more pleasure parents can feel in their role, the better the baby will feel about him or herself. If I had to express one goal for this book, I would hope that it might increase the sense of competence and joy in new parents so that they could pass these feelings on to their new baby.

Infants
and
Mothers

CHAPTER I

The First Week

EVERY NEWBORN BABY IS UNIQUE

There are as many individual variations in newborn patterns as there are infants. Each newborn varies in an infinite number of ways from another—in appearance, in feeling, in reaction to stimuli, in movement patterns, in capacity to develop his or her own individual pattern. This is as thrilling an aspect of having a baby as it is of studying babies. Many parents will remark after holding their second, third, sixth, or eighth child for the first time, "How can he be so different from all the rest!"

A few years ago, at the Boston Lying-In Hospital, a group of four doctors, of which I was one, studied identical twin boys by means of a series of neonatal observations. We spent thirty hours with each baby in the first week, writing down our impressions. At the end of this time, we were all impressed with the differences among these supposedly "identical" babies. We had also asked the young mother to record her impression of each baby after she held him for twenty minutes the first day. We later compared our studied week-long impressions of each baby with hers. Like ours, hers were full of notes about the marked differences between the two boys. But not only was her impression of each boy after twenty minutes more accurate, more clear-cut than ours, she also saw them naturally as potential human beings. We were impressed with the accuracy and depth of insight that is a mother's intuition. This kind of intuition influences a mother's reaction to her infant in the first hours she spends with him or her. Her own capacity to react to his or her individual qualities is predetermined by her past experience, but each baby becomes a special experience to a mother. There are potentials for change and adjustment not only in the baby, but in the mother.

This book will present three different kinds of infants—a quiet one, an active one, and a middle-of-the-road one, all of whom express the variations that we see in "normal" babies. Although it is certainly not true that a quiet infant remains quiet throughout his or her infancy, or that a hyperactive infant necessarily becomes a rip-roaring baby, it may be of value to see the patterns that are possible in infants. As anyone watches a series of new babies, the most striking thing is how different each is from the other. Moreover, each infant's differences affect each observer in a different way. The observer reacts to the different potential within each infant in his or her own way. New parents (or even experienced ones) have deeply ingrained responses and capacities with which they will react to their babies. Because of this, they will begin from the outset to reinforce the differences in each infant. Even more thrilling than the knowledge that we shall give each child something entirely different and special of ourselves, is the fact that he or she will evoke it from us!

AVERAGE BABY

Louis Moore was a seven-and-one-half-pound boy whose mother had two older children, and who wanted to be "asleep" throughout her delivery. Mrs. Moore had been in labor for only four hours, but her doctor had medicated her and had given her an anesthetic that kept her asleep during the delivery. She barely roused to look drowsily at her new infant.

An infant is left with the medication in his blood that is present in his mother's blood at the time the cord is severed. From that time on, his own immature liver and kidneys must detoxify this medication at a slower rate than does his mother. Hence, a newborn is affected longer than his mother, and his immature brain is likely to be more affected by this medication. The marvelous thing to me is that he can appear as wide awake as he does, while under enough sedatives to sedate his mother. Of course, the labor and all of the new stimuli outside the uterus serve to alert him, but sedative effects of this level of medication will be noticeable in him for the next few days after delivery.

As a result of their effect both on the infant, often for as long as a week, and on the mother's recovery, sedatives have been reduced to a minimum over the past fifteen years. No longer are parents asked, "What kind of medication do you intend to have at delivery?" Instead, the question is likely to be, "Do you want any medication at all? If not, are you planning to attend childbirth education courses?" This question is addressed to both mother and father, for we have come to expect fathers to be participants in their wives' deliveries. Their presence during labor as supportive and instructional figures has been found to reduce the duration of labor, the likelihood of complications, and to ease the painful aspects of labor. Now, childbirth education classes are made up for couples, and fathers are expected to participate. As a result, fathers are included in the delivery room in most hospitals and are often the first to hold the new baby after the obstetrician or nurse-midwife delivers it. Research into the effects of this shows an expectable result—that fathers who participate in labor and are present at delivery are much more likely to participate with their wives in care-giving later on. In addition, both they and their wives report feeling closer as a family unit after such an opportunity to share in the excitement of delivery.

The whole delivery scene has changed over the last fifteen years. Parents now expect to participate actively; the mother expects to be alert and awake. Medication is used sparingly. My own research in 1961 demonstrated that babies were depressed for as much as a week after their mothers were given sedatives during delivery, and their mothers' breast milk was delayed by twenty-four to thirty-six hours. Drs. Klaus and Kennell (1976) have demonstrated that when mothers and their babies were alert and responsive to each other at delivery, bonding to each other was significantly increased. The effects of this continued, with significantly improved performance in cognitive and emotional development at two and seven years. There has been a major change in most hospitals toward parent participation at delivery and toward cementing the family by giving the newborns to each parent to hold and for the mother to put to the breast if she wishes while she is still on the delivery table. Parents have an opportunity to get to know the new baby from the first. Both mothers and fathers report that they feel the baby really is "theirs" from the very first. I am sure that having both parents in on all the decisions about childbirth—learning how to manage labor, learning in advance about what to expect at delivery, and then participating with the new baby—must give them an increased feeling of competence and of importance to that new baby. This in turn is bound to affect their feelings about the baby and they will pass on this same feeling of competence to the new infant. (See my book On Becoming a Family *[1981] for a fuller discussion of this.)*

More localized anesthesia—such as epidural or spinal anesthesia —has been demonstrated to affect the baby and the mother minimally; hence they are very much in vogue now. General anesthesia— such as ether or nitrous oxide—is reserved for more complicated deliveries.

The rate of both unexpected and planned Caesarean sections has increased dramatically in the past few years. With improved monitoring of the fetus, we can now detect subtle and not-so-subtle evidences of fetal distress. Rather than taking the risk of endangering the brain of the baby, Caesarean sections are performed. The incidence of brain-damaged infants has decreased significantly. Parents are disappointed when an emergency section must replace their planned efforts to have the baby naturally, and this disappointment should be expected and discussed with the doctor and nurses attending. Otherwise it is likely to affect their future feelings about themselves and the baby.

He was a nicely rounded, sturdy baby who cried immediately after delivery, filling his lungs with air and functioning well from the start. His head was molded into a long melon shape and came to a point at the back.

This molding is necessary to allow his skull to come through his mother's pelvis successfully in the short period of four hours. Her

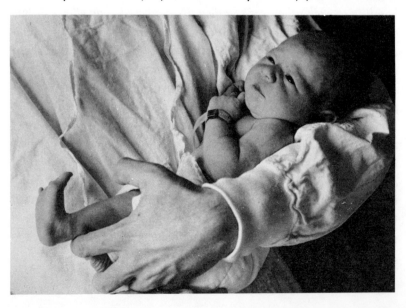

pelvis is usually an inch smaller than his head's circumference and the molding allows the bones of the skull to overlap in such a way that the head can decrease an inch in circumference. The brain is malleable and is not damaged by this change in shape.

Most of this molding had taken place in the days before delivery. His brain and the contents of his skull had also had time to adjust. He was covered with a thick, greasy white material known as "vernix," which made him slippery to hold, but allowed him to slip easily through the birth canal. In addition to a shock of black hair on his head, his body was covered with dark, fine hair known as "lanugo." His ears, his back, his shoulders, and even his cheeks were furry.

Lanugo, a remnant of our monkey ancestry, will disappear in the first few months, leaving the skin smooth and soft.

His skin was wrinkled and quite loose, ready to scale in creased places such as his feet and hands. The hair, matted with vernix, gave him an odd, pasted appearance. Louis was obviously no beauty at this point. His ears were pressed to his head in unusual positions—one ear was matted firmly forward on his cheek. His nose was flattened and pushed to one side by the squeeze as he came through the pelvis.

Before delivery, mothers picture in their minds a baby who looks like the three- or four-month-old infant in a picture book. It is no wonder that a new infant who has "been through the wars" sometimes brings a less than hearty response when he is first shown to his mother.

His face was puffy and somewhat bluish for several hours until his circulation improved. His eyelids were swollen. The lids became puffier, and soon after delivery he was unable to open them easily to look around. However, one could tell that his vision was intact, for when a light was shined in his eyes, or when the light in the room changed, he squinted perceptibly.

The "edema" or swelling of the eyelids is increased by the dependent position of his head prior to delivery and by the manipulation of his lids after delivery when medication is inserted into them. Such swelling disappears in less than a week.
Since his experience with vision has been nil in the uterus, perhaps

the swelling is a form of protection from too much new stimulation in the first few days. A strong blink reflex also adds protection.

When his eyes opened slowly, he gradually tried to focus them, and though they seemed to wander independently, he finally brought them to bear on a distant, not-too-bright object. As the examiner's dull, white mask came over him, he fixed his eyes on it, and when it moved slowly enough he was able to follow it briefly with jerky, slow movements. He even turned his head to follow it to one side, then the other. Up and down seemed harder for him. A fast-moving object was hopeless for him to follow.

From the beginning infants do fix on and track a bright, contrasting object, but it must move slowly.

A pediatrician named Goren demonstrated that, on the delivery table, a newborn infant was already programmed to prefer a schematic black-and-white drawing of a human face that was not garbled. One that had the eyes and mouth misplaced would be looked at briefly by a newborn, but a drawing in which the eyes, nose, and mouth were correctly placed would cause the baby to fix on it and follow it for thirty to sixty degrees to each side at birth. To me this demonstrates how carefully the new baby is engineered to fix on and follow the important face of a care-giver. In this way, not only does he learn about someone who will be important, but he will signal to that care-giver that they are already in communication with each other. How carefully nature has programmed the new baby to adapt quickly to his new surroundings!

His breathing, which had started with a gasping cry at delivery, was reinforced by the obstetrician, who spanked him to make him cry.

Crying serves to fill his lungs and help him make the changeover from a parasitic existence, living off the oxygen from his mother's blood-stream, to dependence on his own independent circulation, furnished oxygen by lungs that need to open quickly. The tiny airspaces of his lungs are collapsed at birth. They open and empty themselves of fluid in an amazingly short space of time. His lungs will continue to open during most of the first week, as his requirement for oxygen gradually increases.

Dr. Leboyer is a proponent of a whole new movement designed to reduce the traumatic aspect of delivery for the baby. He claims that crying at delivery is not necessary to the baby's immediate extra-uterine adjustment and that his lungs will open and fill without the initial cry. As far as I know, no one has proven that he is wrong. However, I have noticed that a new baby will often start crying spontaneously even when the delivery team is trying to reduce stimula-tion for him. And when he doesn't cry, he will have periods of deep, labored breathing that may serve the same purpose. Dr. Leboyer's ideas may be more important to the adults around him than to the baby himself. But any changes that make deliveries more sensitive to the feelings of the participants seem to be important. It is a critical time for young parents as well as for the infant.

Louis cried off and on in that first week, and this crying helped his lungs become better aerated. His color was purplish at first, then changed very slowly from a pinkish-purple, to cherry red, and finally to pink.

Skin-color changes go on for several days and attest to the changes in the circulatory system that are taking place. Infants' hands and feet are bluish for many weeks and remain cold for most of their infancy. This is due to immature circulation and has no pathological signifi-cance. There is no reason that we know of to try to warm them up with booties and mittens since even an immature circulatory system seems to do an adequate job of maintaining the blood supply to the feet and hands.

The breathing patterns that Louis went through were varied and would have frightened a mother who listened.

There are long periods of irregularities, of gasps, chokes, sneezes. For what seems an interminable space of time, an infant may even stop breathing. Then he will take several deep, rapid breaths to make up for the lapse. It may be disturbing to listen to newborns in these periods, but they are perfectly normal for him.

Meanwhile, Louis' equanimity seemed unaffected by all of these irregularities. After he had been awakened, his airway sucked out, and he had been made to breathe deeply, he was tilted head down in his crib to help him get up his mucus.

Since his entire respiratory tree contains liquid and is not even functioning minutes before this, it is no wonder that it takes several days to clear it completely. The amazing thing is that a baby can clear his airway by himself, and effectively!

In fact, with little assistance, he choked, gagged, turned blue, stopped breathing for several long seconds, then was able to spit up a half cupful of tenacious, yellowish mucus from the uterus. After such an episode, he cried to fill his lungs with air, then lapsed into a quiet, restful breathing as if nothing had happened.

These periods of no breath and of low oxygen in the bloodstream, enough to cause periods of cyanosis or blueness, do not cause brain damage in an otherwise healthy newborn. The new baby's brain is not yet geared to consume oxygen at the rate that it will for the rest of his life. With what wonderful checks and balances nature provides us! The head-down position in which nurses place babies after delivery helps clear their airways by gravity. One can hardly choke or smother a newborn. His gag reflex is highly effective, and he uses it rather constantly in the first few hours after delivery.

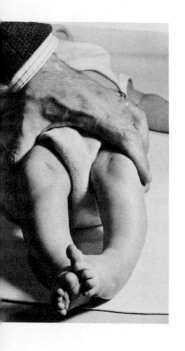

Louis had the usual bowlegs from his position in the uterus, and each foot was cocked in an unusual way. They looked "windblown," with both feet pointing to the right, because they had both been up beside his head.

Awkward intrauterine positions of the feet usually clear up in the first week or so; but they can result in problem feet. If they cannot be flexed and placed in a normal position, the feet should be checked by an expert.

Louis was active from the first. He cried lustily when he was handled or disturbed, reacting to touch, noises, or bright lights with a Moro reflex (see Chapter II). Then he would become active, startling and crying in a cyclic fashion for several minutes until he brought his hand up to his mouth. Then his crying subsided, and he quieted peacefully.

Although his eyes were still closed, he did not seem to be asleep, for he moved in rather free, brief arcs from time to time. His movements were jerky, thrusting, but at times his arms moved in smooth circles. His head turned easily from side to side as he mouthed or seemed to search with his mouth. Rooting with his mouth often preceded a mucous episode and seemed to be a reflex response to his intestinal activity. He smiled briefly before two of these episodes of mucus.

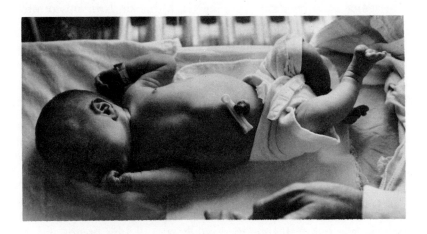

There are a number of "reflex" behaviors with which the new baby is equipped at birth. They are thought to be lower- or mid-brain in origin and are not cortical or "voluntary" in nature. They are set off by stimulation appropriate to each one. Later, they may become, or are superseded by, voluntary or consciously controlled acts that resemble them. One theory is that these reflex behaviors are a kind of practice and pave the way for the complex behaviors. They do serve an observable purpose in many cases. Smiling in a newborn occurs as he is going to sleep or as he is waking up and is often attributed to "gas" pains. However, in a semi-sleepy state, a baby will smile repeatedly if one strokes his face gently or softly croons to him. It seems to reflect a state of peacefulness in the brand-new baby. Later it will become even more meaningful and useful to him.

Bringing his hand to his mouth, rooting or mouthing on it, sucking on a finger—are all examples of "reflex" behaviors that rapidly become incorporated into complex, voluntarily controlled acts and which are used by the baby to serve adaptive purposes for him. Although Louis seemed responsive, alert, and vigorous in the delivery room, responding to all new stimuli, he quieted to a deep sleep on the way to the nursery. When the nurses uncovered him to bathe and dress him, he seemed most disturbed. He cried, became active, with vigorous thrusts of his arms and legs, and his skin color became bluish (cyanotic) from the temperature change.

The temperature-regulating mechanisms of the newborn are not well developed at birth. Exposure of the newborn's body when he is delivered puts an inordinate demand on it. As a result, his body temperature may drop. It is important to wrap him warmly soon after delivery and to protect him from exposure until these mechanisms have had time to adjust. A short period such as this bath will disturb but not injure him in any way.

As soon as the nurse dressed him again, Louis quieted. He contentedly flexed his arms and legs in a curled-up fetal position, relaxed, and seemed to go into a deep sleep. This sleep was interspersed with startles and brief jerks at irregular intervals. He gagged up mucus occasionally but each time successfully regained his breath and returned to sleep. Outside stimuli no longer bothered him unless they were very disturbing—such as vigorous handling. He barely responded to loud noises in the nursery, the only response being a brief change in respiration. He spent the next two days in this kind of sleep, apparently recovering from the effects of labor and delivery and the new stimuli with which he was faced outside the uterus.

The recovery period is a real testimony to the powerful adjusting mechanisms with which a newborn is equipped at birth. In this period, his circulatory, respiratory, and hormonal mechanisms all have an opportunity to achieve a new balance and to begin to function at the increased speed necessary for independent existence.

When Louis' mother saw and held him for the first time in the delivery room, she was prepared for his appearance by her experience with her other two children. She had been dismayed when she saw her first child's battered look. But since Louis was her third baby, she knew that his appearance would improve. She also knew that he would eventually wake up for her.

With Louis, she felt like an "old hand." When she held him, she was impressed by how sturdy he felt. He was a strong baby, and he squirmed vigorously before he settled into her arms in a cuddling position. She interpreted his wriggling as strength and independence, and the quiet periods that followed as "resting" and "saving his energy for important things—such as eating, and getting ready to go home to his brother and sister." She had forgotten how lovely it was to hold a little baby in her arms. Familiar surges of warmth and protectiveness came over her as she watched him.

Mr. Moore had forgotten how nice it was to hold a baby in his arms. When Louis turned his body into his father's and locked his legs against him, Mr. Moore felt a surge of warmth toward him. He had had real reservations about having a third child. Two seemed enough to raise and educate. But when Louis actively snuggled in to him, Mr. Moore felt a surge of warm affection for this new, perfect little being. After a few minutes, he put Louis up at his shoulder to hold him. Louis lifted his head to look around, then snuffled his soft little fuzzy scalp into the corner of Mr. Moore's neck. Louis leaned with his whole body into his father's left shoulder. The combination of the soft head in the crook of his neck and the little body squirming actively to get comfortable against his shoulder made Mr. Moore feel as though he'd always wanted this baby.

A baby's active responses are critical to the bonding process. We as adults seem to be programmed with a whole set of "reflex" responses of our own that are ready to respond to a new infant. For instance, whenever a new baby snuggles up to an adult, the adult responds by clutching the baby closer. When he snuggles into his mother's neck, I have seen nursing mothers let down their milk. So automatic is our response to a baby's plea for nurturing! However, if the baby is too drugged or "dopey," or if he has been damaged at birth and these responses are not available, an adult's natural responses to him might easily be compromised or diminished.

Mrs. Moore wanted to nurse Louis "briefly" in order to "get him off to a good start like the other children." Having nursed the other two, she was fortified by her experiences with them. This time she knew that Louis would survive whether the nursing succeeded or not. She had worried a great deal with the first two about whether she had enough milk and whether it was "any good." This time she found that she had a rather detached feeling that let her enjoy each nursing period in a way she had not been able to before. This time she could look at Louis without worrying about him or her ability to mother him.

There is a well-known quote that bears this out—"Why can't you throw away the first two, and start with the third?" The agony and concern that surrounds the first child are hurdles for him and his parents. But no other child ever has as much caring to fuel his struggle. Once the race with parental over-concern is won by the first and second children, they are eminently fitted for the world.

He was very quiet at nursing periods for the first three days, slept a great deal, or became upset when his mother tried to rouse him. He would try to suck a few times, but then give up and dropped off to sleep. Mrs. Moore found that by prodding him gently, and by rubbing his forehead with cool water on a sponge, he roused again and began to suck.

Years ago, a nursing mother from Ireland taught me this trick of dabbing cool water on a sleepy baby's forehead. As she said, a baby hates being pinched and prodded so much that he either won't respond at all, or else he will end up crying too hard to suckle. A simple temperature change on his forehead is not as disturbing but does rouse him enough to look around and open his mouth to complain. The nipple can then be inserted, and "he'll suck."

A second, more drastic maneuver that helps to wake a baby when he is too sleepy to nurse is to undress him. Very few infants can sleep when they are unprotected by clothing. Their startles are freed up. They get more and more alert. When he opens his mouth to cry, insert the flattened nipple to fit back in his throat. Almost any infant will suck if breast tissue touches the soft palate at the back of the mouth. This maneuver won't be necessary after he has "learned" to suck.

By the fourth day, the battle was won and Louis was nursing effectively. Her milk had come in and his nursing periods became successful.

In the nursery, Louis slept a good deal, but he also had periods of fussing that built up into hard crying. In the first three days these were infrequent, and he spent most of the time sleeping. By the fourth day, when his mother's milk was just coming in, he began to wake an hour before feedings. He cried hard in the nursery, filling his stomach with gas, and fell back to sleep, exhausted, just as it was time to be wheeled in to his mother for a feeding.

How often this happens in the hospital! Not only does the mother have a frustrating time rousing her baby to suck, but she must listen to the nurse's classic report: "He's like this all the time in the nursery, so quiet and good." The inference that they can handle him better than she is hard for a new mother to escape. Mrs. Moore had been duped by such a report with her second baby, and she had been horrified to find him so dissatisfied when she got him home. She had blamed herself for the other baby's "new" crying and questioned her ability to nurse and mother him. After she succeeded in settling him down, she realized that his fussing was a carryover from not having fitted into the hospital's schedule, and that he had cried and been miserable in the hospital, too.

QUIET BABY

Mrs. King had a long labor with her first baby. She had hoped to have no medication or anesthesia, but after twelve hours of hard labor, she and her obstetrician felt it expedient to sedate her. She spent the last six hours of her labor medicated.

After a period in labor, there is reason to feel that medication will assist the progress of delivering the baby. There certainly can be a kind of spasm of the neck of the womb that slows things up, even though the uterus is contracting well. At this point, medication can relax this spasm and allow the uterus to deliver the infant.

If the delivery is slowed up for too long, the baby can become distressed. Her heart rate may speed up or slow down, and either can indicate incipient distress. Fetal monitoring of heart rate detects this.

Each labor pain is an opportunity for determining what the stress of labor means to the infant, as each labor pain is accompanied by relatively less oxygen to the baby. If her heart rate indicates that her circulation is all right, length of labor doesn't really affect the baby. Caesarean sections are performed when the baby is beginning to show real distress.

The actual delivery was performed using an epidural anesthetic, and forceps were applied to the infant's head to speed up the end of the delivery.

Local anesthetics, such as epidural or spinal injection of a narcotic agent, simply dull the local pain of dilation of the cervix for the mother. They may also help the cervix to relax and dilate more successfully. Unless they are injected a long time (thirty minutes) before delivery, their absorption into the mother's bloodstream is so slow that they do not reach the infant in appreciable amounts.

The proper application of forceps does not usually endanger the infant and it can speed up delivery of the head considerably at a time when it is important to institute extrauterine breathing.

Laura was a handsome baby who weighed eight pounds and was well padded and well formed. There were forceps bruises on each cheek, and she had a soft swelling on the top of her head.

This is called a "caput succadaneum," which is made up of fluid under the scalp caused by the head pressing on the pelvic outlet in the last period of labor. It disappears in about a week. It has no correlation with any bruising or bleeding inside the skull or brain.

Her head was molded from the long delivery and looked elongated. Since she was a big baby she had extra stores of flesh and fluid that made her look fat.

Some of this is edema fluid, or swelling which newborns have at birth. It is useful in tiding them over until they begin to get nourishment.

Laura's eyes were puffy and her hands and feet showed extra puffiness. In the first week she lost this extra fluid and became dehydrated and thinner-looking. Her skin, which was furry and soft at birth, peeled and cracked as she lost fluids, waiting for her mother's milk.

From the first moment Laura was striking for her inactivity. She emerged from the uterus sluggishly. After delivery she lay quietly in her crib, looking around with her eyes open wide, as if in surprise. Laura's eyes were her most remarkable feature. Louis had at first resisted opening his, for a variety of reasons. Laura frowned, seemed to concentrate on the overhead lights, and looked as if she were not entirely approving of the change in her status. She had gasped immediately after delivery and had begun to take deep regular breaths, so she needed no extra stimulation from the doctors or nurses. Her color changed from the purplish blue to a pale pink in the first few minutes, and she was wrapped in several sheets to keep her warm. Her hands and feet were purple and felt cold to the touch despite the wrapping. They remained discolored for several days. Only when she was crying did her circulation and the color of her extremities improve. But Laura rarely cried.

Laura's circulation was sluggish as part of her general inactivity. If a baby needs to get oxygen or to raise her body's heat, she will usually cry or begin to shiver. In Laura's case, this slowed down metabolism, and her adjustment to what seemed to be sluggish circulation seemed to be part of her from the first. Although a clinician and her parents might have worried about this, it was just a part of her generally low activity and the lowered demands for oxygen that went with this. Laura is a good example of a baby who is born with an economical set of systems in her body.

While still in the delivery room, her movements consisted of rather gentle, slow, circular motions of her arms within a restricted arc around her face. Her legs were flexed up on her belly, as she had been in the uterus, or flopped out in a frog-leg position on the bed. She mouthed and sucked on her fists. All her movements were gradual, slow, smooth, and, most striking of all, infrequent. Laura remained quiet despite such stimulation as the nurses' injections of Vitamin K,[1] the instillation of silver nitrate in her eyes,[2] her first bath during

---

[1]This is effective in preventing "hemorrhagic disease of the newborn"—bleeding in the first few days that results from immature liver function and an inadequate supply of blood platelets.
[2]Prophylaxis that is used to prevent gonorrheal infection in a vulnerable newborn's eyes. There is some dispute about its effectiveness since we now have other drugs for prophylaxis that are not as irritating to the membranes of the eyes. Researchers in Colorado—Drs. Butterfield and Emde—have demonstrated that silver nitrate causes the infant's eyelids to swell and visual activity after birth to be decreased as a result. Without available eye-to-eye

which the blood and vernix were washed off and she was washed with soap,[3] or the disturbing bouts with her own mucus. She opened her big eyes wider, frowned, but did not startle or cry. She rarely became more active. Her breathing was slow and irregular, but effective enough to maintain her grayish-pink color.

Undoubtedly her mother's premedication just prior to delivery has something to do with Laura's quiet behavior. However, one wonders whether the way it affects her isn't another indication of how different from Louis she is from the beginning. Even the response to a sedative is handled in a characteristic way.

Her mother was too sleepy to share any of these observations. She simply took half-conscious note that the delivery was over and was successful, mumbled, "She's a boy" after the nurses assured her Laura was a girl, and fell promptly back to sleep.

Laura's father was delighted with his daughter. She was what he'd dreamed of. He held her, crooned to her, counted her fingers and toes. As he did so, she closed her first gently around his finger. He was delighted at her gentle softness. He asked if he could wheel her to the nursery in order to be with her as long as possible.

Laura became even quieter as she was wheeled to the nursery. Her eyes closed, her movements virtually ceased, and she lapsed into a deep, drugged sleep. There was little general response to any stimulus. Even the rather rough handling as the nurses removed the sheets and dressed and diapered her did not rouse her for long. Her respiration was slow, shallow, often irregular, and her color deepened to a rather dusky pink. Her eyes had begun to swell from the silver nitrate, and her face began to show bruises from the forceps.

The sluggish circulation in the newborn may delay the appearance of a bruise. All this gave her a look of being battered and drugged. One of the side effects of the depressant drugs is to decrease the infant's circulatory and oxygen demands. The lowering of these demands for

---

contact, their parents' reactions to them are affected. Drs. Butterfield and Emde have strongly recommended that we substitute a less irritating prophylactic medication. It certainly seems timely that we do so, but it is difficult to change long-standing medical practice. There is also reason to believe that silver nitrate causes an unnecessary incidence of chemical conjunctivitis and even plugged tearducts in newborns.

[3]Soap is used initially to cut down on the danger of staphylococcal infections in the newborn.

oxygen very subtly helps her maintain the necessary balance as she recovers in the first two or three days. Laura can thus handle mucus interfering with her breathing with less stress than Louis, who is more active and therefore puts more demands on his circulation for oxygen.

By the second day, she was a little less depressed, though she was as quiet and motionless as before. Her eyes were open again, and her face had become more mobile and firm. She looked less drugged and bruised. Mrs. King was pleased with her mobile face and eyes, but worried by her limp inactivity. She herself felt drugged and guilty that her need for drugs might have affected Laura. She asked doctors and nurses for repeated reassurance that Laura was all right. One question arose repeatedly: "Was Laura really hers?" Not having been awake for her delivery, it seemed unreal, and she kept wondering whether she really could have delivered a baby at all—particularly this little lump of a girl. Laura, with her limp, pudgy body, was not at all what she'd expected before delivery. She found herself wondering whether she'd ever feel positive about this baby. But she dared not express her feelings even to herself.

This conflict in a new mother is a common one and is not to be criticized. It goes back to her struggle with herself about giving up her independent role to become a mother. This is never as easy as it may seem in prospect. The balance a woman has achieved as a woman and a wife must be shaken. She must face a new role—that of having an unknown person entirely dependent on her. Any woman who cares how she meets this responsibility will wonder whether she will be equal to this new role. I am always concerned when a mother accepts her new role too easily.

Instead, she tried to find things about Laura to be pleased with. Only in Laura's eyes and alert face could she find a response to her attempts at mothering. After a session in which she held Laura, talked to her, rocked her, and tried to rouse her to activity, she found herself exhausted. Her fatigue was evidence of how hard Mrs. King was working at an adjustment. Laura wasn't helping very much.

Mr. King was constantly reassuring her that Laura seemed just right to him. Ever since he had held her and she'd responded to him, he'd "known" she was fine. He worried about his wife's constant need for reassurance about Laura. He hoped for and expected a girl to be sensitive and gentle. Mrs. King seemed to need her to be more active.

Mrs. King's being sluggish and "out of it" at delivery certainly is likely to cloud her feelings about this baby for some time to come. This is a real example of how vital it was for Laura's father to be present at the delivery and to see how normal she was from the first. Mrs. King's "normal" postpartum depression is probably being affected by her medication. Mr. King can be a real support to his wife by constantly reassuring her about Laura. For Laura's low-keyed inactivity can certainly be worrisome to anyone who is ready to worry. Her lack of active responsiveness plays right into Mrs. King's fears of having damaged her, which are a normal part of her depression.

Laura's muscle tone was slow to increase. She continued to be a limp, inactive baby who responded very little to stimulation or handling —except with her eyes. When she was sucking, anything visual distracted her, and she would drop the nipple to turn to look. On the fourth day, before her mother's milk had come in, she fussed mildly with hunger, mouthing her fist and crying briefly from time to time. Although she seemed to be upset by her hunger and had lost nearly a pound of body weight, she expressed her disturbance merely with a frowning look and slightly increased sucking on her fist. While she was fussing, a bottle of sugar water was offered her. She sucked on it with vigor. When a bright red ball was brought into her line of vision as she sucked, she frowned, fixed her eyes on it, and stopped sucking. She began to focus on it, followed it back and forth across her line of vision. All the interest aroused originally by sucking seemed to be fixed on this visual object. She was so interested in a visual stimulus that she could be diverted completely from sucking.

This shift of attention and energy in the newborn baby from sucking can also be brought about by auditory stimuli. A baby will turn to listen to a soft rattle or her mother's voice. In this way, she will learn the various signals of being mothered.
    Laura's ability to alert and to suck vigorously are signs of an intact nervous system. Her ability to shift from one system, such as sucking, to another, such as looking, are further testimony. But it is her style

and her low-keyed temperament that make it difficult for her mother (who is also slowed down and depressed) to see her as normal. A baby like Laura, who is perfectly normal, can frighten a new, anxious mother just as much as an overreactive, hypersensitive one can. Laura is at one end of a normal spectrum of temperamental differences.

Mrs. King worried about how difficult Laura was to nurse. She had been determined to feed her at the breast, but had a hard time rousing her enough to suck on the breast in the first few days.

Since nature does not give a new mother her breast milk for as many as four or five days after delivery, it is important for a mother to be aware of how the infant is coping with what appears to be a starvation period. In these first few days, she is reorganizing physiologically. This adjustment uses all her energy, leaving little for eating and digesting. Many babies demonstrate this in that they are difficult to rouse to eat in these first few days. A baby who is fed milk too early gags it up along with mucus; it appears that she is not ready for this kind of complex gastrointestinal activity. When her stores of sugar, fat, and edema fluid are adequate, as they are in normal newborns, she can maintain herself for several days until her mother's milk becomes available. In premature or dehydrated infants, feedings of water and sugar may be necessary to maintain them in this early waiting period.

Mrs. King also worried about how rarely Laura cried and wondered whether it meant that she was damaged. She felt that her medication and the spinal might have "doped her" and felt guilty about Laura's quiet approach to her new world. She was afraid that Laura's normal caput (the swelling under her scalp) was a sign of brain damage.

It would have been easy to assure Mrs. King that Laura was a normal, though quiet, baby. Tests at birth determine whether a baby's reflexes are normal. Wide-open, alert eyes and a responsive face are good evidence of a normal central nervous system.

As she became more responsive to her mother, taking the breast better each day, and responding more to the different kinds of stimulation that her mother offered at feeding time—her voice, her rocking and holding, her face, her warmth and touch—Mrs. King began to accept the fact that Laura was normal. The recovery from birth and delivery seemed complete in this quiet baby after the first few days. She no longer seemed doped, but her disposition was still unusually quiet and even. As she became more effective in sucking at the breast, she sucked less on her fist. She went to work efficiently, bubbled quickly, and went back to rest after a feeding. There was little wasted effort. Her eyes remained open at times after feedings, and she looked up quizzically as her mother made faces or talked baby talk to her. Mrs. King felt she knew far too little to mother this knowing baby. She found she wanted to mother her more than she had ever dreamed. Her inadequate feelings reinforced her determination to do a "good job." She asked questions of everyone—doctors and nurses, interns and visitors. She constantly bombarded Mr. King with her concerns. The house staff began to think of her as a tense, over-anxious girl and predicted a rough time for her at home.

No one stopped to realize that these questions covered up a normal anxiety. Had a doctor or nurse sat down with her and allowed her to "ventilate" her concerns, he or she might have uncovered some of her fears about Laura's adequacy and how she related her infant's quiet affect to possible brain damage. They might have been able to allay her fears that she herself had damaged Laura and hence was already proving herself a bad mother. They would have helped Mrs. King in a more meaningful way, instead of merely turning away her repetitious questions with reassuring answers and a condescending pat on the back. Such an approach could not satisfy a woman as dedicated and as sophisticated as Mrs. King.

Laura's weight loss was accompanied by an increasing jaundice and a dry scaling of her skin—she was somewhat pinched looking by the fifth day when her mother's milk finally came in. Her skin and eyes were slightly yellow with a kind of jaundice that is normal at this stage. For several days, she looked tan, as if she had been in the sun.

This jaundice that occurs on the third, fourth, and fifth days is caused by the breakdown of extra red blood cells that were needed in the uterus with its lower oxygen supply, but are no longer needed in the higher oxygen content of air outside the uterus. The breakdown of

*blood cells produces bilirubin, which must be excreted by the liver,
and in infants the liver is too immature to keep up with its job of
excretion. The jaundice that results is called "physiological" and is
normal in all babies. In some babies it is increased by relative dehydra-
tion and weight loss while they wait for their mother's milk. As they
begin to absorb milk and rehydrate themselves, they wash out the
jaundice.*

*Physiological jaundice need not be a concern unless it gets worse
each day, or unless the bilirubin reaches a certain level in the blood-
stream. Nursery nurses are very alert to this now and are likely to alert
the baby's physician to do a heel-stick to determine the level of
circulating bilirubin. If the jaundice increases, we are likely to place
the undressed baby under the bilirubin lights for a day or more, until
the jaundice begins to recede. It is rare that the lights won't help the
baby to dispose of the jaundice. In the days before light treatment was
made effective, many babies were transfused, and their blood was
exchanged to wash out the jaundice. Now this is rarely necessary. The
danger of damage to the baby's brain from bilirubin increasing to a
level at which it could affect the brain has almost disappeared. Jaundice and the bilirubin lights are likely to make a small baby more
depressed for a few days than she might otherwise have been. This
depression and its accompanying jitteriness usually last only a few
days after the baby is back in balance. For as soon as the jaundice
begins to recede, it won't return and any danger from it is over.*

Laura's mother worried about the pound of weight loss and discussed
giving up nursing on this account. Mr. King was a strong supporter
of breast-feeding. He reminded her that she'd wanted to breast-feed
before Laura came. She'd talked about it all through her pregnancy.
He urged her not to give up because Laura was a bit more difficult.
His determination and his backup came at a critical time. She kept
on trying.

*Mothers need frequent reassurance that newborns are provided with
extra fluid and tissue to live on until their mothers' milk arrives.*

By the end of the first week, Laura had regained her balance in all
respects: (1) she was gaining weight on breast milk, although she still
weighed twelve ounces less than she had at birth and looked smaller

and thinner; (2) her jaundice was decreasing, although her skin was still somewhat yellow and the whites of her eyes were slightly yellow in the daylight; (3) she was no longer dehydrated, but her skin was peeling on her hands and feet, and there were cracks in her skin at her ankles and wrists; (4) the umbilical cord was drying but still present; and (5) her behavior had resumed its quiet pattern—she lay quietly and peacefully in bed, looking around with her wide eyes, mouthing her fists when she was upset, but protesting and moving very little. By this time, her mother was more in tune with this quiet, peaceful baby and could better appreciate her alert eyes and her mouthing without worrying as much about her inactivity. She still felt that the delay she had experienced in getting milk, coupled with the drugs during delivery, might have contributed to Laura's inactivity.

And perhaps they did—in an infant whose personality and particular attributes were all set for a reinforcement of this kind of pattern.

When this was finally discussed with Mrs. King, she realized that she had tended to interpret all of Laura's behavior as abnormal.

Thanks to her husband, she'd been able to attain a balance in the way she accepted Laura.

ACTIVE BABY

Daniel was the second baby of somewhat older parents who were both teachers. The mother had been successful in going back to her part-time teaching after her first baby was launched. She had a nice elderly sitter who did a good job with Mark. Mark was two years older than Daniel. Since he was a "good" baby, they had had a quiet, easy time. Mrs. Kay felt her teaching was important to her and that it helped her maintain her equilibrium as a mother. She, like many highly educated women today, felt she was better fitted to be a mother and a wife if she had an outlet that was more intellectually stimulating to her than just being a mother. The balance in the family had been achieved, and Mark's adjustment as a two-year-old seemed excellent. Now Daniel's arrival was anticipated eagerly, and

Mr. and Mrs. Kay prepared Mark for his mother's hospitalization and the new baby.

Mrs. Kay had been quite active during her pregnancy; in fact, she had been teaching when her labor pains started. During pregnancy the new baby had seemed quiet except for one period a day. When she went to bed at night, he started waking up.

This reported activity of the fetus at the end of the day has been attributed to many things. Perhaps the most likely explanations are: (1) the mother is more conscious of his activity when she herself is quiet; and (2) the lactic acid that a mother generates with muscular fatigue at the end of the day is at a high level. Many doctors feel this lactic acid is transmitted across the placenta and, at a certain level, acts as a stimulus to fetal activity.

Actually the cycles of sleep and alertness in the fetus become clearer and clearer in the last part of pregnancy. A mother can predict when her baby will be active and when he will be asleep. Her own activity cycle very likely determines the fetus' cycling, for they mesh with each other. In fact, my own conviction is that a mother first "gets to know" her baby in the uterus by his daily cycle of states.

Mothers worry whether their anxiety in pregnancy will make their babies tense or anxious. We haven't any idea whether this could be true. Certainly experiences in the uterus are transmitted to the fetus (see On Becoming a Family*), but it is likely that the baby is cushioned too well for this to be a real threat. All mothers are anxious in pregnancy, and all fetuses must be prey to being affected. Any mother of an active, driving baby like Daniel will wonder whether she shaped him to be like this in the uterus—whether something she did or didn't do made him this way. We have no reason to think this is so. Just as Laura is at one end of a normal spectrum, Daniel is at the other. They represent strong but normal individuals who are different from birth, and probably were so even as tiny fetuses.*

The baby bicycled for hours each night after she went to bed and kept her awake in the last few months. So Mrs. Kay was exhausted and thoroughly ready for his arrival. She secretly began to worry that he would be a "difficult" baby, not as easy for the family as Mark had been. She also resented having to break into her close relationship with Mark.

A mother worries about having to give up the balance she has achieved with her first baby. She knows that it will mean an adjustment for him and worries about how she will help him with it. But another concern that may be more fundamental was succinctly stated by Erik Erikson to a young mother: "Perhaps you're worried about whether you will have enough mothering to be able to split in two."

But her husband wanted a family with two children and she knew intellectually that an only child's lot is not likely to be a happy one. So she went into labor with all of her mixed feelings.

Her labor was easy, and she delivered her baby after four hours. She needed no medication and she had only a "caudal" anesthetic,[1] which made the final delivery a painless one. He was a handsome, eight-pound baby who literally "came out crying and fighting." He needed no stimulation to continue breathing, and his color changed quickly to a healthy pink. The obstetrician had had no time to clear his airway with his bulb-suction apparatus before Daniel's first breath and cry.

An effort is made to clear the passages so that the first breath does not carry the fluid farther into the lungs.

Then, because he was so lusty, the doctors and nurses put him aside to care for Mrs. Kay. Daniel gagged, as he lay there, his breathing slowed, and his color changed to a violet-gray before the doctors sucked out his mouth and throat and finally cleared his airway. He began to breathe normally again and to cry. The anesthetist breathed a sigh and held him up to show him to Mr. and Mrs. Kay.

She had been awake enough to sense the commotion and to understand its reason. She looked anxiously at Daniel, who was now breathing normally but was quiet and somewhat limp. She asked, "Is he all right—he looks so limp! I'm sure something is wrong with him!" All those in attendance assured her that he was all right and scoffed at her fears. This clue to her concern about her baby was lost on deaf ears, and whenever she attempted to seek help for her

---

[1]"Caudal" is the name for local infiltration around the base of the spine that deadens the last few spinal nerves and renders the cervix painless as it stretches for the delivery of the baby's head.

anxiety during the next week, she was turned aside with reassurance or condescension by those around her.

This is similar to the concern we had seen in Mrs. King for Laura. Every mother reflects some concern but may focus it on a different aspect of her new infant or his behavior.

Daniel remained quiet, rather pale, and looked asleep as he was wheeled to the nursery. His temperature had dropped below normal from the stress period, and he needed several blankets to bring it back up. As he warmed up, and his respiration remained regular and effective, his circulation and his color improved. By the time he reached the nursery, he showed no aftereffects from his bout with mucus.

Newborns, as has been discussed, are eminently equipped by nature to withstand and recover from such episodes, and Daniel is a healthy example. Even a period of such poor color and low oxygen intake can be withstood well by a newborn who is a good specimen to begin with.

Daniel was ready to cry by the time the nurses bathed and dressed him. He squalled vigorously, thrust his arms and legs straight out, kicked and pushed the nurses' hands away from him. His color improved with each burst of crying, and although he sank into a deep sleep after his bout, he never lost his healthy pink color again. He continued to gag up mucus from time to time, but always effectively, and his breathing continued to be deep and regular. Daniel's mother's lack of medication certainly may have affected his behavior in this first period. He was not nearly as depressed as were the other two babies.

Although premedication given during labor does not permanently affect babies, its presence is easily discernible in the first week. One might wonder in retrospect whether Daniel's activity would have been different had his mother been medicated, and by the same token, whether Laura would have been more vigorous if her mother had not been medicated. We have no real reason to believe either hypothesis. The effect is transient and need not be feared as a permanent influence.

Daniel had a pattern for the first two days that was unusual and difficult for Mrs. Kay to understand. He seemed to shoot from deep sleep to lusty and inconsolable crying with no intermediate states of alerting or mild fussing. She had decided not to nurse him, although she had nursed her first baby. She felt guilty about this, but felt she could leave him more readily with her sitter if he were already conditioned to the bottle. Also, she wanted more time to be with her older boy and felt breast-feeding might interfere with this.

My experience has been that an older child has little memory of any feeding at the breast he may have experienced and minds it less than seeing his mother bottle-feed her new baby. A mother can feed her baby from the breast, can feel she has done a great deal for him in a short time, and can then spend time with the older one, without feeling that she is short-changing the new baby. But women such as Mrs. Kay usually have their own reasons. Though many of these may remain obscure, I am convinced that these are usually well founded and for physicians to try to dislodge such set feelings, with whatever good intent, can be a mistake. I am certain that whether a baby is breast-fed or not is in no way as important to him as is a good start with his mother.

Daniel was hard to rouse from his deep sleep. He was wheeled in to Mrs. Kay, breathing deeply and noisily, moving little. When he was handed to her and she began to rouse him, he seemed to breathe more deeply. Then, as if with a start, he shot from sleeping to an unapproachable state of screaming. He cried with a loud, piercing bellow that continued until he was quieted. Quieting him demanded a vigorous approach on the part of Mrs. Kay.

A first mother, or one less determined to master the situation, could have disintegrated under the barrage of Daniel's screaming.

As he howled, his color changed to a dark purple, his arms, legs, and whole body stiffened, and he became rigid. He could not be quieted with her crooning, with quiet rocking and cuddling, or with a bottle alone. His crying could only be broken into by a combination of tight swaddling of his extremities, plus vigorous rocking, plus the bottle nipple held in his mouth at his soft palate until he stopped crying to breathe and felt it there.

The suck reflex is stimulated best at the soft palate. The interior of the mouth and the lips are next in order of sensitivity. The last is the cheek and chin area, where a rooting reflex is first set off. Then the suck follows it.

His mother felt foolish and unhappy about the means that were necessary to quiet him, but she found they were successful, and after the second day of these maneuvers, she found that he could even be played with and enjoyed after one of his feedings.

By the third day, she had become more adept; he had become conditioned to this determined, matter-of-fact handling and quieted to feed with shorter periods of preliminary crying. His formula was choked down with quick, noisy gulping, and he often spit up some of it as he was bubbled. But after loud bubbles were produced, he lay in her arms in a semi-dozing state. Then she found her chance to play with him, to cuddle him, and to communicate with him. As she crooned to him, he frequently smiled a crooked, fleeting smile —so often that she was convinced it was in response to her crooning. As she stroked his face and watched him, he gradually opened his eyes and looked at her. He seemed to focus on her face and again, on two occasions, he smiled at her. This relieved any guilty feelings she had about him and about damage to him that she might have caused. She felt maternal feelings well up in a way she had not experienced with her older boy, who had been such an "easy" baby. By the fourth day, she found herself awaiting his feeding periods with eagerness and excitement. She began to look forward to the struggle for mastery of his feeding that both she and Daniel had to make.

It is unusual for a mother, at a time when she might understandably see the struggle as between her and her baby, to consider herself his ally in overcoming his driving, upset states.

On several occasions, he came in already wide awake. His screaming could be heard down the hall, and she marveled at his strength. She also felt awed and a bit frightened at this force in him. She realized that she would have been even more frightened if she hadn't been able to master the feeding situation with him.

When he wasn't limp and sleepy, he showed other attributes that thrilled her. He could lie in his crib or in her arms for long periods, looking around the room. He seemed to catch a new object with his eyes, frown, fix on it, and stare with an alert, intent look, as if he were absorbing it.

On other occasions, Daniel seemed to enjoy movement for its own sake. He moved his arms up and over his head and out to the side, and finally over his chest and face—in free, smooth arcs of movement. His legs joined in with slow thrusts in all directions and he twisted his head and trunk from side to side in slow, easy activity.

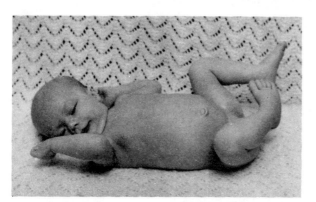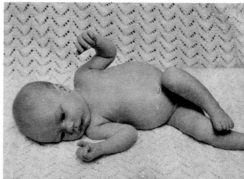

After a while he built up to a more vigorous state and began to cry. As he did, his mother attempted to stop him. Her crooning or her hand placed on him at one of these times seemed to make it easier for him to bring his own right fist up to his mouth. He seemed to need her intervention to help him quiet himself.

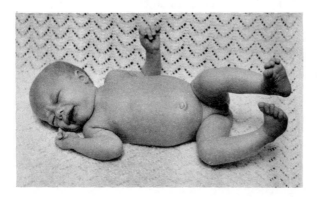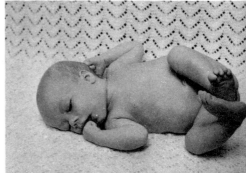

As in the case of an underreactive baby, an overreactive baby can make a new mother wonder whether the baby is intact neurologically.

In fact, Daniel's mother will wonder about this many times through-
out his infancy. So difficult is he, so different from Mark, so overreac-
tive and difficult to quiet, that in her desperation she will either blame
herself for being inadequate or blame him for being "abnormal."
Soon after birth, one can predict that these newborns will be difficult
for their parents. We have found that pointing out this behavior with
parents in the newborn period lets them see early that it's not their
fault. Also, by seeing this overreactivity with a nurse or physician, they
can be reassured that he is neurologically intact. Certainly, in the case
of a baby like Daniel, including the father from the first will create
a very valuable support for the mother—just as Mr. King was reassur-
ing about Laura. In the case of Daniel, it may be even more critical
that Mr. Kay be involved in his care. He will be able to spell Mrs.
Kay at bad times. He will be able to reassure her that their baby's
difficult behavior is not her fault. Two can laugh off the ups and
downs of a Daniel more successfully than one. I certainly have pitied
a single parent who has tried to handle a Daniel all alone. I try to
be available to him or her as ventilation and support daily. The
frustration and the feelings of failure that build up over the first few
months are almost intolerable.

Daniel's progress in the first five days gathered steam, as did his
mother's pleasure with him. By the third day he had lost six ounces
from his birthweight but at five days had regained four of them.
Despite his continued spitting up after his rapid feedings, he became
rehydrated, his color was excellent, and he began to look filled out
by the time he was sent home at five days of age.

CHAPTER II

The Amazing Newborn

Each newly born infant is equipped with a potential for physical, mental, and emotional development. Because the human animal has the longest period of childhood dependency in which to unfold, he or she learns not only how to survive but also how to utilize all of this potential in a complex fashion for learning and thinking. How he does this is intimately dependent on the experiences that he has with the world around him.

The newborn's capacity for reflex behavior resides in the central part of the brain (or midbrain) during the first three months of life. He reacts largely with these reflexes and uses a rather primitive setup by which he receives stimuli and reacts to them. His brain's higher center (or cortex) is playing a monitoring and storage role at best, according to neurologists, not the fully determining one it will play later.

At birth there are pathways throughout the entire nervous system, like electric circuits, that are ready to be set off by the appropriate signals. A mother automatically uses these signals as part of her mothering. An example could be the first feeding. She stimulates his lips and mouth as she inserts the nipple and as she holds him in a way that allows his rooting, sucking, and swallowing mechanisms to start into chainlike action. The infant's cortex is ready to learn with each reaction and to store up the effects of this experience.

THE IMPORTANCE OF STIMULATION

The infant is constantly receiving and reacting to stimuli. Each stimulus adds to the new baby's experience. The stimulus sets off a pathway of reactions. The "receptor" nerves that receive the signal transmit it to the baby's nervous system. A long, complex train of reactions are set off along this pathway that end in a reflex or automatic reaction. Since the newborn's nervous system is largely at the mercy of such stimulus-response systems, many repetitions of this go into the "learning" or "conditioning" that will eventually result in his ability to react with the discrimination characteristic of the human animal. With each stimulus reaction an infant's brain has the opportunity to store up experience for future learning.

How can an infant "learn" in the face of a bombardment of many kinds of new stimuli? He must already have the ability to select which one he will receive and react to. He must have predetermined pathways that will select an "appropriate" versus an "inappropriate" signal. He must have the ability to "prefer" one reaction at a particular moment over another. These assumptions about a brand-new baby may well evoke wonder or criticism from those who have never really looked at or played with a baby.

The infant in the delivery room seems to have strong preferences and strong dislikes. He will react to a loud noise once, but will shut it out the second and third times. Soon after birth, he will alert with a start, control his startle reaction, and turn to a soft rattle or a crooning voice.

More impressive mechanisms are available to him in this selecting process. Even while he is asleep he is receiving stimuli but is able to suppress disturbing reactions to them. He deals with them effectively in sleep so that he need not react in the usual manner to them. In fact, a newborn can be "put to sleep" by a series of strong or changing stimuli that disturb him at first, then begin to quiet him. Finally he goes to sleep in the face of a barrage of disturbing events.

I saw a striking example of this suppressive mechanism in a newborn who was being tested in the hospital. He was brought into the room for a cardiogram and an electroencephalogram or brainwave test. The rubber bands were tightly placed around his scalp like a headband and around his wrists. Both were constricting enough to cause swelling of his flesh on either side of the bands and must have been painful. The infant screamed for a few seconds, then quieted abruptly. He kept his arms and legs pulled up into a fetal position and remained motionless throughout the rest of the testing period. He seemed asleep except that his extremities were tightly flexed. A series of bright lights and sharp noises seemed barely to disturb him.

All those in the room said, "See, he's asleep!" His brainwave showed the pattern of sleep. When the stimulation ceased, however, and the tightly constricting bands were removed, he immediately roused and cried lustily for fifteen minutes. Why hadn't he cried during the ordeal? This apparent sleep seemed to be a more successful way of shutting out disturbing stimuli. The infant's amazing capacity for handling such an upsetting situation makes one realize how well he is equipped at birth to withstand disturbances and insults from the outside world.

This also shows how active is his mechanism for shutting out stimulation, and how much it must cost him to deal with too much stimulation. Overstimulation can be very demanding for an immature organism. Each individual baby has his own "threshold" and his own point at which he is overloaded. We have now defined several behaviors that are a newborn baby's way of saying, "I've had enough." Trying to go to sleep or yawning is one of these. Eyes that begin to "float" or to turn off, so that they appear to be staring off into the distance or to have a membrane over them, are another. Arms and shoulders hanging limply backward try to say, "Leave me alone." And one can see when a small baby is trying to cut out reactions when he starts breathing deeply, regularly, and in a relentless fashion, as if he were an exhausted adult. All of these reactions can be detected and respected in a stressed or otherwise overloaded baby.

Lack of stimulation is a much more devastating kind of experience to the growing neonate. Too much handling and anxious stimulation may create such reactions as excessive crying and even "colic." But as the infant matures, he becomes able to handle and assimilate these stimuli, even though they may not have been the most appropriate. Too little stimulation is worse, for it can lead to subtler forms of interference with development and growth. Just as an infant's physiological growth depends on proper nutrients fed at natural intervals, his emotional growth needs encouragement and a kind of nurturing stimulation. Without them, he will pass through critical periods of development with no progress from one stage to the next. Institutionalized children who are maintained physically, but not fed necessary emotional nutrients, demonstrate the effect of such privation. They may start out as normally demanding babies. They make their needs known by crying and react to attention with smiles. As those around them respond with infrequent, sterile encouragement, the babies' responses become less frequent and their demands less forceful. Their cries become weaker, their smiles fade, and they turn inward. They begin to roll their heads, play weakly with their hands or hair or clothes, or stare at the walls with an empty look. Their social responses to an outside person consist of an apathetic curiosity or faint anxiety followed almost immediately by turning away.

Inner forces that propel an infant from one stage of development to the next are: (1) a drive to survive independently in a complex world; (2) a drive toward mastery, made evident in the observable excitement that accompanies each developmental step; and (3) the drive to fit into, to identify with, to please, and to become part of his environment. The first force comes from within the child and is constantly being fed by the second, his own delight in mastery. The third falls to the mother and father to nurture. It constantly surprises me how early an infant picks up cues from his environment that lead him to "want" to become a part of it. That he can sense the climate around him is by now well known. But the fact that he is able to tune in and out when stimulation is appropriate or inappropriate to his particular state of the moment or to his stage of development can be a reassuring, exciting discovery for his parents. He can choose what he needs from his environment, as long as someone gives him something to choose from.

SENSORY REACTIONS AND REFLEX BEHAVIOR

The newborn shows a capacity to react differentially to stimulation. He will respond in a positive way to a stimulus that is appropriate to him. He will shut his eyes tightly and will keep them shut after being exposed to a bright white light, but he will alert and look intently at a red or soft yellow object dangled before him. As he looks, his face brightens, his body quiets, and his eyes glisten. He will follow it with his eyes, even turning his head when the object is moved slowly from one side to the other. He can even follow it up and down. This complicated visual responsiveness can be seen in a baby in the delivery room, at a time when we know he has had no previous experience with vision. Mothers comment that they can see their new infants looking at them as they hold them, but they have been taught to believe that a newborn can't see. A newborn can and does respond to visual objects that are within a particular range of sensory values that, in turn, are *appropriate* to his particular stage of development.

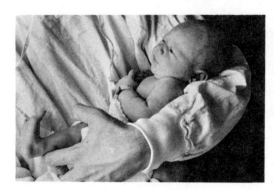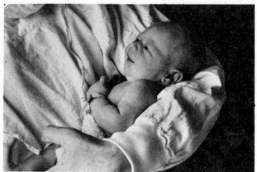

This same differentiation of responses can be seen in his hearing. As was stated before, a loud noise or series of noises causes him to startle or shudder. Thereafter, he can suppress his reaction to more loud sounds so that he seems almost not to hear them. In the newborn nursery, I have been able to produce and reproduce fleeting smiles by the use of soft noises. Research has shown that neonates (before learning can have been a determining factor) exhibit more consistent quieting and alerting to a soft, high-pitched voice than to a low one. Perhaps this is nature's preparation for a mother's voice in preference to a father's. At least it justifies the high-pitched baby talk that many of us use in dealing with babies.

The importance to a newborn of tactile experiences has been outlined by the late Lawrence Frank. He equates touch to a language or communication system for infants and feels that one of the major reasons for defective development in institutional babies is the infrequent handling that they receive. All of us have experienced the thrill of having a baby quiet from active crying when he is picked up or held. Many fussing babies will quiet when a hand is simply placed on their abdomens, or when an extremity, such as an arm or leg, is restrained firmly. Swaddling has this effect, and it is an old remedy for a fussing, "colicky" baby. I think this involves a number

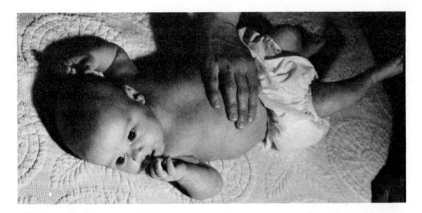

of things for the infant. The quieting, soothing aspect of touch plus the effects of firm, steady pressure join to quiet the baby. By restraining any part of his body, one interferes with a reflex reaction that is called the Moro reflex.

The Moro is a reflex that is a remnant of our ape ancestry. When the baby experiences a sudden change in position that causes him to drop his head backward, he startles, throws out his arms and legs, extends his neck, cries briefly, then rapidly brings his arms together and flexes his body as if to clasp the branch of a tree or his mother as he falls. This reflex is a disturbing one to him, one that he sets

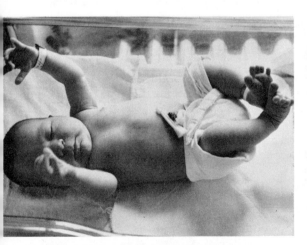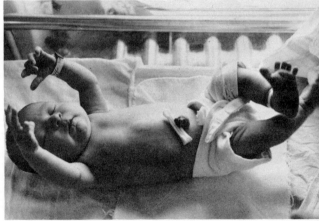

off for himself repeatedly when he is crying. Thus, as he cries, he startles, cries because of the startle, and sets up a vicious circle. Any steady pressure on a part of his body seems to break into this circle and results in calming the baby.

Stroking the infant in special parts of his body will set up special reactions. He will "root" or turn toward the stroking object if his cheek or the area around his mouth is touched. This rooting reflex is important in helping the infant find the breast. The sucking reflex will follow and is intimately tied up with initial rooting. The rooting and sucking reflexes are best stimulated by touching the mucous membranes of the mouth. The inside of the mouth is more sensitive than the area around it. Even a sleepy infant will suck when his soft palate is stimulated.

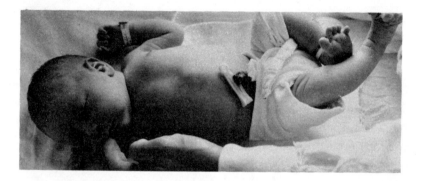

When the palm of the infant's hand or sole of his foot is stroked, he will close on the object in a grasp that is strong and determined. The more premature he is, the more determined and unremitting his grasp may be. Seven-month premature babies can be picked up by their hand grasps and held in the air, clinging to the examiner's fingers, as if they were holding on to a tree branch for dear life. A more mature infant has a grasp that comes and goes with rhythmic

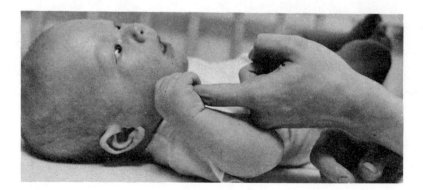

relaxation, but he, too, can support his own weight with his hands, and one can lift his leg off the bed by using his toe.grasp.

Stroking the soles of the infant's foot can set up two opposing reflexes in the toes. One is the grasp, described above, that is set off by pressing the end of the foot at the base of the toes. The other, called a Babinski, is set off by stroking the outside of the sole. The toes spread out and the largest toe extends up in the air.

There is a hand-to-mouth reflex that is set off by stroking either the cheek or the palm of the hand. The simple stroking of one end or the other of this hand-mouth chain causes the infant's mouth to root, his arm to flex, and bring his hand up to his mouth. His mouth opens in anticipation, and he brings his fist up to it. Infants will complete this hand-to-mouth cycle in the first few days, and they need very little stimulation to set it off. In fact, it is likely that hand-to-mouth activity and finger-sucking are common activities for infants in the uterus. It is often reinforced after delivery by their initial fight to clear their respiratory tracts. I have seen a seven-month premature baby suck on her thumb when she was attempting to choke down mucus and clear her airway in order to survive. She was able to bring her fingers to her mouth, to suck on them, and, because of the sucking, to swallow the mucus. The tactile gratification around the mouth and hand is coupled with the infant's ability to reproduce *for himself* the sucking experience that is satisfied every time he feeds. I have come to feel that an intentional bringing of his hand to his mouth during periods of stimulation is evidence of good ability on the part of a newborn.

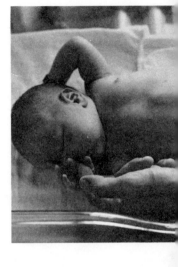

There are protective reflexes that are available to the infant and

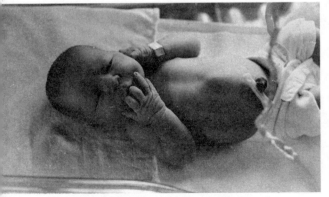

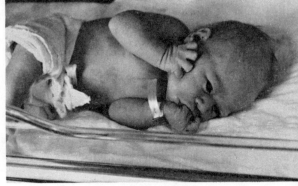

demonstrate his amazing capacity to survive under adverse conditions. When an object that could conceivably stop his breathing is placed over the baby's nose and mouth, he begins to mouth it vigorously as if to displace it, and then twists his head violently from side to side. Finally, if these maneuvers of his head are unsuccessful, he begins to flail; each arm is brought across his face as he attempts to knock the object away.

Stroking one leg causes the other leg to flex, cross over, and push the stroking object away with the other foot. When an upper part of the body is stroked or tickled, his hand comes over to grasp the object. When one applies a painful stimulus to any part of the baby's body he will withdraw from it if he can. Then his hands will try to push the painful stimulus away. He will bat at it over and over again. For instance, when I have to draw blood from an infant's heel, he pulls his foot away. When this doesn't work, the other foot comes over to push me away. The other foot may be quite difficult to keep out of the way.

Placed on his belly, head down, the infant has a set of reflexes that make it almost impossible for him to smother in that position. He picks his head up off the bed, then turns it to one side or the other. He begins to crawl with his legs and can even lift himself up on his arms. Occasionally newborns flip themselves completely over to one side or the other—all as part of reflex responses with which they are equipped at birth.

Temperature changes from warm to cold may be most upsetting to an infant's body equilibrium. When a part of his body is exposed

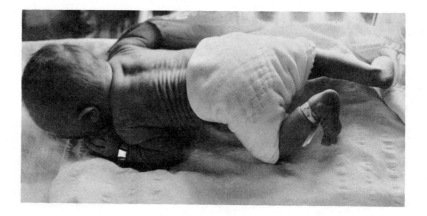

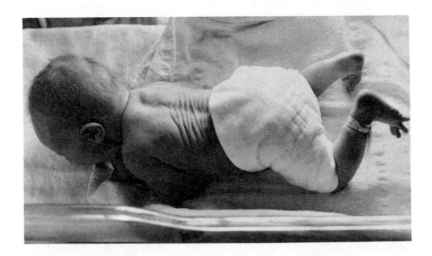

to a real temperature change (and we can see this by blowing cold air from a tube onto a small part of his belly), his whole body changes color and temperature in an effort to equalize the local temperature change. He becomes upset and will pull his legs and arms in to cut down on the amount of exposed body surface. Finally, he begins to cry and shiver in an effort to improve his body's circulation, and to protest the disturbing temperature change. When he is covered and warmed, he quiets down again.

The difference in performance that is apparent in a premature as opposed to a full-term infant demonstrates the importance of time and learning on his movements. The jerky, flinging, flailing of arms and legs that appears in a preemie are precursors to the smoother, cycling, self-monitored movements of a full-term baby. Many full-term babies demonstrate less mature movements. The more imma-ture an infant is, the more such flailing is seen. They are rapid, cogwheel-like thrusts outward of arms and legs, with sudden flexion and return to his body. Twitches and convulsion-like movements are normal and common. The infant's preferred position may vary from a floppy frogleg and arms half extended on the bed to one of com-plete flexion with all extremities pulled into his body, as he must have been in the uterus.

There is a reflex present at birth that is a response to having the head turned to one side or the other. This is called the "tonic neck reflex" or T.N.R. When a baby's head is turned to one side, and even

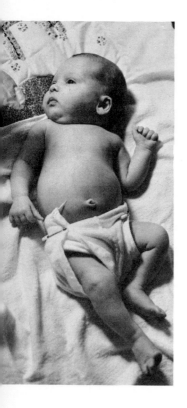

when he turns it himself, his whole body may arch away from the side to which his head is turned. The arm on the face side extends, the other arm flexes in a fencing position, and the leg on the face side may draw up in flexion. This reflex may be used in conjunction with several of the others we have mentioned, such as the Moro and the extension of the head in prone, to assist the baby in delivering himself from the uterus. The T.N.R. influences behavior for several months after delivery and helps him to learn to use one side of his body separately from the other.

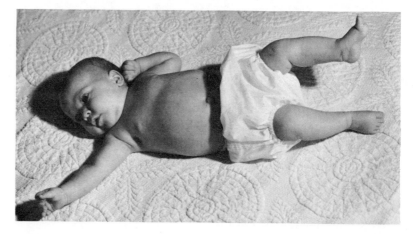

When a baby, lying on his back, is pulled up by the arms to a sitting position, he tries to maintain his head upright. One feels his whole shoulder girdle tense as he helps to pull up his head. When

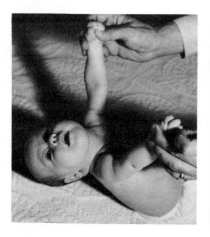 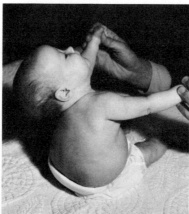 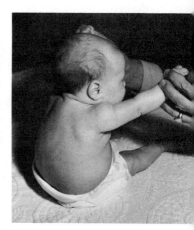

his head flops forward, he will try to bring it up again. It will overshoot and flop backward. He tries to right it again and it falls forward. These attempts to keep his head in the upright position are part of his "righting reflexes." When he is pulled to sit, his eyes open in a "doll's eye reflex"—just like the old baby dolls that had weights attached to their china eyeballs.

When a baby is held in the examiner's hands and rotated toward one side, the infant's head turns toward the side to which he is being rotated, and his eyes also go ahead of the rotation. Rocking a baby from side to side in a moderately upright position may be the most successful way of getting him to open his eyes as a newborn. Most mothers seem to worry about their babies' eyes after delivery. This is a maneuver that may help them to open the infant's eyes.

If a newborn is suspended in the air by his legs, he may assume a fetal position, flexing his legs and arms, curling into an upside-down ball. Then he extends his legs and drops his arms, extending into a straight line, arching his head backward. Babies rarely cry in this position and even quiet when suspended this way. It does not injure them if it is done gently; it must be reminiscent of their position in the uterus.

Another series of reflexes combines to propel an infant across a bed, or even through the water. An infant has available, like any amphibian, a rhythmical extension and flexion of his legs and arms, which can be accompanied by a swinging of his trunk from side to side. This activity looks like that of an amphibian, and relates us to them in the hierarchy of evolution. Added to this is an infant's capacity to inhibit breathing when his head is placed under water for a short period. Mothers who accidentally let their infant's head dip under water report that the babies seem to be less affected by it than they are themselves. Rarely do they choke and aspirate water. Their gag reflexes are still too strong.

The stepping reflex can be seen when a baby is held in a standing position. The sole of one foot, and then the other, is pressed gently on the bed. Each leg is drawn up in succession as he seems to walk. This walking reflex is similar to the voluntary attempts that come much later. A brand-new infant can be helped to walk across a bed. This early sign of the more complex act of walking is exciting to all of us who are interested in the evolution of behavior.

Much of the complex behavior we use later in our human develop-

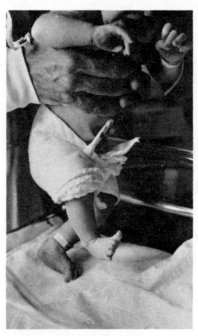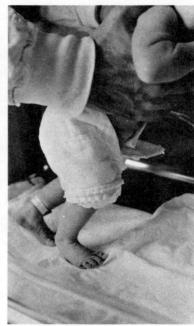

ment is anticipated in early infancy in the form of reflexes. The infant builds upon these reflexes. After they appear, they may go underground and, with a lapse of time, return as controlled, voluntary behavior. Walking is an example of this. Long after the newborn's walk reflex has disappeared, it reappears in the voluntarily controlled, complex act of walking.

Since every new parent is presented with an infant whose repertoire is made up of reflexes and poorly understood response systems, I hope that this sketchy documentation of some of them will increase his pleasure in watching and caring for the infant. As I stated in the paragraph on the importance of stimulation, any is better than none. However, stimulation geared to an understanding of the infant's own style is bound to be even more productive. Mothering is too complex and instinctive to teach, but understanding of what is going on in her infant can reinforce a mother's best judgment and instincts and, above all, add to her pleasure. When parents enjoy interacting with their new baby, he, in turn, becomes more rewarding. This circular process can only add luster to each of the participants.

CHAPTER III

The Next Three Weeks

AT HOME

The three sets of parents have made the first hurdle and at last are on their way home. These new creatures whom they have held and fed and who have begun to seem real are suddenly all their own. All the softness, the gentle movements, the appealing responsiveness are theirs to play with by the hour. The routines of the hospital and the shared responsibility tend to place a barrier between a parent and the feeling that this is really their own baby. Once at home, this barrier disappears. All the stored-up longing to hold her, to play with her after feedings, to watch her as she sleeps and stirs, to show her off to friends—all of this can now be satisfied.

But they must gird themselves for the adjustment to parenting. In my experience, it may hit harder at home than in the hospital. The father may be handling his baby for the first time. Grandmother may be on hand—or suffering in absentia. When there are other children, each has his own adjustment to make. The newborn must go through a period of disorganization of her own, in the transit from the overwhelming nursery to the gentle, caring home atmosphere. This disorganization may not be an easy one for a new parent to handle. By the second or third baby, a parents know she will survive in spite of their mistakes. The first one is hard to face without extreme concern. But this concern is part of caring and will be put to use. Caring concern will become the foundation for learning to be a parent.

When new parents are feeling overwhelmed by the sudden, momentous responsibility and the anxiety that this responsibility creates in them, they must remind themselves that they are not alone. All new parents have been through some degree of it. They can console themselves with the fact that plenty of the others were more inexperienced and cared less than they do—and they made it! A baby is not as fragile as she looks and has tremendous capacities for adjusting to a changing, disturbing world. The mistakes they make at first will bother them more than they will the baby.

The physical adjustment that a new mother is making after delivery lasts for many weeks. It is a strain on her resources—both physical and emotional. It is largely responsible for her inability to sleep well, to eat properly, to keep her emotions in control. Many young mothers have told me that they feel like weeping most of the time in the first few weeks at home. They wonder if this is a sign of inadequacy in them, or if they are indeed "going crazy." It must be reassuring to know that this is a common result of the physical and psychological readjustments that follow delivery. These will pass. They may even be an important part of her ability to become a different kind of person—a "mother," rather than a young girl.

The new father is anxious to do his part, to become the parent he has been dreaming about. He may wonder how he will ever get to be a parent, and if he does, will he have to be like his own parents? He has been trying to divorce himself from that, but his own childhood is likely to be his only experience with parenting. He wants to "mother" his wife, but she is likely to be withdrawn into her own world. When he tries to reach her, she may snap back at him, or she may fall apart with unexpected weeping. She may swing from moods of extreme dependency to detachment. And she is likely to be locked in a sort of cocoon with "her" baby. He is likely to feel shut out of it and even angry at being excluded. Certainly this feeling doesn't help him mobilize a necessary feeling of self-confidence in handling the new baby. His wonder at her responses helps him at first. And as the responsibility of taking care of her grows day by day, his feeling of understanding her must grow also. That is the big job of adjusting that a father will feel. Many young fathers are trying to take responsibility for the new baby equal to that of their wives. It is entirely a real learning experience unless the father has been in on the raising of his own younger brothers or sisters. Few young people have. So a man today feels he may have to go into this new role with no or at least inadequate experience. The more he cares, the more frightening it may be. And, to add to the responsibility, he may be the only real support his wife has as she learns her new role. Too many of our nuclear families are lonely and isolated at a time when the structure and supports of an extended family could be a major blessing.

Our present social structure does not help much in this period. Grandmothers and helping family are either too far away or are not acceptable as help in our emancipated generation. Hired help for new mothers may be an emotional, as well as a financial, strain; many feel a nurse is an intrusion. Physicians can hardly take up the slack of dependency, and many women feel deserted at a time like this —with no one to turn to. Even the books that are written about this period state glibly that parents should love and enjoy their baby and must always think of her first. Since no one can feel this way throughout such a difficult time, the new mother can only conclude that she is hopeless as a mother and the father that he will never make it. But there are better times coming; the first few days are a necessary slump before the exciting surge ahead. It may help to know that most other parents go through a similar blue period at this time and to know that they gradually recover their physical and emotional resources.

One mother in my practice wrote down her feelings at this time for me: She found she was quite exhausted at home. Everything she did took more out of her than it should. Anything out of place in the house bothered her more, and she wanted to straighten everything out. She was exhausted when she did and irritated if she didn't. Her food was tasteless, and yet she hadn't the energy to fix exotic dishes. She wished she could complain about her husband's cooking, but she realized that she should feel lucky that he was helping at all. But it seemed as if everything he did was wrong in some way. Every time he helped with the baby she resented him. If he did anything for the baby, the baby cried and in the end she had to console them both.

She knew her husband could use a bit of attention, but she resented this. The nurse who came to help did things all wrong, and for some reason, she resented this more than she usually would have and felt like fighting with her. Her own mother told her to rest more, and she knew she was right, but she felt like fighting with her, too. And the baby—he cried so much, he ate for so long each time, he seemed so demanding and yet at the same time so frail that her anxious mind pictured him just drying up and blowing away. The worst of it was that she found herself wishing he would at times, and that frightened her even more. She dreamed of doing something to him without being aware of it—of rolling over on him in bed as she nursed him, of dropping him as she picked him up, of falling downstairs as she carried him—all ghastly but possible in her weakened condition. And then she remembered her pregnancy fantasies of what being a mother would be like, and she wanted to cry! She was none of the things she had wanted to be, or that other young mothers are with their new babies. She felt she was a *failure*!

The baby, meanwhile, must make equally radical adjustments. He has been busy adapting to life in the newborn nursery at the hospital. He has erected his own inner defenses to the continual bright light; to the constant new noises—the clatter of cribs, the chatter of nurses, and the caterwauling of other infants; to being wet and dirty for long periods; to being hungry at times that do not fit into hospital routine; to being handled roughly at times by vigorous, busy nurses. His ability to handle such inappropriate stimuli was discussed in Chapter II. In spite of the unkindly aspect of the hospital environment, I am sure that during this period in his life he is best fitted for such a mélange of "disturbing" stimuli. He needs to be awakened physically and psychologically, and these harsh stimuli probably do just that. Further, with his exquisite inborn ability to shut out the disturbing aspects of his environment, he may sort out better responses. The experience in handling these early disturbances may enhance his capacity to protect himself from unavoidably disturbing influences at home. It may also be reassuring to any young mother who worries about the kind of environment she sets up for her new baby to know that few are as inappropriate or as overstimulating as a newborn nursery.

At home, he becomes surrounded by a protecting and nurturing atmosphere. His desires are anticipated, even encouraged, and each person is geared to lavish affection upon him. Each parent is waiting for an opportunity to demonstrate this affection in the first few days at home. In fact, a wise young mother will capture this desire on the part of her husband by pushing him to do some of the ordinary but, at this point, exciting things for their infant—let him feed him water or an emergency formula if she is nursing. She should urge him to help at bathtime and at the changing of his diapers. When a nurse or grandmother is showing her "how to," he can learn "how to" also. Fathers want to be included.

Learning how to do these things will not only capture and encourage his wishes to be with the baby, but it will give him a feeling of "doing something"—perhaps as important to him as to her by this time. He may feel lost without a way to reach out to his new offspring. I shall never forget a young father who hung over me eagerly as I examined his new baby at home. As I finished the examination, I handed the undressed baby into his waiting arms. He sagged and grew pale as I clutched the infant back. This, I realize now, was a bit more sudden responsibility for a new young father than was necessary at that moment.

We are past the attitude that I grew up with—that fathers were likely to be incompetent, even dangerous. When our first baby came, I was sent home because I'd be in the way. When I wanted to see and handle her in the newborn nursery, I was told that of course, I couldn't, I was her father. I was asked to inspect her through the glass window shielding the nursery. That glass said to me that, as a father, I was dirty and dangerous. And yet I was a pediatrician who was "safe" for every baby but my own. Fortunately, these practices have been replaced in most progressive hospitals by active programs to include fathers. But a new father is still likely to feel incompetent and overwhelmed in much the same way as the new mother. Together they can learn their new roles, cementing the family for the future as they do. Men will learn about themselves, just as their wives will, as they learn to nurture together.

The danger in a new situation such as this one, in which all the adults are tensely involved, is that they will overwhelm the new infant with too much fluttering attention. They may overstimulate the infant at a time when he needs to readjust his regulatory mechanisms. Most newborns cry a lot the first day at home. They eat poorly and need frequent feedings. They do not quiet with handling as they might at other times. I am sure they sense the tension in the air. Since a baby can be so acutely in tune with the feelings of the person who handles him, tense handling administered to "shut him up" at a time when a desperate parent or grandparent doesn't know "what else to do" may work in just the opposite way. The baby may be crying to let off his own tension and, with such handling, has a double load with which to cope—his own and his parents'.

AVERAGE BABY

Louis became the center of attention on the way home. His father brought Martha, aged five, and Tom, aged three, to the hospital with him when Mrs. Moore was discharged. Martha rushed to see "her" new baby and ignored her mother. Tom clung to his mother's knees in the reception hall of the hospital.

A hospital nurse carried Louis to the car, placing him in Mrs. Moore's arms for the ride home. The two older children immediately climbed over the seat and swamped mother and baby with their attention. Both children stuck their faces into his, smacked at him, and talked to him. They soon began to fight over him with loud voices. The loud argument and the jostling of his mother upset Louis and he started to cry. He let out a wail that came like a shotgun blast into the noisy car. The children quieted immediately and looked with awe at this new infant. His insistent wails drowned out their bickering. He had already asserted himself as a person in their eyes. Martha's lip quivered as she watched her mother attempt to comfort Louis, and she added her own soft cooing in imitation of her mother. Tom squeezed even closer to his mother, put his thumb in his mouth, and closed his eyes to shut out the commotion.

Louis cried most of the way home. His mother gently rocked him in her arms, attempting to soothe him. As he continued to cry, her rocking became fiercer. By the time they reached their four-room apartment, all the occupants of the car were strung on tight wires. Mrs. Moore felt that she could hardly wait to put Louis away in his crib. She had intended to feed him as soon as she reached their house, but she realized that she had very little milk. Her breasts did not seem as full as they had at feeding times in the hospital.

Tension surrounding the homecoming interferes with milk production. A mother must rest and relax at home in order to keep producing.

Safely at home, things only got worse. Mr. Moore began to storm around the apartment, complaining of all the things that had gone wrong while his wife was away. Martha and Tom began to make incessant demands of her—Tom alternately showing off and dragging at her skirts; Martha pulling her this way and that. Mrs. Moore changed the wet baby, swaddled him in a sheet, and put him in his clean crib by her bed. He continued to wail. She rushed to make some sugar water for him. She filled the bottles with a teaspoon of sugar and four ounces of water and set them on the stove in several inches of water.

It suffices to sterilize them by boiling around them for fifteen minutes. In many communities, where water is carefully tested for pathogenic bacteria, it is perfectly safe to use unboiled water in the bottles.

Mrs. Moore then realized she was exhausted, sat down in a chair, and began to weep. As she wept, the household quieted down. Her husband crept up to the baby's crib and began to rock it gently. Louis gradually quieted. His eyes opened wide and he looked around. Mr. Moore talked to Louis in a low soothing voice, and Louis responded with a softening of his face and a brief smile. Mr. Moore was so delighted with the smile that he shouted to the children to come and see. The shout frightened Louis and he was off again with loud wails. But his initial success gave Mr. Moore courage. He picked up Louis and rocked him in his arms. The infant quieted and alerted for his father. Tom felt that both his parents had deserted him. Martha wanted to participate in this close unit of her father and Louis and so climbed into his lap. Mrs. Moore found herself watching her husband's success. Her spirits revived. She leapt to her feet as she remembered the bottles, which were boiling dry.

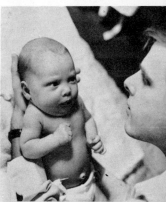

With the sugar and water, Mr. Moore quieted Louis until his mother's milk came in. In half an hour more, she gave him a good feeding at the breast with everyone watching wide-eyed.

I have never been convinced that sugar water interferes with successful nursing, unless it is given too close to the next feeding. Both sugar and water are so quickly absorbed and utilized that they could hardly "fill up his stomach" for very long. Nor can they really dull any hunger he might work up.

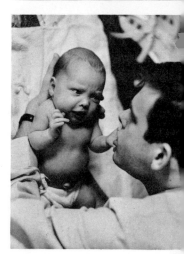

Louis was a responsive baby. He quieted to handling, to changes in position, to crooning. He learned quickly to quiet himself by bringing his fist to his mouth and sucking on it. As time went on, he differentiated the two first fingers of his left hand and learned to suck on them for comfort, showing how early a lasting pattern like this is established. As he inserted his fingers and began to suck, his arms and legs relaxed. His face became serene and peaceful. From time to time, he jumped with a startle as Tom fell against his crib or let out a war whoop, or as Martha stomped around singing.

He cried every evening. He lay for hours during the day, looking around quietly, but by the end of the day, he seemed determined to have his say. He began slowly building up with intermittent whimpers, as the children began to settle down for their supper. He quieted when his father played with him or rocked him, but as time wore on, his cries became more insistent. In the beginning he could be talked to, would alert and fix on his father's face with his eyes for several minutes at a time, his face softening and his bodily activity ceasing in the process. He loved to be rocked, and either of his parents could rock him for thirty minutes at a time before he built up to crying. But after half an hour he seemed to tire and began to cry with loud wails. Then no effort to comfort him would succeed. He was jostled, picked up, rocked again, swaddled, and played with. His diapers were changed. He was fed sugar water and occasionally even formula. This was offered him to be sure he wasn't hungry in spite of its being far too soon for his next feeding. (Mrs. Moore knew she had milk, but felt that at the end of the day it might have diminished in quality or quantity, so she used an "emergency" formula for bad evenings.) He was not crying for hunger, and he continued to cry for 15- to 20-minute stretches, ending with deep wracking sobs as he tapered off.

The cyclic timing of such crying periods, plus the infant's "determination" to cry them out, are strong evidence to me that he is expressing some inner need to cry or let off tension. No effort to quiet a baby in this state really works for more than a brief period.

Every evening Mr. and Mrs. Moore found it necessary to remind themselves that Tom had also screamed every evening as a new baby. They needed the reassurance that they were not neglecting Louis, whose wails seemed to them so much more insistent and demanding than they remembered Tom's. Mrs. Moore found that, after long tortured evenings of trying everything, her mother's advice was the most comforting to both of them. Her mother had raised six children and was philosophical about crying babies. She had said, "Tom just needs to cry. He doesn't like being a baby any more than any strong, smart boy would. He puts up with it all day, but he can't stand it all night, too. Let him cry some. Then pick him up and love him, and you'll see that it will work better." Mrs. Moore had worked out a system of letting him cry for twenty minutes, then picking him up and cuddling him, getting bubbles up with sugar water, and putting him back in his bed to cry again. She had found that when she had handled him calmly in this routine he seemed quieter and cried for shorter and shorter periods.

His fussing lasted from one to three hours, the longer periods invariably following a noisy, disturbed day, or a weekend when Mr. Moore was at home, or when Mrs. Moore was blue or upset.

There are studies on infant crying that demonstrate that environmental tension adds to the duration and intensity of these periods. They suggest that the timing of these crying spells at the end of the day is not entirely by chance. The tension of a tired family and the expectant excitement around a father's homecoming are certainly contributing factors.

The rest of his twenty-four-hour day was beautifully organized and easy.

I am convinced that this fussy period may be an organizing force. Infants who don't fuss rarely sleep for long periods at night. It looks as if these periods serve the purpose of discharging stored-up tension for the rest of the day.

Louis took his feedings well. He sucked for long stretches of thirty to forty minutes at each breast on some days, but for only ten to twenty minutes at other times. Mrs. Moore fed him on a demand schedule that suited both his and her demands. The other children were so noisy and active that nursing Louis seemed a grateful release from the turmoil around her. Few feedings were really quiet and relaxed, but Louis seemed to manage the intrusions. Tom climbed into his mother's lap and tried to push Louis out. At other feedings, he dreamed up all of the annoying mischievous things he could in order to draw Mrs. Moore away from feeding Louis. Once he climbed up into Mrs. Moore's lap and tried to imitate Louis' nursing at the breast. Though startled and shocked, she realized the reason, and therefore cuddled Tom to her breast and comforted him. As she did, he lost interest and climbed down. He never tried it again. Mrs. Moore had been wise in not shoving him away, as she might have.

If a mother accepts such investigative, intrusive behavior with a certain amount of understanding and humor, a child can satisfy his curiosity. Shoving him out of this intimate situation only increases his feelings of jealousy.

Martha's five-year-old reactions were less easily discernible. She was not openly antagonistic to either Louis or her mother. In fact, she imitated her mother more fiercely and tried to mother Louis whenever she was allowed to.

This attempt to identify with her mother is characteristic of a five-year-old. A fierce sort of imitation is an attempt to handle ambivalent feelings about the changed household or the mother's preoccupation. Children use this to work out some of their negative feelings.

Martha saved her real vengeance for Tom. She kept after him all day, stimulating him to be a bad boy, teasing him until he cried, racing round and round the apartment after him.

Relief came when Mr. Moore arrived home. Both of the children seemed to wait for him, and by the end of the day they were getting higher and higher in anticipation. When he finally arrived, Martha and Tom vied for his attention. Tom showed off. Martha thought up all the stories she could about their day. He had to sit down on a sofa, flanked by each older child, in order to fill them up with hugs and attention. Mrs. Moore felt as if the balloon of tension that had been building up all afternoon was suddenly deflated. She wondered how a single parent would ever make it through a day without the relief of the other parent to divert and balance the tensions in older children.

Being a single parent is one of the most difficult jobs I know of. The feelings of being isolated, of being at the mercy of one's children, and of having no other adult to balance the tensions and the demands can be overwhelming. I respect single parents tremendously. Raising a child or children alone is an entirely different order of responsibility.

Louis seemed to be more responsive after a feeding. At as early as three weeks of age, his face brightened when the children talked softly to him. When his mother talked to him, he often seemed less contented. He would mouth his fist, or squirm, or fuss at her voice.

Perhaps a mother's voice is too much a part of the feeding situation to engender a contented response. It is surprising how early these associations are made, remembered, and manifested in infants.

Mr. Moore could produce the most prolonged period of responsiveness. Louis often tried so hard to focus on his father's face, or toward the sound of his father's voice, that his eyes crossed. He shivered with a wracking shudder or began to hiccough with the effort. All of these antics pleased the children, and Mr. Moore felt a tremendous closeness to his baby.

The children found that Louis could be picked up by his hand grasp. He grasped a finger with his whole fist and clung tightly as they pulled him to a sitting position. When they dropped him back, he startled and flung out his arms, crying. When they turned his head, he assumed a definite position of "fencing," a "tonic neck" pattern (see Chapter II). The children loved to see him walk as his father stood him to perform. He picked up each foot in a slow cycling walk as he was propelled across the bed.

Nevertheless, several things bothered Mrs. Moore about Louis. She did not remember that they had occurred with her older children. He had a triangular pink area on his forehead between his eyes, which blushed when he cried or was hot. This area became quite red at times, but grew pale at others. He had a similar area at the back of his neck. Mrs. Moore was afraid that they were birthmarks.

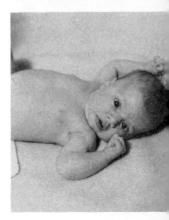

These areas are called "stork bites" and will disappear in time. They are areas in which there is a collection of tiny capillary blood vessels close to the surface, showing through the transparent skin at this age.

As a baby grows older and his skin becomes thicker, these areas are no longer apparent. Many babies have them at the nape of the neck; others have them along the midline of the scalp. They disappear in the first two years. A few very blond adults still show them when they are angry or flushed with heat. There is also a vein, which crosses the bridge of the nose, that can be seen as a blue area when an infant is flushed or straining. Mothers commonly mistake this bluish discoloration for a birthmark. It, too, will no longer be visible when his skin becomes less transparent.

Louis' right eye drained tears constantly. When he cried, the tearing increased. The eye seemed to have a film over it most of the time. Very often there were what appeared to be creases over the blue part of the eye. These creases moved around but they looked to his mother as if the lens of the eye were defective. She also noticed that when specks of dust or eyelashes settled in his eye he didn't blink them away. In his left eye none of this happened.

These are signs of a blocked tearduct in the right eye. The tearduct carries tears from the eye into the nose. This either may not be open at birth or may be irritated by the silver nitrate instilled in the baby's eyes in the delivery room. The blocked tearduct does not function to clear the tears, which wash the eye. Since the tears cannot drain properly into the nose, they remain stagnant in the eye or drain down the infant's cheek. They cannot wash away the mucus that forms as a reaction to dust or lashes. It is the mucus that gives the appearance of creases over the eyeball.

Mrs. Moore was told to wash Louis' eye with sterile water when it looked irritated. She was assured that this condition could in no way hurt Louis' eye and that, if necessary, the duct could be probed open later in a very simple procedure. She was told to press and massage over the tearduct in order to help open the duct into the nose. She gathered her courage each morning, pressed hard over his tearduct despite Louis' protests. By the end of the week, she realized that his eye no longer teared except when he cried, and his eye remained clear during the day. She had opened the tearduct by her massage.

Louis' swollen breasts began to produce little droplets of a milky substance.

Many breast-fed babies have enlarged mammary glands from their mothers' hormones. Even boy babies can produce "witches' milk" from these functioning breasts. Since this engorgement makes them somewhat more sensitive to damage or infection, Mrs. Moore was told to call the doctor should the breasts become hot and inflamed.

At the end of his first month, Louis seemed to have settled down already. Mrs. Moore was amazed at how easy he now seemed. He had begun to sleep more at night. The four-hour stretches between feedings were regular during the day, and at night he slept five or six hours after his mother wakened him for the ten P.M. feeding. The sleep periods seemed more defined and he slept more deeply. Aside from the regular evening fussy period, he lay quietly on his back much of the day, alert and listening. He fussed when he was ready for the daytime naps and went to sleep when he was turned onto his stomach.

QUIET BABY

Laura and her mother came home to an eager father, and a grandmother who had just arrived to help. Although Mrs. King's mother had had two children of her own, she had not had any recent experience and was prepared to help with the housework, but to stay away from the baby's care.

Mr. King expressed his longing to get them home and to become a family. He shyly voiced his desire to hold the new baby in his arms. Since he had seen her mostly in the nursery or in her mother's arms, he hardly felt like her father yet. He had not expressed his own concerns about the baby to anyone. He had noted that she was always sleeping when he went to look at her through the nursery window. The other babies appeared to be more active, and he magnified the reports he got from his wife about how quiet and difficult to feed she was. He woke at night twice with dreams of holding her and finding she was incomplete. As he dreamed, he had broken out in a cold sweat. He wondered whether he would "act like" a father even though he didn't feel like one. He was eager to prove to himself and to his wife that he could assume his new role.

The efforts today of most hospital staffs to include fathers in adjusting to the new baby are certainly encouraging. Since I first wrote this book, they have changed dramatically. But the job of adjusting to the new baby is still seen to be that of the mother, not that of the whole family. A father who cares is likely to have been through a turmoil similar to that of his wife in pregnancy as he adjusts to wanting to become a parent. He may long to "make it" with this baby.

Since this is a period when support from the hospital staff will strengthen these inclinations in him, it is timely that we are doing more and more to encourage fathers' participation.

He really saw Laura for the first time when the nurse undressed her to put her in her "going home" clothes. He was amazed at her perfect little pudgy body. Her peeling skin and her disappearing jaundice were missed by his inexperienced eyes. What he did see were her legs and arms, moving slowly and smoothly—in what seemed to him magic perfection. As she was undressed and handled by the nurse, she began to rouse. She came slowly to a wide-eyed state. Her eyes looked around the room, appearing to focus on objects. He hung over her in open admiration, hardly daring to touch her.

When she was dressed in her fussy pink clothes and ready to go, the nurse picked her up to take her to the car. Mr. King felt jealous that he could not carry her. He realized suddenly that he'd almost forgotten about his wife for the first time in months. He looked around guiltily and found she needed a supporting arm to help her down the hall to the elevator. He realized that she was anxious about this next step. Squaring his shoulders to help her, he assumed his new role.

Mrs. King's mother was waiting at the car. She had left her husband and her job at home to come to help. She felt torn between wanting to be there for her daughter but needing to be at home. When she arrived, she had found a cluttered mess of an apartment. She spent a day cleaning it, washing stacks of dishes, sorting out baby things, and buying the necessary equipment from a list that the hospital gave Mrs. King. As she talked to her son-in-law, she realized how tense he was, and she began to feel that she would be of real help. Now she rushed to her daughter in the corridor to welcome her.

Mrs. King stiffened and barely allowed herself to be patted. She had been weeping on and off for the past two days, often unaccountably. (We have seen that such moods are not unique to Mrs. King during this period.) She felt that if she could make it home without actually sobbing, she would be all right. She looked with longing at the nurse carrying the baby and wished she could take this competent girl who was a symbol of hospital protection home with her. She felt confused and helpless. She contrasted the nurse's competence with her own confusion and her heart sank.

When they finally reached the car, everyone helped her in and the nurse handed her the baby. She felt as if Laura were some strange baby and wondered vaguely whether she might drop her. Her husband climbed in beside her, thanking the nurse profusely. Her mother began to chatter to fill the tense silence.

Laura slept peacefully. She had closed her eyes as her clothes were put on, and she appeared to sleep ever since. She seemed not to notice her mother's awkward way of holding her. As her grandmother chattered away, Laura's eyes fluttered from time to time and her respiration changed pace. Now and then, a slight shudder would run over her body as she slept. When her mother clutched her more closely, Laura startled slightly but then cuddled down into the blankets.

During the drive home, each adult was beginning his or her adjustment to a new role. It seems important to point out the attempts each of these three were making to handle their feelings in this adjustment. After what seemed an interminable trip to the three adults, Mrs. King's mother jumped out of the car to take Laura. As she took the baby upstairs, Mr. King helped his wife out and up the stairs to the apartment. Mrs. King felt jealous of her mother carrying the baby. As her mother calmly handled Laura and took off the baby's outside clothes, Mrs. King felt herself resenting her mother as though she were interfering.

This is a common reaction in new mothers and is most often aimed at their own mothers or a competent nurse. Obviously it reflects the mother's yearning to be as easy and competent with her infant as the others.

Laura opened her eyes and fixed on her grandmother's face with her brightening gaze. Mr. and Mrs. King both stood still and watched this scene, each feeling as if he or she would like to interrupt it. Laura and her grandmother communicated for many minutes before Mrs. King broke into it. She took Laura from her mother and hurried her into their bedroom to feed her, in an effort to have her to herself. Her mother felt she had made an error, but couldn't quite understand what it had been. Mr. King felt flabbergasted by all this emotion on the part of his wife.

Laura began to fuss, to stiffen, and to root around at her mother's breast. She seemed to sense her mother's tension and actively began to demand a feeding. As her mother put her on the changing table to clean her before the feeding, Laura let out a wail. Mrs. King had never heard her cry like this before and was stunned into helplessness. Mr. King and his mother-in-law rushed in to see what had happened. Both of them fussed around the baby and tried to quiet her. Finally, Mrs. King sat down heavily, unzipped her dress, and put Laura to her breast. Laura quieted and began to suck immediately. She and her parents relaxed as her effective sucking continued. Even her grandmother had a chance to remember her earlier resolve to stay out of the baby-care situation, and she crept out to the living room. As Laura continued to feed, Mrs. King began to feel strength returning to her and she looked down at Laura gratefully. Laura had pulled them all together.

The tension and drama in the King household may seem exaggerated, but they are not. Most families go through some equivalent of this upheaval. Some turmoil is inevitable as everyone's energies are reorganized toward a new goal—that of being a family.

After the feeding, Laura's father asked whether he might change her, and Mrs. King went to bed.

This is an important time for a nursing mother to rest. Her milk may have come in, but just barely, and the balance is tenuous at best. Too much activity is certainly one of the things that will tip this balance away from adequate milk production. My experience has been that a large part of the early days spent with "feet up" may make the difference between success and failure in breast-feeding. Therefore it behooves a mother to allow the grandparent, husband, or sitter to help whenever possible and not waste precious resources worrying or trying to do everything herself.

Her father was easy with her. He handled her so gently that Laura virtually slept through her diaper changing. When she was clean and dry, he wrapped her up again in the same receiving blanket in which she had come home and put her on her side to sleep, "just like they did in the hospital."

This position on the right side after feedings is used on the assumption that milk may then pass more easily and quickly, by gravity, out of the stomach into the intestinal tract. Actually this probably makes very little, if any, difference, for the stomach is very effective in emptying itself without gravity. In the hospital, the nurses leave infants in this position until they clean and change them for the next feeding. At this time, they are turned to lie on their left sides. In this way, a head nurse can tell which babies have been attended to before they are sent out to their mothers. The positions have no significance for home use. Most babies are too active to stay on their sides anyway unless they are kept as swaddled as they are in nurseries. I do not recommend this kind of swaddling for babies over the long run—for I feel that their free activity is an important aspect of their development.

Laura slept for four hours without stirring while Mr. and Mrs. King waited eagerly for her to awaken. They wanted to get started in their new jobs, and they wanted to play with Laura. Finally Mr. King wakened her timidly. Mrs. King was even more nervous about it and admitted that she was afraid Laura might not be "all right." Mr. King had no doubts about Laura so he pooh-poohed his wife. When Laura finally roused and became alert, Mrs. King's anxiety subsided but it was obvious that she still equated this baby's quiet pace with "something wrong."

This is a common fear for a mother to have. Any deviation from what she has imagined her baby will be revives her old fears of "something wrong."

Laura's quietness continues to be a drain on Mrs. King, although she might well have found something to be fearful about even if Laura had been entirely different. Mr. King sees this quietness for what it is, a gentle personality who looks and listens rather than using activity as a communication system. This kind of person is not necessarily linked to being female, but it probably is easier for a parent, especially a male parent, to accept these attributes in a girl baby. We are loaded with unconscious and well-indoctrinated expectations for sex-linked differences; it is hard for a mother or father not to press a girl to be quiet and gentle and a boy to be active and aggressive. Insofar as possible, it is infinitely preferable to look for and respect the individuality of the child rather than building on our expectations. I hope the women's movement has started us on such a quest—to respect the individual strengths of each baby, regardless of sexuality. In this way, we are more likely to pass on to children an appreciation of themselves as worthwhile individuals and to prepare them for the struggles for equality in our society.

Laura's diapers were changed by her mother this time. As she changed her awkwardly, Laura began to squirm, stiffen, and push out her legs, her whole body changing color. Laura passed a soft, green bowel movement, and her straining subsided. Mrs. King looked with horror at the grass-green bowel movement and turned to the phone to call her doctor. Mrs. King's mother reached to the changing table to put a hand on Laura, whom Mrs. King had deserted. She said, "Mary, hadn't you better wait a while and see whether Laura is really ill? I hear from my friends that breast babies have very odd bowel movements." Mrs. King was vaguely irritated by her mother's calmness but also reassured. She resumed her cleaning of the baby. Two more forceful squirts of green and yellow liquid from Laura upset her temporarily, but she remembered her mother's quiet assurance that "there was time."

Many newborns have green or yellow loose movements in the first few days after the black meconium has passed. These loose, often mucous, stools are called "transitional" and do not last beyond the fifth day in formula-fed infants. However, breast-fed babies may continue to have loose and green bowel movements all along. Since breast milk is laxative but is also so perfectly digestible by the baby, I rarely worry about the number, color, or consistency of breast babies' stools.

Laura became more alert than she had been before. She fixed her eyes intently on her mother's face. She kicked with her legs and airplaned slowly with her arms as she was undressed. One or two slight startles interrupted her cycling arms, but her pace was markedly slow in comparison to what we saw in Louis. Laura had a doughy feeling to her fat little body when she was held. She blended into one's arms as if she were molding herself to the cracks and crevasses. She assumed what mold there was and forced very little change in holding position from the parent who held her. Mrs. King asked her mother whether she felt that Laura was really all right. Her question carried so much anxiety and dependency that the grandmother at last felt her presence was justified.

One of a grandmother's main assets in such a situation is to be ready to shore up her daughter at each turn. An inexperienced mother who cares about doing a good job with her baby needs this kind of "sounding board" from an old hand.

Mr. King called to them from the other room. He had been trying to find his pipe, which his mother-in-law had carefully put away. As he called, Laura's eyes widened, her face brightened, and her cycling activity ceased. She turned her head in the direction of his call.

In the next four-hour interval before Laura was awakened for her feeding, tension began to grow again. Mr. King found many more things out of their usual places, and, since he was a young man of habit, it got on his nerves that his mother-in-law had felt it necessary to intrude her neatness into his way of life. He felt it as a personal criticism. Mrs. King felt her own tension mounting as she realized that her homecoming was in no way what she'd expected. In place of her anxiety about her ability to take care of Laura, she began to feel an emptiness, a sense that Laura didn't make enough demands on her.

The grandmother wished that she could do more to help the two young people. She, too, felt Laura's lack of demands and wished that the baby might wake up sooner and show herself more of a helpless infant. This smooth pattern of sleeping and eating was just too easy and left very little for her as the "sore thumb" to do. She tried to fill up the silence by chatting about the difficulties they might have encountered and how lucky they were to have such a good baby. She caught herself giving advice in spite of having promised herself to stay in the background.

Laura's easy cycle continued for the next few days. She had to be wakened for most feedings during the day, but she roused herself at night. She ate well, sucking efficiently for twenty minutes on each breast. She bubbled with some difficulty and often had no bubble at all.

Breast-fed babies are often so efficient that they do not gulp down any air with their feedings.

After she was put down again, she occasionally spat up. On one occasion, after she spat up "the whole feeding," Mrs. King broke down. Mr. King attempted to measure the vomitus. He realized it was not over a half ounce although it covered a four-inch diameter. His wife's overreaction puzzled him before he realized that she took any deviation on the part of the baby as frightening. Laura often hiccoughed about the time a bubble was due, and this, too, disturbed her mother.

It must be obvious to the reader that Mrs. King is unnecessarily anxious about Laura. How could we help her so that she doesn't give this baby a feeling of being a "failure" or of being deviant? She needs a chance to ventilate her fears of having damaged this baby. Whether they are based on reality or not, they are common ones in new, inexperienced parents. In addition, it would help her to share some of her fears about Laura's personality with a professional who could show her that it lies within the spectrum of normal, healthy personalities. Alexander Thomas and Stella Chess instituted a longitudinal study of such temperamental differences as these in the 1950s. Laura fits a prototype of theirs—a watchful, quiet, sensitive, slow-to-act kind of person. Laura's behavior is not abnormal, and she won't become a deviant person, unless her parents see her that way and reinforce her to become more deviant.

Hiccoughs are set off by bubbles returning and are perfectly normal. They rarely bother a baby, but can be stopped by putting the baby back to suck or offering a bottle of water.

Other than these few deviations, Laura was easy. Mrs. King began to feel more confident about her mothering. She put Laura to bed in the times between each feeding and rarely felt inclined to play

with her. She stayed in bed a lot, read a good deal, watched TV in
the living room, and argued with her husband and mother. She did
not feel at all challenged by Laura. She began to wish that her
mother would go home and her husband would go back to work. She
could not get herself mobilized to do any housework or anything
constructive. She called all her friends to come and see Laura,
although this was against her doctor's wishes. He had warned her
about the danger of visitors—wearing herself out as well as exposing
the baby to infection. But she was bored and not a little depressed.

Mrs. King is going through postpartum blues—common to many
women. Without realizing it, they are bored, depressed, angry, and
jealous of those around them. All of this is the psychological counter-
part of the physiological recovery period in which a woman's body is
reorganizing itself after delivery.

Her mother sensed this brewing discontent and could see that Laura
was becoming quieter, rather than more active. She sensed that this
might be due partly to the lack of stimulation between feedings.
Both young parents tended to leave any overture for attention to
Laura, who seemed not to make such gestures. With trepidation, she
decided to suggest a more active approach to her daughter. She
wished that she could be certain she was right in feeling that this
baby should be played with more than she was. She remembered
that with her own babies, she had been so relieved to get rid of them
that when they slept, she never wakened them. But she also remembered that they wakened and demanded attention for themselves.
Laura was perhaps too good.

She discussed this with the parents. Both of them reacted at first
as they did to any of her suggestions—with a certain amount of
defensiveness and irritation at her intervention. Nevertheless, each
one latched on to the idea of playing with Laura. Mr. King had been
longing to, but had often been put off by his wife's protectiveness.
Mrs. King was relieved to be urged to do more with the baby and
by now was ready to make a few mistakes.

Mr. King played with Laura often. As he would pick her up, he
would feel her body tense and put her back down. If he pulled her
up by her arms to sit, her head would flop backward, then forward
as she came to a sitting position. He was sure that her head would

snap off in one of these flops. His mother-in-law urged him to put one hand behind her head as he handled her. Until he got her nested in his arms, he did not feel that she was safe. At first the worry Mr. King felt as he played with this relaxed baby made it difficult for him to enjoy her completely. But his steps were in the right direction, and he persisted.

Mrs. King was becoming more and more accustomed to handling Laura. The umbilical cord had finally dropped off in her crib. She cleaned the stump with alcohol several times a day as she'd been told by her doctor. Then she was ready to try the next and one of the biggest steps—a bath.

She tried to remember all the advice she'd heard at the Red Cross course. None of it came back. She could remember such admonitions as "Don't let her slip out of your arms" and "Support her head at all times." But she had forgotten the simple-sounding tricks they had passed on to her to make these possible. She gathered all the necessary articles for the bath, including her mother and husband. She gathered up Laura. Laura seemed even more floppy than she had before. She seemed to be made of disjointed rubber arms, legs, and a head attached only by a wire spring. Everything seemed to fly in separate directions. As she undressed Laura for the bath, which she'd felt for temperature with her elbow, she looked at Laura as if she had never seen her before. Laura's arms and legs turned a mottled color as she was undressed. Her skin was dry and scaling, her lips peeling, and a blister was forming on her upper lip from sucking.

This is common in babies who are working at their sucking and it does not bother them. Vaseline will protect it.

Her head seemed particularly lumpy and the soft spot larger and more vulnerable than ever.

A baby is not very vulnerable to injury via this fontanelle. It has allowed for molding in delivery, and now it serves as a protection so that the skull can let the brain enlarge more rapidly than the bones can grow. Actually, it acts as a cushion and allows the many bones of the skull to give with a blow to the head. Since our adult skull is inflexible, a blow cannot be cushioned and our brain must bounce off the skull. Because of this, we will suffer a concussion more easily from

*a head injury than will a baby. The anterior fontanelle or "soft spot"
does not close until eighteen months, when the period of rapid brain
growth is over. By this time, the toddler is less likely to fall on her
head. But she has needed this cushion effect many times during this
first year and a half.*

*The pulsations that one can see in the soft spot reflect the beating
of the baby's heart and the blood flowing through her body. When
she is active or has a fever—either of which events increase her heart
beat—the pulsing becomes more rapid. Although this pulsation
makes the soft spot seem even more vulnerable, the blood vessels are
not near enough to the surface to be easily damaged by any ordinary
blow. Certainly mothers need not fear to wash or scrub over the soft
spot. Nor will a sibling hurt the baby with the usual sort of pokes and
pushes. The size of the fontanelle can vary in all directions. Unless
it is bulging outward, its size and shape may be assumed to be normal.*

As her mother held her, Laura's chin quivered and she shivered,
yawned, and sneezed—all in rapid succession. Mrs. King was so
unnerved that she quickly put her back on the changing table and
covered her. Laura's eyes had been wandering around sleepily
through all this. As she was covered, she seemed to waken and looked
around. She looked at her mother, stared at her face, as if to say,
"Have courage, I'm all right." Mrs. King pulled herself together,
retested the bath water, which had now turned cold, and ran in more
warm water.

As she placed her in the tub, she felt Laura's body slip out of her
hands. Laura hit the bottom of the bathinette with a splash of water

that covered her face and head. Mrs. King paled. She managed to hold on to Laura's head to keep it out of the water. Laura became more active in the bathinette, squirming and kicking as her mother tried to soap her legs and arms. The soapier she was, the more active she became. Soon Mr. King was holding her head, Mrs. King her legs, and Mrs. King's mother her body. Laura seemed to enjoy all this handling by the three adults. They seemed to enjoy it less.

The bath finished, all three adults lifted her in unison onto the changing table. By then, her body was a purplish pink. Her arms and legs were shivering and jittery as she was dropped back onto the table. Mrs. King thought she was convulsing and was sure they'd given her pneumonia. As they dried her rapidly, her pink color returned and her jittery movements ceased. When Laura was dressed and back in her crib, Mrs. King fell in a heap on her bed, exhausted. Mr. King poured himself a drink; his mother-in-law joined him.

Laura stared around the room with a wise, wide-eyed look in her eye, caught a ray of light from the window, and stared at it for a long time. As her parents talked, she turned her head to the sound and seemed completely at peace.

Feedings were Mrs. King's main contact with Laura. At first they went easily and well. Mrs. King seemed to have a lot of milk, and she felt confident that Laura was getting enough. After the first two weeks, Laura began to take only five minutes of sucking on each breast, then turned away as if she were full. She sucked her fingers more and more after each feeding. Mrs. King noticed that when Laura started sucking, she made choking, gasping noises. After the struggle of the first few minutes, she would bring up enormous loud bubbles. Spit-up milk followed the bubbles, and she would often hiccough after them for ten or fifteen minutes.

Laura was being choked with too much milk and was having to drink it too fast. A nursing mother can remedy this by gently expressing the first streams from her breasts until her milk is just dripping. Then the baby does not have to struggle to swallow it. Noisy gulps contain air with each mouthful and contribute to a bubble in the stomach that will come up, bringing milk with it.

After using this method of manual expression, Mrs. King found that

Laura could drink more easily and comfortably. The sucking became more gratifying to her, and she was able to suck for longer periods. She seemed more contented with the whole process.

A baby who continues to spit up after feedings can be propped at a thirty-degree angle for thirty minutes after feedings before she is bubbled. This gives the milk a chance to settle by gravity and the ingested air time to rise to the top of the stomach. When a baby is bubbled after this period, the milk stays down, the bubble comes up without it, and hiccoughs often decrease.

Laura was not a crybaby. She fussed for brief periods about three times a day. Two of these were usually at the time she was trying to have her daily bowel movements. At that time, she strained, pushed, changed color, and acted as if she were in agony. Mrs. King called her doctor to see whether she should use a suppository when she began to do this, and she described Laura as constipated. He assured her that it was almost impossible for a breast-fed baby to be constipated. Since Laura's stools were liquid, this was not an accurate appraisal. He predicted that as Laura grew used to the gripping that preceded her bowel movements she would stop this fussing behavior.

I have never seen a constipated breast-fed baby. Many breast-fed babies strain this way with each stool, and there seems to be nothing that needs to be done to relieve this. As is the case with many of the discomforts of infancy, they "outgrow it." This is an instance in which it seems to me that infants show us two things: (1) the line between discomfort and pain is a fine one for them, and (2) as they get older, they either become used to the discomfort of an imminent bowel movement, or their maturing intestinal tract no longer registers it as painful.

Stool color is a source of concern to caretakers of babies. The green often seen in them is due to bile from the upper part of the gastrointestinal tract. As it passes through the lower tract, it changes to yellow, orange, and then brown. Greenish-black is also undigested bile. The color, then, reflects the speed with which it comes along this pathway.

Fluid is absorbed from the stool in the large intestine, or colon, and hence a liquid movement also means a rapid movement through it.

A loose, wet, green movement simply implies this rapid transit. Breast milk commonly is laxative in its action on the infant's intestinal tract. Sugars are laxative. New solids are also responsible for loose, greenish stools until the digestive system becomes accustomed to them. Infection and gastrointestinal allergy are the two pathologic conditions to be concerned with. When the stools are frequent (that is, five or more, except for breast-fed babies) and are wet, foul-smelling, and green, it is time to consult your physician. Mucus and blood are further signs of irritation. Blood turns black as it is digested and is a reddish-black when it comes from high up in the intestine. A greenish-black is less significant. With these guidelines in mind, one can distinguish between important and unimportant intestinal upsets. Mild diarrheas occur frequently—when they persist, they may be indicative of a more significant intolerance to some aspect of the diet. One need not worry as much about breast-fed babies—human milk is too easily digestible by the human infant.

These patterns began to stabilize more and more. By the time Laura was three weeks old, there was a definiteness to her and to her schedule that seemed eerily reliable. Laura could be predicted to be awake and ready to eat every four hours, day and night. Since her spitting up was settled, she ate and bubbled on schedule, then lay in her chair looking around and sucking her fingers with loud smacks. Her fussing continued to revolve around her bowel movements. Laura seemed so quiet and self-sufficient that she was rarely picked up or talked to by her inexperienced parents. They felt that she seemed "to know best" and left her in her crib or sitting in her chair a large part of her day. Her grandmother didn't entirely approve of this, but whenever she attempted to prod the young parents to play more with her, they bristled. She herself found it easier to leave Laura alone, too, since Mrs. King hung over her whenever she handled Laura, as if she were jealous. Indeed Mrs. King did feel jealous of any responses that could be drawn out of Laura, for they were rare. The grandmother returned to her own home at the end of the third week, feeling pangs of sadness at her inability to help the tension that was present in the household. This is often the result of a grandmother's attempt to help at such a tense, important time. Neither she nor the young parents needed to have felt guilty about her "inability to help." She had helped immensely by supporting them when they needed it and by being there to offer support and to be angry with. Probably the most important thing she did was to plant a seed for the future, that is, she suggested that the parents should play with Laura more and not leave the cues entirely to the baby. Her sensitivity to the situation in not pushing her ideas on Mrs. King was great, and she played her role beautifully.

The element of time, which gives the parents a chance to make their own adjustments and to mobilize themselves to mother and father a baby, is an important factor here. No third person can make their adjustments for them half as well as eventually they will themselves.

ACTIVE BABY

Mrs. Kay had begun to feel that she would never get out of the hospital. She had developed difficulty with her bladder function and had had to remain an extra day. She had planned to go home with Daniel on the fourth day. By the fifth day, his weight gain was good, and she had learned to master his feedings. He was spitting up less than he had in the first few feedings in the hospital, although he continued to spit a little after each bottle. His progress was deemed eminently satisfactory by the pediatrician.

She sat on her bed, dressed and ready after the ten o'clock feeding, waiting for her husband. He had promised to arrive at eleven with Mark, aged two, and the sitter. (The sitter had been with him since birth, during each day while Mrs. Kay worked.) By eleven, Mrs. Kay was pacing the floor. By 11:30, when her husband still hadn't arrived, she was upset. She telephoned home to see whether he had left. He answered the phone, saying they had been delayed but were starting right away. As she put the phone down, she threw herself across the bed. She felt lonely, forgotten, and unwanted. Why hadn't they been eagerly ready and waiting for her at the stroke of eleven?

This kind of sensitivity is a common symptom of the emotional instability characteristic of this "blue" period.

When her husband finally arrived, he left Mark and the sitter in the lobby. Sheepishly, he sidled into Mrs. Kay's room, expecting the outburst he received. He had little excuse for being late, except that he had overslept, and the sitter had kept Mark out of the house all morning.

Daniel was wheeled to his mother's room to be dressed for discharge. He was already screaming. He cried in loud, piercing wails, furiously kicking and thrusting his arms out. While he was being undressed, this activity rose to a new peak. Startles and Moros were interspersed in the fussing activity. The nurse held his arms down as she changed the diaper with one hand, and he responded to this restraint by quieting. She pointed out to Mrs. Kay that when a newborn is undressed and free, he can become upset.

As an example, many newborns seem to "hate" their baths, but in reality are reacting to this exposure and freedom from restraint.

The nurse showed Mrs. Kay that Daniel would start this cycle as soon as she freed his arms. On the other hand, when she held one arm tightly flexed at his shoulder, he quieted even though he was still undressed and free from any other restraint.

Daniel was finally dressed, the hospital bill paid, and the family on their way. Mrs. Kay found herself eager to see Mark again. Mr. Kay held Daniel, although the nurse objected.

In most places, the hospital rules state that a nurse must accompany the baby and discharge it to an appropriate person at the hospital door.

Mrs. Kay wanted to run down the hall to meet Mark, but she restrained herself. She felt tears welling up as she walked toward him. Mark heard her call him, but refused to move from the couch beside the sitter. He gazed intently at his mother as she came up to him, but he looked at her as if she were a stranger. Mrs. Kay felt panic rising as Mark seemed to ignore her. Mark's father pushed him to go to his mother and explained that maybe Mark was feeling a little left out. He had been deserted by his mother for nearly a week and might naturally turn away from her. Mrs. Kay gathered Mark into her arms. She asked him whether he wanted to see his new brother. Dutifully, he peeped at Daniel in the midst of all the

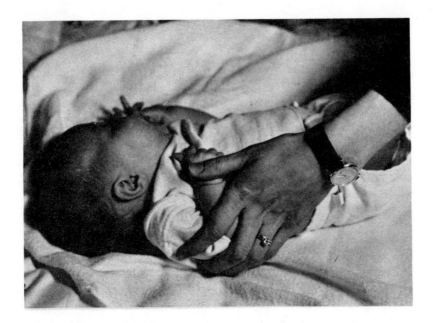

wrappings, but he returned quickly to hold his mother's hand.

Mrs. Kay began to recover at home. It was good to see the familiar furniture, the objets d'art she loved, and her books. They made her feel more composed as she looked around her. Her impulse was to get busy with household duties. But her doctor had urged her to rest, so she sat down in a comfortable chair. Mark came up to sit next to her, and Daniel was handed to her. She cuddled him in one arm, and Mark with the other. Her husband flopped in his chair across the room. The older woman busied herself in the kitchen, while the family became a unit again. Even though this peaceful scene lasted only fifteen minutes, it refueled Mrs. Kay and gave her a warm glow.

Daniel was not an easy baby. He continued to be extremely sensitive to the moods of those around him. When Mrs. Kay was tired or tense, she found Daniel impossibly fussy and jumpy. When she was rested and could sit down to feed him without something else on her mind, he responded with an easy feeding. His responsiveness made her blame herself when he was exceptionally fretful, and yet she did not feel capable of maintaining a strictly even temper. She thought of Daniel as some sort of retribution for Mark's placid and easy infancy.

Daniel was always active when he was awake. He slept only about twelve hours, the rest of the day being spent in active squirming, kicking, sucking on his fist or nightgown, and plain yelling.

Recent studies show that from their earliest days babies sleep as little as twelve hours a day. While their eyes may be shut for more than that, they are receiving and capable of responding to stimuli.

Daniel still seemed to jump from a deep sleep to a state of vibrant activity. At times his mother saw him draw his legs up onto his belly, turn red in the face, and finally expel large amounts of intestinal gas. Reminded of descriptions of colic she'd read, she added another worry to her list. Often Daniel held his breath when he was crying, long enough for his color to change from pink to dark purple.

Mrs. Kay called the doctor many times during these days, until she felt him getting as desperate with her calls as she was with herself. They tried a pacifier and swaddling, but Daniel continued to cry for long periods each day. They changed Daniel's formula a few times, but with no apparent effect.

Some babies are sensitive to the ingredients in a particular formula, for example, to one of the sugars, or even to cow's milk. These infants respond to a change in formula. Usually, however, crying as a symptom of intolerance to food is accompanied by other evidences of intestinal sensitivity, such as (1) forceful vomiting that increases over a period; (2) mucous, frequent, loose stools; and (3) if one persists in feeding them the sensitizing agent, a sensitivity rash, or "eczema."

Daniel accepted the pacifier at first, but soon spat it out in favor of his fist, which he was beginning to suck on for longer periods. Mrs. Kay uncovered his fists so that he could reach them more easily.

Fists are covered in newborn nurseries so that a baby can't scratch himself. The nails are not cut in the hospital for fear of causing an infection around the nail if it isn't cut properly. There is no reason to cover the infant's hands at home. Nails can be cut when he is quietly asleep.

As Daniel's intolerable crying persisted, Mr. and Mrs. Kay tried to analyze the reasons for it. They realized that he was an extremely sensitive baby who quickly reacted to any tension arising in the household. His makeup was that of a high-strung baby who could not easily calm himself. He was a greedy eater whose rapid feedings allowed him to gulp down a great deal of air. Also, as he cried, he seemed to "cry down" more air. Both of these habits left him full of gas. As he became active, this gas became mobilized and his intestines "gurgled" constantly. Together with the doctor they figured that Mrs. Kay could counteract some of this ingested gas by offering him sugar water every twenty to thirty minutes to help him burp.

She then found that as she picked him up to give him the sugar water, he calmed from his wild state to look around in alert interest. He remained quiet and watchful for a short while after burping, before he gradually built up his crying again. The fact that he could quiet and alert for even a little while was the clue she needed to reassure her that his crying (like Louis') did not mean that anything was seriously wrong. She saw the crying was inevitable and maybe even necessary; but she also knew that the interested periods would lengthen and the fussing shorten. Realizing this, she was able to let Daniel work out much of his fussing himself.

His total crying time began to decrease as her newly found resolve helped her handle him with more understanding and less anxiety. She found he had two patterns of crying in a day. On some days he cried for twenty- to thirty-minute periods four or five times a day after feedings and just before he went off to sleep. These periods seemed to represent his attempts to let off enough steam so that he could settle down. When she picked him up to calm him and feed him his sugar water after these twenty-minute intervals, he took it, bubbled, and dropped off to sleep. On other days, he had more prolonged periods of crying. For two or three interminable hours at a time, he could cry, squirm, turn red and purple, push and expel gas. She now knew there was nothing she could offer but the mechanical comfort of helping get up bubbles. In time Daniel shortened the crying time himself and seemed to eat and sleep better after his explosive bouts.

Mrs. Kay has avoided real colic—which can consist of this same screaming, thrashing, inconsolable activity accompanied by a parallel hyperactivity in the intestinal tract. Colic can build up to twelve or fourteen hours a day and can last solidly through the first three months. I am convinced that it often starts out with spells such as we have seen in Daniel. The infant susceptible to colic is an active, driving baby who is hypersensitive to the climate and stimuli around him. As his exasperating period of fussing creates tension in those around him, they overreact. They try too many ways to quiet him, feeling there must be a magic way or that there must be something wrong that they should correct. Often there are three generations at work on each other. The tension around the infant builds up, he reacts to it with more of his own, his intestinal tract begins to reflect his increased tension—and what starts out as a two-hour period of crying rapidly grows to four, eight, ten, twelve hours. His intestines are as hyperactive and hyperreactive as the rest of him to the increasing fatigue and breakdown in the family. This pattern becomes a vicious circle, and we call it "colic."

Mrs. Kay felt like a new person after her increased understanding of Daniel's fussing. He was an exciting baby in many other ways. When he was awake and not fussing, he remained alert for long periods, watching everything around him. She put him in a semi-sitting position in his infant chair and carried him around the house with her and Mark. He could turn his head to look at Mark and seemed to watch him from whatever the distance. Although his eyes could not change focus easily, nor could he move his eyes to follow a rapidly moving object, he could maintain an alert interest in his brother for ten or fifteen minutes at a time. Then his eyes would cross, he would begin to be restless and soon cry. Before he disintegrated into hard crying, he could be placed on his belly in bed. This position helped him gain control over the startling that still accompanied his crying. He often went off to sleep for a brief nap in this position and awakened refreshed, ready for more active participation in his world.

Daniel's motor activity was as intense as his looking and listening. He could lie on his back for long periods, cycling with his arms and kicking hard with his legs. He turned himself from his back to his stomach in these first three weeks. On his belly, he pushed and pulled his legs so hard that he virtually swam like a frog. Meanwhile, he could raise his head up from the bed, turn it from side to side, and he often brought his fist to his mouth. As he sucked noisily, his whole body tensed, and he changed color with this activity. His face

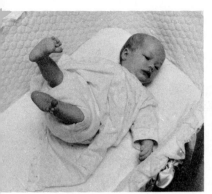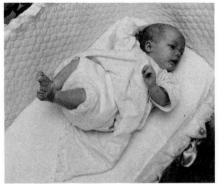

was intent, and he seemed to invest a lot of energy in it. His sucking lasted for ten or fifteen minutes before he lost his fist and other more random activity took over.

Mrs. Kay had noted that Daniel fussed about any change in his intestinal tract. He fussed just before he spat up, he cried before he had a bowel movement, and his mother thought he strained and fussed before he urinated. As his circumcision healed (with Vaseline applications every time he was changed), this straining and fussing associated with urinating eased. Occasionally Daniel shuddered just as he began to urinate. Daniel's bowel movements were loose and expulsive. They smelled more strangely than Mrs. Kay remembered Mark's bowel movements had.

These may be normal since many prepared formulas cause loose stools. One can cut down on the sugar in the formula to make them less loose. Mucus may be present in early stools but should not recur too often without a consultation with the doctor. Four to six stools a day are not unusual, and they certainly can be smelly on formula. The straining and complaining about movements and urine was just another sign of Daniel's sensitivity to any stimulus.

Daniel's cord stump remained solidly in place for three weeks after he came home.

Unless there is a foul odor or inflammation around the cord stump, there is nothing dangerous about the cord's remaining in place. The dye disinfectant with which it is painted in the hospital is to kill the bacteria that could infect the cord. The dye works so efficiently that it eradicates normal bacteria that would cause the cord stump to degenerate and fall off more quickly.

Mrs. Kay continued to wipe around it every day with alcohol and only sponge-bathed the rest of his body. Washing upset Daniel and he thrashed furiously. Characteristically, he overreacted to exposure as he did to other stimuli. When Mrs. Kay restrained his arms by wrapping them in a diaper, he would calm down. She did the same with his legs when sponging the upper part of his body.

Daniel continued to gather steam. He ate ravenously, taking five to six ounces at a feeding in fifteen minutes. His mother was conscious of the importance to him of the sucking time spent with each bottle.

These intense babies may need crutches such as sucking more than babies who develop resources of serenity for themselves.

Mr. Kay had to buy blind nipples and puncture them with a hot needle stuck in the end of a cork, in order to make them small enough so that he would suck at least twenty minutes with each feeding. When he gulped his bottle down, he invariably spat some up. During his fussy periods, he often vomited several mouthfuls of the last feeding. Despite this, he gained well and seemed rosy and healthy. His mother tried to feed him on a schedule, but he woke so irregularly and required such different amounts that she soon found a modified demand schedule was better. When she tried to feed him and he wasn't ready, he either took very little or was almost impossible to feed, and then woke early for the next feeding. If she let him show her he was ready—by restless motion, mouthing his fist, and finally by screaming and searching for the nipple—he ate well and was satisfied. He asked for feedings every two and one half or three hours in the daytime, but he stretched out to four or five hours at night.

Mr. Kay took Daniel over at the end of the day. He loved to play with this sturdy, reactive little boy. Every time he picked him up, Daniel would tighten up all over, his head would come up, his eyes would open and his face would brighten. He looked as if he loved every bit of handling. By three weeks, he would look quietly alert when he heard his father's voice, as if he expected to be played with. When his father failed to come to him, he let out a fussy cry as if to say, "You've forgotten me!" Mr. Kay loved his responsiveness, so he spent most of the evening bouncing Daniel or rocking him up and down. Mrs. Kay insisted that this was why Daniel had to cry and fall apart at the end of each day.

Perhaps it contributed in part to his disintegration, but a baby like Daniel would have a fussy period no matter what. His father's learning how to play and excite him is pure gold for Daniel's future. They will know and adore each other from now on.

We have found that by four weeks of age a baby can show by his behavior that he is recognizing and distinguishing his mother and father by face and voice from other people around him. Daniel is already showing clearly how attached he is to his father.

The three weeks since leaving the hospital had been long and exhausting. The parents looked back with some yearning to the corresponding weeks of Mark's life. On the other hand, some of that calm had been due to Mrs. Kay's virtually turning him over to her kind, elderly sitter. She was less frightened with her second child and determined not to miss the opportunity of mothering him. Her relief at having the more experienced woman take care of Mark had, she realized, been mixed with a certain amount of resentment. Mrs. Kay was honest as well as intelligent. She had, after all, dealt successfully with Daniel's difficult feeding situation in the hospital, had worked out a modus vivendi for the excessive crying—had done this, furthermore, with an admirable objectivity at a time when a woman's physical and emotional resources are pretty low. Reflection strengthened her resolve to carry on with this baby a little longer before she considered going back to work. Daniel was a demanding, driving baby, but his sensitivity could also be fascinating and produced highly rewarding responses.

CHAPTER IV

The Second Month*

AVERAGE BABY

The second month was one of leveling off. Louis was part of the family now—not a new plaything. Mrs. Moore was beginning to feel like a person again. Often she even felt rested and organized after a night's sleep or if Louis took a long nap. However, these moments were short-lived, indeed, for the rest of the family reminded her of her responsibilities to them. Whenever she sat down, one of the older children made some demand of her. Nevertheless, everyone was beginning to feel back to normal again. Mr. Moore could concentrate on his job again without feeling as if he should rush home to referee or pick up the pieces of his household. Five-year-old Martha continued to help her mother with the baby and enjoyed this role. She also continued to tease her three-year-old brother, Tom. She went to kindergarten each day with reluctance. She balked at being "away from everybody" and was openly jealous of Tom, who could stay at home with his mother and the baby.

Tom flourished while Martha was away—alternately showing off and teasing his mother for attention. He rarely left her side. When he did, Mrs. Moore found him in Louis' room lifting the baby out of his crib or poking him with a toy, as if he wanted to find out what would make him cry. Mrs. Moore reacted to his investigations as if he were attacking the baby. She screamed at Tom, who dropped the baby, and both began to cry. After she'd done it, she knew that this was not an ideal way to help Tom with his feelings about the new infant.

*Chapters are laid out to subsume the development expected over that period. Many of the developmental steps will not have occurred at the beginning of the month but will begin after the month has started.

Such interest as Tom shows in the baby is not all bad; these simple "assaults" can also be interpreted as investigations, an attempt to find out what makes the baby tick. The new infant does not become the object of an older child's jealousy until his mother is openly protective toward the baby. When she first comes home, the older child is depressed and upset at her having "deserted" him. The baby does not usually become the object of his anger until he realizes that she has deserted him for the baby. Also, when she shows him how upset his investigations make her, she focuses his attention on the new infant and shows him a way of "getting back at her." This sets up sibling rivalry as a way of involving and getting back at mother in one very simple act—attacking the new baby.

There is no question as to whether a mother should supervise an older child's investigations, but she can do this subtly. When she overreacts as we have seen above, the whole episode takes on a heightened value. The older sibling is more likely to repeat the sadistic part of his investigation. A child Tom's age cannot be allowed to play with an infant without supervision. It would frighten him too much if he really hurt the baby, and of course he might.

Mrs. Moore began to include Tom in her play with Louis. She showed him how to rattle a toy for the baby. She showed Tom that when he talked, Louis would stare and smile. Tom said, "I want him to play with me." She realized that Tom was expecting an equal, had not anticipated that a brother meant anything but a playmate. Now Tom began to call Louis "my baby."

Bursts of fury from Tom still appeared around nursing times. He thought up new, destructive methods for drawing his mother away from any peaceful feedings. Being equipped with a free hand since she was breast-feeding, she found ways of keeping Tom interested with this one hand. She found that she could draw a fire engine on his blackboard with her left hand. She could hold him next to her and read to him or feed him a cookie as the baby fed.

These crazy feedings made her wonder whether she should wean the baby. She felt that she would be freer to devote herself to Tom. She also felt that, since Tom was so jealous of these nursing periods, he might be better off if she were bottle-feeding Louis. She even wondered whether poor Louis, too, might not be better off with a bottle propped up for him in a quiet room alone.

An older child will still feel left out no matter which method of feeding a mother uses. As long as she is involved with the baby, he is bound to feel "left out." However, this is a necessary part of his adjustment to the new situation, and avoiding it helps no one. Propping the bottle for a small baby and leaving him alone can seriously interfere with his chance for normal development. Propping a bottle is the surest way of depriving a baby of all of the accompanying warmth that a mother can add to the simple act of feeding. It is a "cold" way for an infant to experience such an important event in his day as feeding. It forces an infant to rely on his own resources at feeding time. This in turn is apt to prolong and intensify his attachment to his bottle, since he has had to turn to it as the sole source of gratification in his most important experience.

Learning to live with Tom was a large part of Louis' future. She realized that Tom's intrusions did not disturb Louis as much as they did her. The greatest asset to her in breast-feeding him was that she found herself at peace after nursing Louis. She felt that she had given Louis a real part of herself, had really communicated with him on his terms for a short time, and she did not have to feel guilty when she left him for the next few hours to tend to Tom and her other responsibilities. This became her most important reason for continuing the breast-feeding.

The feedings were increasingly pleasant. She gave him fifteen to twenty minutes on each breast, as this gave him a period for sucking in addition to what milk he needed.

Although an infant can get at least half of the necessary milk in the first five minutes, he will continue to suck for two reasons—nutrition and the pleasure he receives from the act of sucking.

When he was three weeks old, Louis began to suck his two middle fingers after breast-feedings. His mother worried about whether he was having enough sucking, for she had read that if an infant sucks his fingers, he is not getting all the sucking he needs.

This finger-sucking is very common among babies who are having a happy time at feedings and is not a reflection of inadequate mothering. The happiest babies often do the most sucking after feedings. It seems to be the baby's attempt to reproduce the pleasant situation for himself. The sucking seems to become a symbol of the pleasant situation and an infant soon learns to reproduce this important and gratifying aspect of feeding all by himself. When the finger-sucking is invested with the memory of the satisfying feeding, the contact with the mother, the gratification of the need for sucking, it can become very important to the baby.

She noticed that Louis returned to this finger-sucking even after the more peaceful, pleasant feedings, as if he were making up for losing her. She found herself jealous of this first evidence of his self-sufficiency, but she also felt impressed that he had such an ability to satisfy himself.

Louis was regular in his demands. He wanted his feedings at four-hour intervals. Mrs. Moore had been afraid that she might become engrossed with the other children and forget to feed him. Louis was not one to let this happen. At three and a half hours he began to stir, whimpering off and on, until he built up to real crying at four hours on the dot. By then, his strength and insistence could be heard everywhere in the house, and everyone responded. Mrs. Moore's breasts dripped milk, Tom became cranky, and Martha ran to Louis to comfort him. Even Mr. Moore became grouchier at these times if he was home, and he found himself going to the ice box.

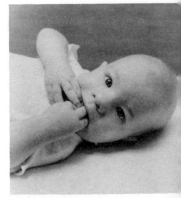

Feelings of competition with a nursing mother are common ones for fathers. Not only do they identify and compete with the baby but also with the mother's role in satisfying the baby.

Louis stretched out the time after his late evening feeding and by the fifth week was sleeping as much as seven hours each night. At seven weeks, he slept from ten-thirty until six in the morning. Mrs. Moore looked on these seven hours as a gift from the gods.

Babies will usually sleep through a night feeding when they are around eleven pounds. Some will do this earlier and some later. Solid foods may contribute to this, and certainly a conditioning push from the environment helps them sleep through the night.

Louis loved to stay awake after feedings. With his belly full, and his fingers in his mouth, he lay for a long while on the floor or propped in his chair. When Tom or Martha came up to him, he stopped to stare. The stare was accompanied by release of his fingers from his mouth. Open-mouthed and wide-eyed, he fixed on their faces and followed them with his eyes. He was already able to follow them several feet across the room.

Although studies on newborn vision indicate that a baby at this age does not have the visual capacity to follow a moving object six or eight feet away, Louis demonstrates that they are wrong. When the object is invested with the libido that his siblings have for him, he will use all of his capacity for vision, attention to cues of all kinds, head-turning, and concentration in order to keep them in sight. A testing object in a sterile laboratory setting is hardly likely to interest him in the same way—hence inaccurate test results.

When the others remained nearby, Louis gradually worked himself up to cycling activity with his hands and to a slow smile when they were particularly quiet and gentle in their approach to him. Martha learned quickly that if she was quiet, he responded for longer periods, and she was able to keep him responding to her for as much as twenty minutes at a time before he broke down with fatigue. Tom could not allow Martha and the baby to play with each other very often, and he broke into their play with noisy bouncing up and down or loud shouts.

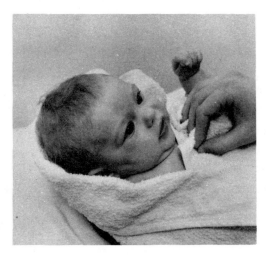 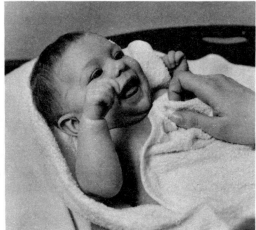

Second children seem to be as much disturbed when the older sibling turns to the new baby as they are when the mother does. This added desertion is the crowning blow.

When Louis was left alone in his crib or propped in the corner of a sofa, he could stay awake for as much as an hour and a half. He looked around the room, sucked on his fingers, and responded to many things. He watched the overhead light or the open window. He particularly liked to watch a fluttering curtain and the mobile of many-colored butterflies that his father constructed for him. When he heard a voice, he turned to it quickly. He seemed to recognize his mother's voice particularly, and even in a noisy crowded room, he would frown as he heard her speak and slowly turn in the direction from which her voice came. In spite of Louis' preference for his mother's voice, Mr. Moore could produce a smile more easily than she. He interpreted this as a preference for him and was secretly pleased.

Actually this is more likely to be based on the infant's early association of cues, which may amount to a kind of discrimination—father means play, but mother means business (feeding). All of the cues of the feeding, her voice, her smells, and even her presence have taken on heightened significance by this time. Just as a breast-fed infant will not take a bottle from his mother by now, because he smells her milk and associates her with a different kind of feeding, fathers tell me that they can succeed in feeding a bottle to their babies only when their wives are out of the room.

Martha and Tom had fun making Louis perform his infant acrobatics. Martha pulled him up to sit by each of his hands and was delighted by his attempts to hold up his wobbly head as he sat. He often smiled as she pulled him up, which so delighted her that she laughed and smiled back.

The positive reinforcement of the infant's smiles that comes from older children shows why second and third children are likely to be gayer than first children. Although parents are just as delighted with an infant's smiles, their reactions are not as free or spontaneous as are those of children. Here we have just one more instance of how much a baby gets from his siblings!

Tom gave the baby his fingers, and Louis hung with a strong grasp
to each of Tom's forefingers. Tom pulled him up to a sitting position
before Mrs. Moore stopped him. Louis' grasp had been strong
enough to support his body's weight in sitting.

*Mrs. Moore is right to protect Louis. As long as an infant is pulled
up slowly and steadily, the wobbling of his neck will not hurt him.
But when pulled up too abruptly, he can conceivably dislocate a
shoulder or an elbow. His head can also snap forward too abruptly
in the sitting position. I have never heard of an infant dislocating a
cervical vertebra in this fashion or even "hurting his spine" in any
way, but I have no doubt that it could happen. A child as young as
Tom might tire of this and drop the infant back on his head suddenly.
Again this probably would not hurt him much, but it would hurt his
mother if she saw it.*

When the children rolled him over on his abdomen, Louis immediately lifted his head like a turtle to look around at them. On his belly,
he made crawling movements with his legs, and Martha found that,
when she placed her hands against his feet, he pushed against her
hands and propelled himself forward, as if he were trying to crawl.

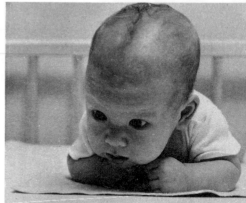

*This is an inborn crawling reflex and has little to do with an infant
being aware of propelling himself across a space. The latter is a
learned addition to the inborn reflex and will be added to it at a much
later date.*

His movements became smoother each day as they watched him play. Very soon there was little of the jerky, staccato quality in his quiet activity. But when he was upset or when he was hungry, his movements immediately reverted to the jumpy, jerky activity he had shown when he was younger. When Tom jumped across the room, screamed at Martha, or slammed a door down the hall, Louis' whole body startled. The Moro reflex, which he had demonstrated so frequently in the first weeks, returned out of the blue, and he threw out his arms, arched his back, and began to cry.

He still cried in regular periods every day. At the end of the day, he was likely to be fussy on and off for an hour or so. By the end of the second month, he was wide awake for as much as ten hours during the day. He could be amused by his brother and sister during his fussy periods, so that several days often went by without much fussing. Then there was usually a third or fourth day of almost constant crying, as if he were making up for the good days. During his fussy periods, his chin still quivered and his legs and arms trembled. When he cried Mrs. Moore would have liked to carry him or play with him to quiet him, but she couldn't devote this much time to him at the end of the day, when the rest of her family was also falling apart. Mrs. Moore found that, when he was left alone as he built up to loud wails, he could find ways of quieting himself—such as sucking on his fingers, turning on his side, or finding his mobile on which to fix his eyes. Sometimes one of the children would rock him or push him in the carriage, and this could quiet him. When he cried, his face rash became more prominent. Pimples came to the surface whenever he was hot, and they went away when he was not.

From four to ten weeks there is a rash on the face and neck that comes and goes spontaneously. It is thought to be associated with hormone changes as the infant loses his mother's hormones. The rash is a red, raised, scattered "acne-like" rash that consists of pimples with white centers. They are oil and sweat glands, which are beginning to function. As they do function, they discharge their white centers and disappear. But other pimples come out, and the rash characteristically changes from day to day. It is worse when a baby is kept too hot or has been crying. Oiling this rash will make it worse. Leaving it alone is usually the best treatment. It disappears spontaneously by eight or ten weeks, as the glands of the skin become more efficient.

It was a relief to everyone in the Moore household when his fussing began to change into sociability by the end of the second month. The change was almost imperceptible, and only in retrospect was it apparent to Louis' mother and father that this change began before the eighth week. Mr. and Mrs. Moore found they still waited tensely for his fussy periods each evening, even though Louis had given them up.

By the end of the second month, Louis weighed 11½ pounds and was 23½ inches long. He was a handsome, vital baby.

QUIET BABY

Laura continued her steady, independent course. She ate well, slept much of the time, was quiet when she was awake. There seemed little for a mother to complain of. However, both Mr. and Mrs. King wanted her to "wake up." They continued to feel that she was quieter than they wished. Mr. King rationalized this feeling by thinking that, because she was a girl, she just wasn't what he'd expected.

Even though society might find such quiet, watchful inactivity more appropriate to a girl than to a boy baby, it is not sex-determined. I have seen many little boys with this same makeup who are sturdily masculine as they develop. There are few clear sex differences at birth. The ones that have been reliably determined seem to be subtle and need reinforcing from the environment if they are to last. For example, boy babies do seem to be slightly more active and more vigorous in their motor activity. Girls do seem to be a bit more wide-eyed and watchful as newborns. If a girl baby watches you, she watches for a longer period. A boy will watch intensely but lose interest more quickly and tend to get involved in motor activity. These differences are subtle ones and do not necessarily pertain to all babies. The interesting thing to me is that society's expectations seem to have shaped them or to have been shaped by them. By the time the baby is older, these differences have been reinforced by parents' behavior. Mr. King would be very unlikely to pick Laura up to throw her into the air. If she were a boy baby, he probably would. Mrs. King would probably automatically be pushing a boy baby to get more actively responsive. Hence, Laura's quiet, watchful inactivity is probably being perpetuated by their expectations for her "as a girl." The danger in our society is that we value hard-driving, competitive behavior and underrate Laura's kind of low-keyed, highly sensitive approach. One could predict an artistic bent in Laura. But if she grows up feeling this sensitivity is devalued, it won't help her to seek its fulfillment.

Mrs. King blamed herself for Laura's inactivity. She felt depressed and weary a lot of the time. She thought that, because she didn't feel like playing with her, Laura wasn't making as much progress as she should. When she talked to her friends and heard that their babies were smiling or crying or demanding, she was envious. She felt guilty about this envy, but it didn't make her reach out for Laura. In fact, when she did, Laura's quiet, slow responses discouraged her, and she found herself avoiding play with Laura at times.

She needs someone to tell her that what she is feeling is not too uncommon. This is known as poor "feedback" from the infant to the mother. Since the mother instinctively expects a rewarding response from the infant, when she doesn't get it the cycle becomes an empty one. A quiet baby like Laura becomes less and less gratifying to a mother's competitive expectations. Unfortunately, the American mother's game of comparing her own baby with her friends' babies in order to keep up with them adds another hazard to this—a mother begins to question her own, and her baby's, adequacy.

This poor feedback is seen even more dramatically in damaged babies—those with neurological defects, deafness, or blindness. Babies with such handicaps will respond to mothering, but it takes extra stimulation from the mother to reach them. Unless a mother is properly geared to reach out for them over and over again, she may get discouraged, and the infant will stay locked in a shell. Once they are reached, the babies will gather steam, then the communication cycle will generate more and more reward for each participant.

Laura became more definite in many of her patterns. She preferred the left breast, and often fussed or cried when she was put to the right one. She sucked easily and steadily on the left. On the right, she ate for five minutes, then turned away as if she didn't enjoy it. Mrs. King found that she needed to empty her right breast more completely, for she became lopsidedly heavy on the right. She grew as determined as Laura was and put her on the right side first. When this didn't work well, she found other ways of making Laura perform on the right side. She could nurse her lying down and get her to take both breasts more easily. Sometimes when she held her in a more vertical position, Laura was willing to suck better at the right breast.

Some babies show such definite preferences. The preference for one breast may have to do with an inborn cerebral dominance or a strong preference for head position. In these infants, it usually reflects their wish to keep their heads to one side or the other. A baby who prefers the left breast probably prefers having her head to the right. She may already be showing a right-sided dominance, or it may simply reflect her position in the uterus, in which she became accustomed to having her head to the right. In the latter case, she will outgrow it.

This same preference for a head-to-right position persisted for Laura in her crib. She obviously preferred to keep her head turned to the right. She sucked her right fist and looked to the right out of her crib whenever she was in bed. Propped in her baby chair, she also kept her head turned to the right. By the sixth week, her skull was beginning to flatten at the back on the right, and her pediatrician intervened. He ascertained that there was no muscular or neurological reason—such as a shortened, tight muscle in the neck, or damage to the nerves in her neck—and he gave Mrs. King some suggestions. He pointed out that it was because Laura preferred her right side. He urged Mrs. King to turn the crib around so that Laura would have to look out to the left to see out into the room and to see who was approaching her crib. He suggested that they hang toys over her slightly to the left so she would have to turn her head to look at them. He also urged them to raise the mattress an inch or two on the right side so that gravity aided Laura in turning her head downhill to the left. In these ways, Mrs. King could prevent the flattening that might result if Laura was allowed to continue her constant head-right position.

A flatsided head is not attractive to see in a baby, and it can usually be prevented. A mother need not worry about permanent head flattening, however. A baby's head rounds out over the first year and a half as it grows. Later, when she sits up, the pressure on the flat side will be less constant and this will give the head a chance to round out.

Laura had an equally strong preference for a particular sleeping position. She preferred sleeping on her stomach and could stay awake on her back for the entire day unless she was turned over. She rarely fussed, and her preference for a sleep position became apparent only when she would not nap unless she was turned over onto her stomach.

Most infants do have a strong preference for a sleeping position and many of them show it at birth. Mothers often try to change this urge in their infants to sleep in a preferred position. They change the infant because they read that one position is not safe and another may hurt her legs or feet. Since the literature is full of advice about sleeping positions, I shall add to it. I feel that it is much more important to satisfy the infant's natural urge to repeat a comfortable pattern in sleep than to worry about some of the pros and cons that are presented for each sleep position.

Infants will not aspirate and choke on their backs unless they are sick. Nor will they bury themselves in their bedclothes when laid on their stomachs, unless a mother foolishly puts too many in the crib. (Heavy pajamas and sleeping bags preclude the necessity for many bedclothes.) The concern of orthopedic doctors about foot problems resulting from sleep positions seems overrated to me. Most foot and leg problems will follow an inevitable course, and a sleeping position will add little impetus to this course. The course can be altered in other appropriate ways—such as exercising the feet and legs at the hips, and, when necessary, giving early attention to more severe problems. Even severe defects can be treated early with casts—at a time when the infant is not yet held back by them.

Laura refused anything out of a bottle. When her mother offered her sugar water, she gagged, choked, and turned purple. Mrs. King thought there was something wrong with the nipple and tried another.

Laura is demonstrating the discrimination in taste differences that is strong in many breast-fed infants. A bottle should be offered from time to time early in the game so that the baby is familiar with it. Otherwise one may be in the predicament of having the infant refuse a complementary formula. In spite of such a refusal when it is not vital, most babies seem to sense when it is a real emergency—and will take a formula if their mothers are ill, out of milk, etc.

When she was offered a bottle of milk by her mother, she acted as if she were injured. She took one gulp, choked, and spat out the nipple. She frowned and clenched her jaws. Then she turned away from the bottle to her mother's breast. Mr. King could feed her a bottle when Mrs. King was not around. On one occasion, he was feeding her a formula successfully when Mrs. King spoke from the kitchen, and Laura heard her voice. She stopped sucking on the bottle, made a face, turned her head toward her mother's voice, and refused to accept the bottle again. This demonstrated her strong orientation to all cues that reminded her of the "gestalt" of the feeding (the atmosphere around the feeding that includes all the usual associated stimuli.)

When Mrs. King went out, leaving Laura with a sitter, Laura became fussy and inconsolable. For the three hours that Mrs. King was gone, Laura was actively fussing in a way that she had never done before. The sitter tried everything to quiet her. As she rocked and jiggled her, Laura became more upset. She refused the proffered bottle. Not until her mother returned and nursed her did she quiet. Then she settled peacefully and cozily into her mother's arms and quieted immediately. For the first time, Mrs. King felt herself needed by Laura. But she also felt trapped.

She need not have. This strong reaction to the change in handling is due to an infant's sensitivity to all the cues around her. With an infant as sensitive as Laura, it is wise to have one sitter who under-stands (and likes) her, and who can offer her gentle cues appropriate to her particular makeup.

Laura's feedings began to last for over an hour. She nestled in and sucked for as long as forty-five minutes until her mother took her off the breast. Since her mother had built up extra milk with this stimulation, Laura often ate too much as she sucked for these long periods. Most feedings were followed by spitting up as she was bubbled. Often Laura spat up several more times between feedings. Nothing Mrs. King could do, such as propping her after feedings or stopping her after shorter intervals of sucking, seemed to change this pattern.

Many infants spit up some after feedings until they begin to be more upright, that is, until seven to nine months of age. As long as it isn't projectile (gushing out forcefully) and they gain properly, it isn't necessarily a sign of pathology. It may be a function of eating too much or too rapidly. It may also be a symptom of an inadequate sphincter at the top of the infant's stomach that allows milk to come back up. Whatever the reason, some infants are "spitters" and there is no explanation for it. They continue to spit no matter what one does, and do well in spite of this. They stop spontaneously by the age of nine months, but sometimes before that. Since breast milk doesn't smell when it is vomited, this is not as hard to live with as it is with cow's milk.

Laura continued to eat every four hours, day and night. She gained rapidly and was thirteen pounds at her two-months' checkup. But she had not relinquished her four-hour pattern at night. Since she was so quiet and good, she did not tire herself enough to move into a lengthening pattern of night sleep. Her mother thought of torturing her for a period in the evening so that she would cry. One of her friends had undressed her baby and made him fuss for a period each evening. Following this active period, he slept better at night. Mrs. King wondered whether she should push Laura to this extent. She tried feeding Laura solids in the evening, hoping that they would "fill her up" and tide her over. Laura refused them as definitely as she did bottles. She tasted the first few spoonfuls, then closed her mouth tightly, frowned, and turned away. None of these maneuvers changed Laura's definite pattern of eating every four hours, day and night.

Most babies are not as stubborn and difficult to change at night. I would find it difficult to justify a deliberate attempt to make a baby fuss, at least from the infant's standpoint. However, if a mother is

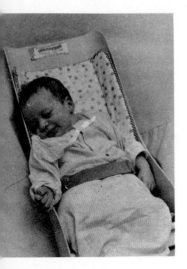

*desperately in need of rest, some sort of forceful push toward accultu-
ration might work.*

While she was being held, or when she was propped in her chair,
she began to smile. At first, this was a "surprise" smile out of the
blue. When Mr. and Mrs. King saw it, they were so excited by it
that they reacted with attempts to draw her out more. Laura reacted
to their activity by becoming serious and by frowning. When they
tried to elicit another smile, she would turn away and look at her
mobile, or at one of her hands. They felt shut out by her response.
Mrs. King mentioned this to her mother, who had known Laura in
the newborn period. She suggested that maybe Laura was overwhelmed by so much stimulation, and that a gentler approach might
be more appropriate. The suggestion to stimulate her with a quieter
approach worked well, and it became apparent that she enjoyed
gentle stimuli. As Mrs. King realized this, she became more effective
in drawing out responses from her. She and Mr. King began to feel
that they had understood Laura. They began to feel like parents!

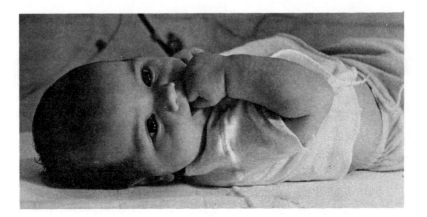

Laura's crying seemed limited to two different kinds—one kind
accompanied unpredictable short bursts of activity, and the second
occurred around the time of a bowel movement. The sudden bursts
of activity were not associated with any obvious internal or external
source of stimulation and seemed mostly to be triggered by fatigue,
or after long periods of lying awake, or by looking around. In these
bursts, she became active, waving her arms and legs jerkily and

frantically. Her motor development was less mature at eight to nine weeks than that of the other two babies. Usually she lay in a froglike position with her arms and legs flexed on the bed. In active periods, she waved all four extremities in full arcs of motion in all directions. Her chin quivered, and she yawned frequently. She shivered as she became active and sneezed as if to clear her nose. When her mother held her, she quieted immediately and looked up intently into her face. At these times, the tone of her body was better, and her mother responded gratefully by holding her more and more.

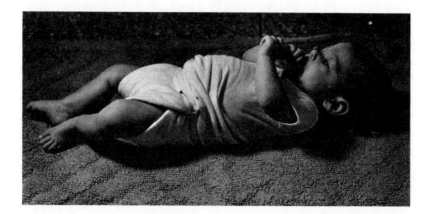

When Mrs. King took her out in the carriage, Laura demonstrated her usual sensitivity to cues. She loved the wheeling motion and lay looking around at everything that passed. When her mother stopped to talk to someone, she began to pucker. When the passerby leaned over to talk to her, she frowned and turned her head and her eyes toward the side of the carriage. Such a negative reaction to strangers made it unpleasant for Mrs. King to show her off on her walks, so she lost some of the pleasure of them.

Mothers often ask me whether getting a baby out is a necessity. I answer that it may be for the mother, but I doubt that it is for the infant. At best it may "tone up" her circulatory system, but an open window in her room that changes the temperature will do that. So I know of no reason from the baby's standpoint that makes it important.

Her bowel movements had been frequent (six to eight a day) when she first came home from the hospital. In the fifth week, she skipped three days before Mrs. King realized that she hadn't changed a dirty diaper. She inserted a thermometer rectally, and Laura produced a liquid normal stool.

Many breast-fed babies go for several days without a bowel movement. I have had three who did well for eight weeks with one soft stool every ninth day and nothing in between! This can be a normal pattern for an entirely breast-fed baby. Unless the stools become hard, it need not be treated as constipation. The pushing and straining seen with these liquid stools cannot be eradicated by manipulation or laxatives. I am sure that many normal intestinal tracts have been ruined by overatten-tion.

Laura seemed wheezy at times and sneezed as if she needed to clear her nose.

Stuffiness or mucus in the nose and upper airway can be due to dry air, to dust, or to wool lint from fuzzy blankets. Spitting up adds to the irritation, with milk residue left in the posterior nares, which can be irritating and needs to be cleared away by sneezing or coughing. A humidifier in the room helps. It is especially important in the winter, when dry heat inside and irritating cold outside are factors. Although the mucus and milk in the back of the nose make for noisy breathing and a "rattle" with each breath that is transmitted through-out the chest, this does not harm a baby. She will not choke on the mucus. However, an infant usually will not open her mouth to breathe unless she is desperate, and she may lie for long periods breathing noisily through her nose. Elevating the head of her bed a few inches helps her swallow these secretions. Sugar water helps her suck them down. A few drops of a solution made out of salt (one quarter teaspoonful) and sterile water (eight ounces or a glassful), boiled for three minutes, can be used as nosedrops to wash out the nose.

Laura's forceps bruises had not completely disappeared. There seemed to be lumpy scar tissue in the bruised areas.

There are often tiny, pea-sized, fibrous tissue lumps in the fatty tissue beneath these bruises. The bruises and the underlying scar tissue will disappear in time without leaving a mark.

Mrs. King's question to Laura's doctor seemed almost naïve: "When can I play with her?" Had he not sensed the anxiety underlying her request for help in establishing a relationship with her baby, he might have laughed at her. Instead, he answered, "She's yours, play with her whenever you want to." He should have given her more support. Mrs. King needed guidelines and a push to play with her baby, to break through the kind of quiet isolation with which Laura surrounded herself. Laura's delayed, slow responses to stimulation were accompanied by a sensitivity that demanded a certain kind of stimulation and a limited range of stimuli. Outside of this range, she either didn't respond or would turn away—either reaction was a rebuff to an eager set of parents. The fact that Mrs. King was able to pull herself out of her own postpartum blues to ask for advice as to how she might reach Laura was a testimony to her desire to be a good mother. Laura was not an easy first baby, and at this point her parents could not feel as if they were really on the way with her.

ACTIVE BABY

Daniel's repertoire of accomplishments increased daily. His parents felt they were on a toboggan with Daniel in control, the rest of the family hanging on desperately, while he raced downhill.

His wiry, constant activity filled ten hours of each day, and his parents marveled that he slept so little. Mrs. Kay and Mark spent a large part of their day watching him perform, chuckling at him. Mr. Kay found him at his worst each evening, for it was then that Daniel had his fussy periods. He therefore found it difficult to share their excitement about Daniel's achievements.

Since the regular fussy periods nearly always start at the end of the day and often are coincident with father's coming home, they tend to be a real deterrent to a father's developing a relationship with the baby. I used to feel "shut out" or even responsible for my babies' fussy time. Fathers need to understand these cyclic fussy periods as part of

*the twenty-four-hour cycle just as mothers do, so that they don't take
them personally. Part of wanting to do a good job as a father means
that one cares too much. If a new father can accept the fussiness but
go on to play as much as he wants with the baby at that time of day,
it can be gratifying. That certainly is an alert period, and as a three-
month-old baby "outgrows" the fussing, it will become his most
sociable time. Fathers should either play then or find another satisfying time. Often, after the fussy period, babies are alert and playful.
Or, if there are no other times, I would urge a father to wake the baby
up for a play period in the morning before he leaves the house for
work. It is critical to both that the baby knows his father as a special
person different from his mother.*

When Daniel was placed in bed on his back, he began to whirl in
motor activity. His arms cycled like windmills in wide areas around
his head. He swiped his face, scratched himself, and sometimes even
scratched his eyes. His mother cut his fingernails repeatedly (always
when he was asleep!), but this did not eliminate the scratches. The
whites of his eyes occasionally had tiny red hemorrhagic spots in
them from nicks made by his fingernails. Mrs. Kay wondered
whether she should put mittens or socks over his hands to protect
his face.

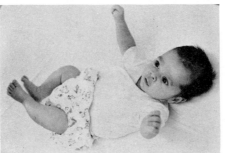

*These scratches heal quickly and well. Even the eyes are so rarely hurt
by an infant's own scratch that it is not necessary to worry about them.
A scratch on the conjunctivae of the eye from an outside source such
as a mother's fingernail can cause trouble, but usually a scratch by the
baby himself does not cause any infection as it seems to be handled
by his own immunity. It heals quickly, without any scar. This is*

fortunate, for infants are constantly scratching themselves. It seems preferable to take the chance of such a scratch and allow an infant to have his hands free. When his hands are covered, a large sector of his experience is cut out. He needs to explore his universe with his fingers, to watch and look at his hands, and to explore his own face and mouth with them. All this is an important part of the early exploration of himself and of his world. There are studies on animals that demonstrate that unless a baby animal can watch its limbs as it uses them, its motor development is severely impaired. This is un-doubtedly true of human infants also.

Mrs. Kay decided not to interfere with Daniel's activity since she felt it to be such an important part of his makeup. His cycling arms eventually zeroed in on his mouth, and he made repeated stabs at his mouth before he finally reached his goal—that of sucking on his thumb. When he finally achieved the contact, he sucked it into his mouth with such vigor that Mrs. Kay could hear the pop in the next room. She wondered that he didn't choke on it. Vigorous sucking continued as Daniel looked around the room. His whole body was oriented toward the sucking and the tension of his body demon-strated his fervor. As he sucked, he was able to quiet his other activity, and it was apparent that this was an important time in his day. In that period of relative inactivity, Daniel was freed to look around the room, to absorb visual experiences in the way that Laura and Louis were freer to do a large part of each day. Without a way of slowing down the rather frantic activity that absorbed his ener-gies, Daniel might not have been able to add to his important visual development. In these active, driving infants, one feels inclined to "teach" them how to relax.

As he lost interest in his thumb, or lost the thumb in a startle response to an outside noise, he began his cycling activity again. His legs went round in a bicycling motion as his arms wheeled overhead. He twisted his body from side to side and often turned over onto his belly with this twisting. He was surprised when this happened, became upset, and cried, until his mother rushed to turn him back. He propelled himself to the top of the crib. There he quieted for a moment, then continued his activity. After a few minutes wedged in the corner, he screamed out in frustration, and once again his mother had to come to the rescue. She pulled him to the center of the crib to start over again.

Some infants seem to seek a corner or the top of the crib and will not settle down until their heads rest against a solid object. Analysts have likened this to an attempt to return to the uterus with the head engaged in the pelvis. It is similar to other attempts on the part of infants as they try to reproduce fetal positions in sleep. But babies as active as Daniel are not easily comforted, and a crutch as simple as a sleep position is no real source of calm to them.

By the end of the second month, Daniel seemed to have learned that when he screamed a particular kind of scream, his mother would appear. She began to realize that he was "trying her out," for he relaxed and broke into smiles when she came. She felt "used" by him, but his smiling response was so charming that she melted every time. Mrs. Kay enjoyed Daniel's vigor. If she had not, it could have been their downfall. If she had been irritated by his rather obvious ways of calling for her when he had had enough, she might have ignored his cries for help. Daniel needed her to help him get out of the binds he got himself into—just as he needed her to pull him out of the corner. She responded to this need and thereby was able to do two things: (1) to enhance his and her pleasure in his motor activity, and (2) to show him ways of extracting himself from his frenzied predicaments.

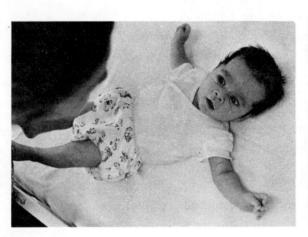 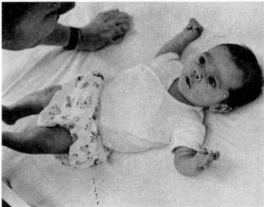

When she could allow herself time to stand over him and watch him, he responded by putting on a show for her. He arched, turned, twisted, kicked, and built up to such a peak of activity that even Mrs. Kay felt exhausted.

He learned to "talk" to her. As she or Mark watched him, he would gradually work his face up into a smile and a gurgle. The smile seemed to activate his limbs and trunk, and quickly his whole body was "smiling" at them. He gurgled and cooed for long intervals if they stood over him. If this went on too long, he became over-wrought and the smile would change with lightning swiftness into frustrated crying.

His father strung a series of spools on a string across his crib for him to play with. He soon learned to swipe at them with his hands. At first he missed them, but gradually he hit them more squarely to make noise. When he sensed he could make these noises himself, he worked with concentration. He worked his body up into a kind of total activity so that he could hit out at the spools with his arms.

The need to use the whole body in order to accomplish any segmental activity is characteristic of learning at this age. It is one of the delightful aspects of infancy. As an older infant becomes able to isolate an activity from this total reaction, he loses some of his early baby charm.

Such awareness of what causes the noise and such determination to repeat the swiping and banging rarely comes as early as the second month.

Putting him down for a nap or at night brought on a tantrum. Daniel was furious when he was placed on his belly. Since this was the only position in which he would sleep, his mother knew he interpreted being placed in this position as being put down to sleep. His head reared up to a forty-five-degree angle as he looked around for help.

He roared as he reared up. His arms pushed into the bed and he arched his body upward. His legs pushed vigorously in thrusting, crawling activity. He propelled himself forward fiercely. Since this was an inevitable part of his activity during the night, Mrs. Kay found it hopeless to keep him covered.

The mother of such an active infant has two choices: to harness him to one spot, or to put him in a sleeping bag, in which his arms are free but in which he can move freely without needing extra covering.

Mrs. Kay and her husband chose the latter. They felt that activity was an important outlet for Daniel and that at least half of his twenty-four hours were to be spent in this sleeping position. They did not feel they could interfere with his activity to the extent of tying him down—even at night.

Daniel was a light sleeper. He whimpered off and on through the night. He seemed to rouse in regular cycles three hours apart. He would cry out, raise his head, whimper, move to the top of the bed, bring his fingers to his mouth, and then settle down again to sleep. When he was in the parents' room they roused with him, and he woke them frequently through the night. They found that both he and they were better off if he was in a separate room. He sensed their presence during these semiconscious periods, responded by coming to full awakening, and cried out for them. As soon as they isolated him, he slept more peacefully.

He took one- to two-hour naps during the day. Three times a day he would wear himself out and begin to scream with fatigue. When his mother realized he was tired, she would turn him over on his abdomen, and he worked himself to sleep.

Mrs. Kay wished she could sleep while Daniel did. She was tense and exhausted most of the time. She thoroughly enjoyed all of his activity, found him fun to play with, and exciting to observe; but he was not easy.

He hated the infant chair. His arms and legs seemed to be too restrained in it, and he would struggle until he arched himself out of it. One day she placed him on it on a table near her in the kitchen while she worked. She heard a noise, turned around in time to see him pull himself and the chair over, off the table and onto the floor. He hit the floor face forward and immediately started screaming.

Fortunately, Daniel had not been knocked unconscious. When

she got to him he was actively using his extremities. As she felt him all over, he appeared to have no tender areas on his body. Her doctor told her what to watch for to rule out a concussion.

Periods of unresponsiveness, pupils that do not shrink down in re-sponse to a light, and/or repeated vomiting are signs of a possible concussion. Most babies do fall like this at one time or another, and most survive. If a baby is unconscious or develops any of these symp-toms, a doctor will want to check him for a concussion.

She felt terribly guilty and shaken by this experience, but Daniel seemed fine. She never put him on a table in his chair again.

There are sudden reflexes that can turn a baby over in a chair or on a table. A mother should get in the habit of keeping her hand on the baby whenever she turns to do something, if he is on a table or bed. I have seen a four-week-old infant flip off a flat table to the floor, fracturing her skull, while her mother's back was turned. With a hand on her this need not have happened.

Daniel still disliked his bath. He scrambled and struggled fiercely whenever he was undressed. His arms and legs flailed, he startled, began to cry, and finally worked himself up to such a screaming pitch that his mother dreaded each ordeal. She found she was bathing him only every other day, then twice a week, and leaving him dirty in the creases as she rushed through these baths.

Baths are not a necessary part of each day. Many children who have dry or sensitive skins cannot be bathed more than once a week—and they survive. In certain cultures—such as the Eskimo or Indian in the mountains—children and adults never bathe completely. With some attention to cleansing the buttocks and genital area at changing times, bathing certainly needn't be performed daily. I am sure that regular times make it easier for mothers to remember and children to become accustomed to the routine of the bath, but there is no other rationale for all the attention to bathing that we pay in the United States.

In his crying periods at the end of each day, Daniel quickly built up to a steady, demanding, piercing wail. As he cried, he stiffened, cut down on other bodily activity, and seemed to put all his energy into deep breaths that ended in long bursts of high-pitched sound. His color changed to purplish. He often built up to periods when he seemed to stop breathing. After a period of such apnea (absence of breathing), Daniel would quiet. He then might yawn and, after the yawn, start crying again. His parents picked him up and tried to hold him on their shoulders. He stayed there stiffly, not allowing himself to fit into any position they offered him. He wriggled out of their arms. He seemed resistant to being held. If one of them rocked him vigorously or walked rapidly with him, he would quiet for a short period, but he gave them the impression that he was not really happy being carried on their shoulders. As soon as they gave up their attempts to comfort him, he built up again to his vigorous crying.

They offered him a pacifier. Mrs. Kay had always hated seeing children with "plugs" in their mouths, as she called them. She had sworn she would never resort to one. But Daniel had changed many of her predetermined ideas about childrearing in the few weeks he'd been with them. Daniel accepted the pacifier at first, mouthed it, sucked briefly on it, then spit it out forcefully. When he was peacefully active during the day, he could be conned into sucking on it for periods of fifteen minutes at a time. But Mrs. Kay did not feel he needed it then. In his evening fussy periods, he was intractable and refused this crutch with characteristic and definite vigor.

Mothers wonder about the use of pacifiers. My own feeling is that the point is not which crutch a mother "pushes" but how she pushes it. Nearly every infant will need some extra sucking. If he is allowed to, he will find it for himself on his thumb or fingers and will be independent of his environment in the process. A pacifier will replace his interest in his own fingers, but it is not an independently mastered crutch. Hence it can become used by the mother when he may not need it. Many mothers tend to overuse pacifiers and do indeed use them like "plugs" from early infancy on. It is no wonder that, as their children grow with this plugging from the environment, by two years they may be big, fat, passive babies who need to have their mouths filled to be happy. In these cases, they reflect their mothers' need for a crutch, not their own.

Feedings were reviewed with his doctor to see whether his regular crying could be attributable to hunger. Daniel ate well during the day. He tended to gulp down a bottle with the same vigor that he showed in all other areas. When he did, he spat back a large part of it. His mother had learned to slow his nipples, to make him take at least fifteen to twenty minutes of sucking. He seemed satisfied with each bottle and had fallen into a rather regular four-hour pattern in the day. In the evening, he could be fed an ounce or two of formula from time to time as he fussed, but he showed the same lack of interest in it that he had in the pacifier. He was very likely to spit up the milk he took in this period, as he became more and more active. At the end of the crying period, he would take six or seven ounces with his usual gusto, then drop off to sleep for an eight-hour stretch. It was difficult to blame his fussing on a need for food.

Mrs. Kay tried to feed Daniel rice cereal in the evening before his fussy period to see whether this would shut him up. He accepted a soupy consistency from a demitasse spoon. He seemed interested in it the first few days, and she felt she might have hit on a solution. He ate as much as two tablespoons of the dried cereal mixed with enough milk to make it liquid. But his crying was not affected. After the first few days, Daniel began to choke on the cereal when she offered it. He would swallow, then spit, choke, stop breathing, and wiggle in his reclining chair. He obviously did not enjoy it. Finally, as he was able to bring his fingers to his mouth, to insert his thumb and suck on it, he ended by sucking the cereal down and seemed happier to eat it. At one point, Mrs. Kay attempted to restrain his hands so he would not get so messy, but Daniel then absolutely refused the cereal. He twisted his head, clenched his mouth, and screamed. When she let his hands go, he took the spoon and cereal again and followed a mouthful of cereal by sucking it down with his fingers. Although he accepted the cereal each evening, he continued to cry, and it became apparent that hunger was not the reason for his crying.

Their visit to the pediatrician at two months reassured the Kays about his progress. He had grown an inch and a half and had managed to gain one and a half pounds in spite of his active life. She asked about two "defects" in Daniel that worried her and her husband. The first was an inequality of eye shape. His left eye looked smaller than the right. The physician explained to them that this was due to his immaturity and the inequality of muscle tone in the muscles of the eyelids, and that most of this appearance would change as he matured. Daniel's bowlegs bothered the Kays, and they wondered whether this was normal. Since his feet were flexible and his hips well placed in their hip sockets, the pediatrician could reassure the Kays that the bowing of the lower legs was the normal result of having had his legs up around him in the uterus. With the axis of weight bearing as he stood on them plus adequate vitamins all along to prevent rickets, the bowlegs would straighten out later.

They reviewed Daniel's excessive activity and his demanding day. As they did, they found their pride and excitement in his progress superseding their complaints. The doctor was as delighted as they were with Daniel's drive toward motor achievements—his early swiping at objects, his smiling and vocalizing, his turning over, the creeping locomotion in bed, and his ability to hold on to an object that was placed in his hand for an extended period. The doctor called him precocious and said he seemed a month ahead of himself.

He confirmed the Kays' feeling that the fuss period went along with this intense drive to perform—an inevitable disintegration at the end of the day. He warned them that there was no magic way to interfere with this period. Time and his maturation would take care of it and by three months he would turn this energy into other outlets. He urged them to play with Daniel and enjoy him as much as they could. He attempted to assuage their guilty feelings about not being adequate to him in their desperate periods.

CHAPTER V

The Third Month

AVERAGE BABY

The third month made the earlier two seem worthwhile. By the end of this period, so much had happened, life was so much easier and more rewarding, that Mr. and Mrs. Moore felt a kind of euphoria. Louis was already an exciting, responsive individual. Indeed, his responses seemed out of proportion to the stimulation he was offered, and he was so delicious that they felt they didn't deserve him. As she looked at him with his rounded, full face and body, and as he responded by smiling and vocalizing back at her, Mrs. Moore felt she could go on having babies forever.

Mr. Moore called him his "dish of ice cream" and constantly played with him, cuddled him, and nuzzled him now. Louis gurgled with glee at all of this attention. Earlier, his father had felt chagrined at his lack of feeling for this new infant. He had wondered when he would begin to feel about him the way he remembered feeling about the others. Now, when he came up to Louis, who would be lying in his crib or baby seat, the infant immediately turned to his father's face. He searched it briefly, focused on his father's eyes and mouth, and became more active. He smiled almost immediately, began to kick his legs, wiggle with his body, and reach outward with both arms.

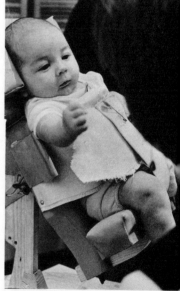

This bilateral reaching out to each side is a precursor of the reaching forward for an object that will come later. Stretching of arms out to the sides is a way of incorporating a part of the earlier Moro reflex into a more voluntary activity such as reaching.

All of his body seemed to become involved in a kind of movement of joy at seeing a smiling face. As he became active, he chortled and squealed. His mouth formed in a round oooh and he gurgled at the

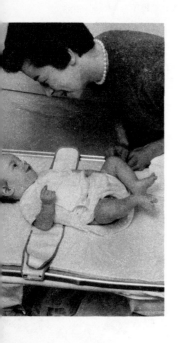

back of his throat. As each new sound came forth, he stopped with surprise and began again. All of this was so pleasant for his father, that he found himself leaning over Louis for long periods, bobbing his head, smiling at him, and imitating Louis' sounds. Occasionally, Louis would stop his activity, watch his father, and try to produce a slow gurgle. When his father finally left him, Louis squealed with frustration. This attracted Martha or Tom, who began to reproduce the interplay again. A large part of their afternoon and evening could be spent in this kind of interaction with Louis.

Parents with more than one child express their sadness and guilty feelings at not having enough time for the new baby. They feel he gets cheated in comparison to the first, for whom they had so much time. To see why this need not be a concern, all one needs to do is to watch such interplay as this with Tom and Martha—how many times they take up the slack, how many different kinds of stimuli they offer a baby, and how much he loves to watch and play with his siblings.

Infants seem to show a preference for other babies or children. Given a choice, they will often choose a child to observe rather than an adult. This is surprising in that the child or infant is full of sudden noises and startling changes in activity. But infants seem to prefer to communicate with someone who is close to their own age level. Do they have an inborn tendency to identify with the activity of the smaller person? There must be ways in which they sense the similarity of a younger child to themselves. Certainly, a small child learns a great deal from the older children in the family and seems to learn it more easily. Perhaps all of the cues given from child to child are more appropriate than are the ways an adult tries to "teach" a child.

In the end, Louis seemed to go to pieces and would cry or suck his fingers as he turned his face away. At this point, his mother could put him to bed. He wiggled in bed in a few scrabbling attempts to make a nest for himself in the bedclothes, put his fingers in his mouth, and settled down for his nap or the night.

He also has established a definite pattern for going to sleep. His preference for his stomach was probably evident at birth, but by now is a necessary part of settling down. The nesting activity of finding a comfortable spot, gathering in his fingers in order to settle down, is followed by the capacity to give up to sleep. Some infants need to cry themselves to sleep; for them, crying is the last evidence of disintegration before sleep can be achieved. These patterns are of great importance, and one sees this behavior repeated in the middle of the night when an infant comes up to semi-consciousness and must get himself back down to deeper sleep again.

Louis' crying periods had almost vanished by three months, and his parents had forgotten about them, too.

There is a magical turning point in crying behavior around the three-month birthday. Something happens that takes the place of this need for crying. It seems to be related to an increased capacity to reach out for and participate in the world in other ways, for example, cooing, gurgling, looking at his hands, reaching out for an object overhead.

He slept quietly for two hours in the morning and for an hour and a half in the afternoon. His night sleep stretched to a ten- and occasionally to an eleven-hour period by the end of the third month. Mrs. Moore had set this up. By waking him during the day for his feedings in the early weeks, she had organized him to stretch out when he could, i.e., at night.

When parents feed a baby entirely on a demand basis, they tend to let him pick his own part of the twenty-four-hour cycle to stretch in. This seems like an unnecessary kind of masochism to me. Few babies are not willing to adjust, to be perfectly satisfied with their long stretch at a time of night when it is a blessing for the rest of the family. But this may well take effort on the parents' part to bring about.

Louis' feedings were just as organized and effective. He now whimpered in a special way when he was hungry. When he listened to Mrs. Moore's footsteps as she came to feed him, he learned to wait. He lay in bed expectantly as she prepared herself and her rocking chair. When she picked him up to change him before the feeding, he looked serious and attentive, but he did not cry. But if she had to go off and leave him strapped to the changing table at such a time, he could contain himself no longer, and he began to wail.

The ability to wait for an expected reward such as feeding is quite an achievement and demonstrates a lot of learning and trust in the environment. Compare this to the animal world. How many animals can learn to trust and to wait for a feeding that is in preparation? Louis shows how fragile this new accomplishment is when his mother must leave him after he has been waiting. Then his resources no longer maintain him, and he disintegrates.

This demonstrates to me how much an infant learns to depend on a kind of pattern or consistency in his parents—when the parents are too easily distracted from what they have led him to expect from them, he suffers in his ability to build up this kind of trust in his environment.

After the feeding had begun, and he had gulped down the first part of it, he stopped in the midst of the feeding to look around, to smile up into her face, or to watch his own hands. She could jiggle his head and get him going again, but the feedings were interspersed with bits of play. When one of the other children came into the room, he stopped briefly before he continued.

All of these bits of play at feeding time may be exasperating for a mother who is in a hurry. They are solid gold for the infant. It is his most receptive time. His physiological needs are being met. He is in a satisfied, receptive state, and each experience that occurs at this time must take on a heightened value. A baby savoring these moments is like a chubby old man savoring his cigar at the end of a delicious, filling meal.

By the end of the third month, he was no longer satisfied with just her milk, and he looked around afterward as if he expected more. His mother interpreted this as time for the introduction of solids.

Babies are not always so clearcut in showing when they are ready. They may seem ready for a period, then stop eating almost entirely after solids are started. Infants take spurts in hunger and eating. In these spurts they can hardly get enough to eat for days at a time. Then they drop back again and no longer want all they had demanded before. Their physiological requirements are not organized on a constantly ascending slope, but on a much more jagged line of spurts and regressions.

She remembered her earlier discussions about solids with her pediatrician. He had not been an advocate of early solid feeding, for (1) he felt they could interfere with breast-feeding by filling him and dulling the infant's interest in sucking at the breast; (2) he did not feel that infants digested the complex molecules of solid food in the first few months, and quoted stool analyses in small babies that contained largely undigested particles of the complex carbohydrates, fats, and protein from solid foods; and (3) he felt that there was some indication that sensitivities to foods could more easily be triggered in the early months without any external evidence of their sensitizing effect, and that as an infant's gastrointestinal tract matured, he was better able to digest and react directly to sensitizing agents. Hence, when she started Louis on cereal, she chose a one-grain cereal, i.e., rice.

This is in order to offer him only one challenge in foods at a time. Should a baby demonstrate a sensitivity to this one food, a mother can be sure of the agent immediately. If she offers him a mixture of new foods, she cannot tell which is responsible for any difficulty that might arise. Sensitivities to new foods can be indicated in several ways. An immediate reaction occurs frequently to orange juice—the infant vomits it and continues to do so every time he is offered orange juice. His stools become frequent and loose that day or the next. He may be quite fussy and gassy for several hours. A more delayed reaction to solids can be demonstrated by a sensitivity rash—a dry, scaling, red rash (usually on the face, but occasionally on the body), which begins to appear as much as a week later.

The Academy of Pediatrics has recently recommended that solid food be postponed until the fourth to the sixth month, for the reasons given above. There are few reasons for starting them earlier, unless the baby seems to need "fillers" in addition to milk. In Louis' case he may be showing that need, but he may just be getting more active and demanding around feeding time. At any rate, it certainly would be wise to start solids slowly and to increase them very gradually. There is no reason to let them interfere with the baby's milk consumption or to reduce his demands on the breast. It would be too bad to let the introduction of solids interfere with nursing or cause the baby to cut down on nursing too abruptly.

At first, he balked and choked, so she tried a sweeter baby food, applesauce. He continued to balk and seemed to resent the new

taste. She had experienced this same resistance with the other babies, so she plowed through the first few days to reach the end of the first week. At this time, as she expected, he began to accept her spooned-in foods.

The balking and its ultimate resolution does not seem to me to be based on the kind of taste as much as on the novelty of the whole situation—the new way of being fed, the new texture and taste, the need to actively swallow food instead of suck it down. Until about ten to twelve weeks, swallowing is largely a milking and sucking that involves the entire mouth, esophagus, and upper gastrointestinal tract. At this time a more voluntary swallowing becomes possible. As is often the case with a changeover from reflex to voluntary mastery, there may be a period of delay before the voluntary act is entirely mastered. Infants show their preference for the earlier kind of swallowing or sucking when they bring their hands to their mouths to suck after each spoonful of solids is given them. Without a finger to suck on, they may refuse solids.

Mrs. Moore waited a week before adding each new food, to allow for a sensitivity to each one to show itself. Martha had developed eczema in infancy, and Mrs. Moore wanted no more of that in her babies.

I am convinced that many sensitivities can be circumvented in infancy by such careful introduction of new foods and sensitizers. If the allergic mechanism is not activated, each month raises the threshold level for it, and it becomes more difficult to set the allergic reaction off. Many infants are sensitive to eggs before six months but will not be after this age. There seems to be a real reason for avoiding reactions to allergens rather than setting up an allergy and then trying to cure it.

As Louis began to eat better, he began to gulp down the solids. He could have eaten as much as she would feed him, but when he did, he refused her breast milk. So she began to watch for cues to let her know when he had had enough. When he spit out more than she spooned in, she realized he was not swallowing effectively any longer, and it was time to stop. She began to limit him to two tablespoons

of each solid and found that he then still had room for her milk after he finished.

Milk is much more important than solids at this age. Babies do not always indicate when they've had enough solid food. Some will eat all that is offered. Then they refuse their milk. So it is preferable to limit solids in order to emphasize their intake of milk.

The days were easy and full of fun at three months. Louis lay on his back for long periods, playing with his hands, watching his mobile or his fingers. He found that he could grab one hand with the other and play with the fingers on the other hand as if they were toys. At one point, he became aware that his whirling arms made his mobile move. His efforts to whirl and move the butterflies became more deliberate. At another time he caught sight of his feet and began to watch them for periods as he circled them in front of his eyes. His parents were amazed at his ability to realize his role in making the mobile go and in bringing his feet up to watch. They did not remember that the other babies had been as quick as this.

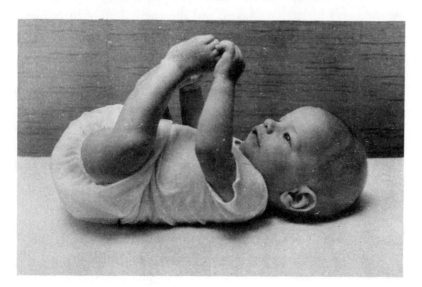

He is demonstrating a marvelous train of associations. The fact that he can associate his action with the result of it is a big step in learning. One of the first examples of this comes about with the hand-to-mouth organization we have already seen. As the baby closes this circuit, he

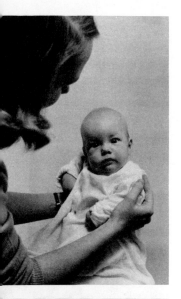

begins to sense the gratifying stimulation at each end—the mouth and the hand. Then he holds out his hand and adds seeing to this circuit, as he sees his hand as an extension of himself. When this appreciation of his ability to extend himself includes his feet and a mobile in the distance, he is surely beginning to demonstrate an awareness of himself that is sophisticated. Not only is he learning the extensible properties he has, and the limitless possibilities these offer, but he is also getting a preview of his own boundaries. These are all part of early ego development.

When he was picked up, he responded by bringing his whole body up in one piece. As he came to a sitting position, he could now hold his head up easily with a minimum of bobbing. He could sit in Martha's lap like a compact doll and help maintain himself. He loved to sit in his mother's lap and watch the children play around him. As they grew noisy and he more tired, he startled more easily and began to cry. Then his mother put him in his room in his crib where he could go to sleep.

Mrs. Moore felt she had never enjoyed a baby as much. She worried very little about Louis, and she enjoyed all of his achievements more than she ever had been able to with the other children. She began to tell all her friends that they should have a third baby.

This is a common statement from mothers. The first baby is such an experimental proving ground that few mothers can enjoy their first unequivocally. As a result, they wonder how a first baby survives all of this anxious handling. In the long run, however, there are advantages, as well as disadvantages, to being a first child. I am sure that the high correlation of success in adult life and coming first in a family of children is no coincidence. The first child certainly has to learn to deal with the parents' conflicts about his rearing, but he also gets the major slice of his parents' positive concern. The second or middle child is often more "left out" as the family recovers from the first. Everyone feels the pure joy and freedom of the third.

QUIET BABY

Laura remained quiet and seemed as if she were insulated. She was perfectly content to lie in her bed for most of the day, and she made few demands on her parents. As she grew, she seemed to become more placid and more watchful.

The contrast between our portrait of Laura and that of the two boys is so marked at times that the reader may question her normalcy. She has an entirely different makeup—her apparent lack of investment in motor activity, the obvious gratification she receives from using her sensory apparatus, coupled with a high degree of sensitivity to the outside world, lead to a different pace of development. She is well within normal limits.

She is on her way to becoming an entirely different kind of person. An interested reader should refer to Thomas, Chess, Birch, Hertzig and Korn (1963) for their longitudinal studies of the outcomes for these different kinds of temperament. Laura could become an artistic person, a sensitive observer, or she could turn her strength into intellectual pursuits in which she could become a very competitive kind of person. Many intellectuals have been described as babies who were like this.

Her even disposition was unruffled by any of the usual events. Mrs. King found she often forgot to go to Laura at the end of four hours to feed her. Laura never minded. When she did appear, Laura turned to her, brightened, and smiled as if she were happy to see her but had not really expected her. This annoyed Mrs. King, and she felt again the gnawing feeling that Laura really did not need her very much.

This may be the most difficult aspect about such a self-contained child. At a time when the mother is having to give up a large part of herself to a new baby, she expects the reward of feeling the baby's cuddly dependency on her. "Independence" may seem like a kind of barrier between them.

Laura whimpered in the middle of the night for a feeding. She gradually stretched from 10 P.M. to 4 A.M., but she regularly demanded a feeding at that time. By the time her mother arrived, Laura was awake and glad to see her. She grinned with a beautiful wide smile in which her entire face participated. This kind of spontaneous smiling response seemed so rare that Mrs. King felt it made up for getting out of bed at that hour. After such a feeding, she felt more intimate with Laura, and she cuddled and crooned to her in a way that made Laura come alive. She could smile, gurgle, and wriggle with her shoulders as she obviously enjoyed this play period with her mother in the early morning. Her mother loved it, too. She reproached herself that the feedings during the day could not be more like this.

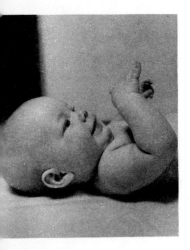

During the day, when she was awake, Laura lay in her crib on her back with her legs bent and frog-legged, her hands up by her face. She watched her mobile, listened to noises around her, and followed her mother around the room with her eyes. As she lost sight of her, her hands came up in front of her face, and she played for long periods, watching her fingers move slowly back and forth, catching the light. She seemed to be experiencing some sort of exquisite pleasure in combining the feeling of motion of her fingers with watching them as they moved. She would look at one hand and bring it up to her face as she watched it. Her eyes widened as her hand approached, as if it were some strange new object. Then, when it came too close to observe any longer, she would push it back out to arm's length and start over. Often she brought the hand close and gently touched her face, eyes, and mouth, exploring them with her hand. As she reached her mouth, her fingers played gently around it, gradually entered, and she began to suck on them. All of this seemed an exploration of the many facets of motion, of sight, and revealed the importance of her mouth as an ultimate goal for exploration. During this period, she demonstrated how the infant learns about herself, exploring more minutely than did Louis.

As she sucked her fingers, she was free again to look out into the room. She explored each source of light with detailed care. She listened for her mother's step in another room, stopping her sucking to do so. As she heard familiar sounds, she settled down peacefully to suck again.

She already recognized her mother's sounds in the distance. She watched her mobile as if it were a new experience each time. She slowed her sucking as she shifted her attention to each new object on the mobile. She seemed to explore the facets, the color changes, the shapes as it moved. She followed it gingerly with her eyes, dancing with it as it swung.

It may seem adultomorphic to credit her with this much ability to

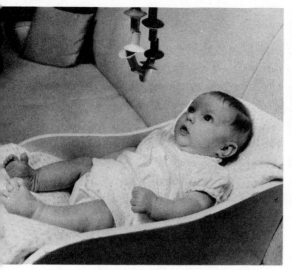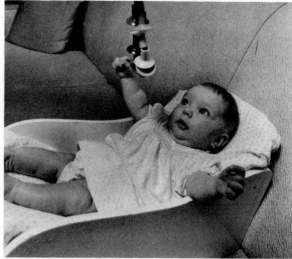

appreciate minutiae. However, this kind of visual exploration is possible as early as the third month.

When her mother realized her investment in her hands and in her mobile, she felt a bit jealous. She attempted to draw her out by cooing and smiling at her. Laura would watch her in a solemn way, sucking on her fingers and exploring each part of her mother's face. On one occasion Mrs. King was not satisfied, and she pulled Laura's fingers out of her mouth as she attempted to force her to react. Laura frowned and became more solemn. Her expression changed from curiosity to a sagging lack of interest.

Laura was extremely expressive in her motor reactions to stimulation. This sagging tone as her mother interfered with her pleasure in looking and sucking was just as active as Daniel's increased activity to refuse a stimulus he did not like. It is just as expressive. Unfortunately for Laura and her mother, Mrs. King felt rejected by it and could not understand Laura's reactions. As her mother lifted her by the shoulders, she felt like a sack of meal. Her head fell backward, her arms and legs hung loosely. There was so little reponse that Mrs. King felt like dropping her back into her crib and leaving her. But she was encouraged to play with Laura by her pediatrician's warning. He had pushed her to play with her baby and had quoted studies that indicated that babies in institutions who did not get stimulating attention at any but feeding times showed signs of deprivation as early as two months. At home this was not as likely. But he urged Mrs. King to be more active in drawing her out.

Mrs. King was afraid that Laura's quiet self-sufficiency was a kind of withdrawal from her. She did not notice the intense, quiet interest that Laura mustered whenever she was presented with stimulation that suited her. Her style of response was certainly not an appealing one to those around her. It would take a confident, resilient mother to pull Laura out of this.

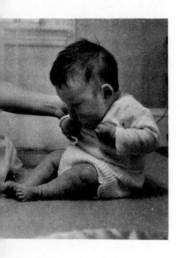

When Mrs. King played with Laura, she pulled her to sit and held her floppily supported in sitting. Laura seemed to accept this pushing and pulling as if she were a rag doll. When she was placed on her abdomen, she raised her head off the bed to look at her mother, as if to ask what was expected of her now. When Mrs. King got down on the bed with Laura, she could draw her out to play a little. When she placed a bright object near her hand, Laura would slowly and dutifully reach out in its direction. Finally, after a few frustrating minutes of this play, Laura would put her left thumb in her mouth and lay her right cheek on the bed, subsiding into a floppy heap.

Mrs. King felt she was making too little progress with Laura. Mr. King was better at it. She urged him into this role of "stimulating Laura." When he placed her on her back and watched her as she explored her universe, he realized, more than her mother did, how much Laura invested in her watching, listening, and slow movements. He put a toy into her hand. She automatically grasped it, but then she actively held on to it. She quickly learned to wave it, and to watch it as she waved it. She turned it in several directions, watching each new aspect of it. Finally, she brought it to her face, stroked her cheek with it, and brought it to her mouth where she explored it. Her father was delighted with this demonstration and began to brag about how thoughtfully sensitive Laura was.

His eager new interest only provided Mrs. King with another source of frustration in her attempts to mother Laura. She felt herself a failure. She phoned her mother to report this, ending with: "All I do with Laura is experimental, everything she does to me is not."

ACTIVE BABY

Tension dominated the Kay household. Mrs. Kay felt herself keyed up to a taut pitch most of the day. Mark was becoming more active and demanding than he had ever been, as if he were reacting to Daniel's activity with some of his own. Mr. Kay found he was working later at the office out of choice and finding things to do on weekends that would take him away.

This is a time for some "sitting" help. A mother needs a chance to get out of the house, and both parents need to feel together again. This is a common time for fathers to pull away. They tire of their wives' involvement in the infant and in the minutiae of the household. Each parent could be refueled with a little pleasure together, which is now important to their lives as a family.

Fathers who have been more involved in their babies' care are not as likely to pull away. They see each step in the baby's development as their own. They are getting feedback each day from the infant, which feeds their involvement. Even if competitive feelings develop between the mother and father at this point, as they may, they are focused around the baby's development. In our research we have been able to distinguish four levels of development of self-awareness in mothers in the first five months as they learn about the babies, and themselves as nurturers. So far, we have not examined this same kind of development in fathers, but I'm quite certain that it is there in the fathers who are intimately involved with care-giving. By having to learn about a baby at each stage, one is bound to learn about oneself.

But the danger of unconscious, competitive feelings is also likely to be there, and young parents do well to be aware of it as normal, and probably inevitable. It needn't be a divisive force between them, but it can become one. That would be too bad for everyone, especially the infant.

Such competitive feelings are common around small babies. Day-care personnel feel competitive with parents. Doctors and nurses tend to exclude parents for these reasons. Grandparents criticize young parents because of them. All people who care about small children are likely to become competitive about them.

Daniel continued his activity—increasing his repertoire daily. He lay on his back in a playpen, kicking, cycling his arms, twisting his head and body. He had learned to turn around in a complete circle by kicking hard with his feet and bouncing on his buttocks. He moved his legs together and cycled his arms together in unison.

The one-sided alternating and mirrored movements that are character-istic of earlier cycling are being replaced with the new ability to use both sides of the body in symmetry. Turning over is less frequent as a result of this symmetrical use of the body. At this stage, a baby rarely twists over to one side. The tonic neck reflex (see Chapter II) is losing its force in dominating his body postures.

He batted at his cradle-gym with both hands, delighting in the noises he produced. The first time he found he could bring about a noise by hitting the string of toys, he sobered, concentrated, and gingerly batted at them again. He remembered this, and he tried it over and over again as soon as he was placed in his playpen.

Determined repetition plays into the ability to learn quickly. The memory a baby carries over from one day to the next makes it unnecessary for him to relearn each day. He can then add a bit more each time and gather steam quickly as a result.

Mark brought a rattle to him, placing it in his hand. Daniel's hand closed over it. He waved it. The rattle of the toy surprised him and he dropped it. Mark's mother joined the game. She replaced the object in Daniel's hand. As he waved both arms in unison, he rattled the toy. The realization that he was responsible for the noise seemed to take hold, and Daniel's activity increased. When he dropped the

toy, he blinked, his face sobered, and he waited for his mother to
put it back in his hand.

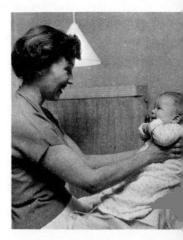

*Waiting for the mother to help him repeat this activity demonstrates
another dimension. A baby begins to realize that there is a limit to
his own ability to reproduce the activity. But he becomes conscious
of his mother's role in making up for this inability. Daniel is precocious in these associations.*

Mrs. Kay attempted to pull him up to sit in the middle of this
activity. Daniel arched his back and refused to be placed in a sitting
position. She found it difficult to break into these long play sessions.
Often he would scream with frustration when she did. She found
that she must make a transition for him to other kinds of play. For
instance, she could distract him with a toy held over his cradle-gym.
When she moved it slowly, he would follow it in full 180-degree arcs
from one side to the other many times in succession. As she drew
his interest away from his motor activity to watching the toy, he was
readier for a transition to another kind of play, or a diaper change,
or whatever she wanted for him.

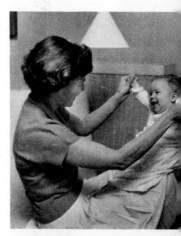

*A kind of inflexibility is noticeable in these infants who work so hard
and long at mastering an activity. It reflects the degree of investment
they are putting into a task and leaves them relatively insensitive to
distractions around them. This can be a major asset to rapid early
learning.*

On his abdomen, he could now hold his head up for long periods.
He would concentrate on a picture at his cribside or on a toy in the
distance. As his legs became active, he made active crawling movements. These were symmetrical, and he pushed himself along on the
mattress.

There were periods of sociability with his mother and Mark that
were delightful. He fixed on their faces over him, became active,
then quickly calmed down in order to look at them. His concentration on their faces was as intense as his motor activity had been. He
seemed to arch his head in order to reach for them with his eyes.
His mouth formed a circle as he stared.

He found he could produce sounds and practiced over and over.

His face screwed up, his arms and legs became active as his whole body became involved in the effort. As he became more intense, motor activity broke up the vocalizing. He could not continue both at this pace, and Daniel was at the mercy of his motor activity. He built up to a peak of movement, which resulted in fussing and disintegration. At this point, Mrs. Kay had to step in, pick him up, and comfort him with cuddling or rocking. He would relax in her arms and look up at her. This monitoring was Mrs. Kay's major role as a parent for Daniel.

Daniel and his mother still dreaded his baths. When they were necessary, she used all her ingenuity to help him with the transition from being dressed to being undressed. Usually, he broke down crying anyway. She found she could take him in the tub with her and wash him successfully while holding him in her arms. Washing his hair was painful for them both, and he had a patch of cradlecap that exactly reproduced his soft spot. This soft spot seemed so fragile to her that she was particularly afraid to scrub over it.

Daniel's feedings were more fun. At mealtime he was propped in his chair for his solid feedings. He had been taking cereal for two weeks and was used to the taste and to swallowing it. When his mother started fruit, Daniel's eyes widened as he tasted it. He smacked his lips and broke into a broad grin. Then he began to arch forward to reach for it with his mouth and face and head. He was so eager that it was hard for Mrs. Kay to keep up with him. She felt she should pour it in.

The early settlers in colonial days had "papcups" for pouring in liquid solids. Maybe it makes more sense than spooning in food, although I feel there is value in the baby learning about the spoon at this time. Some mothers put solids in bottles with a big hole in the nipple. This allows the infant to suck it down. It seems to be avoiding the issue of "teaching" him to swallow.

When she finished the allotted amount, Daniel let out a wail. He jammed his right thumb in his mouth and sucked furiously on it.

She returned with his bottle. Daniel looked up, brightened, arched his neck forward, opened his eyes and mouth, and waved both hands, as if he recognized it. He gulped it down greedily at first and finally relaxed in his mother's arms as he reached the halfway mark. She could rarely stop him long enough to bubble him in the middle of a bottle. This meant that he had accumulated an enormous bubble at the end, and he usually brought up milk with it.

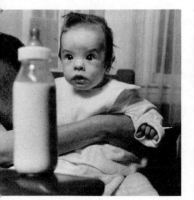

Air is swallowed with each gulp of milk, and the noisier and more rapid the feeding, the more gas the baby collects in his stomach.

Bedtime was still difficult, although he was sleeping ten hours regularly by three months.

According to recent studies of sleep, sleep cycles in infants are regular and are characteristic of them. An active, noisy baby like Daniel may be active and noisy in his sleep. Three- to four-hour cycles usually make up the night's sleep. Each cycle can be broken down into various types of sleep. In the middle of each cycle is approximately sixty minutes of deep sleep. The hour on each side of this deep sleep may be a lighter, dreaming state in which movement and activity (or dreaming) comes and goes. Then, at regular intervals through the night, an infant comes to a semi-conscious, semi-alert state. In this period, he may suck his fingers, cry out, rock or bang his head, move around the bed, practice his newly learned tricks, fuss, or talk to himself, and then settle into his conditioned sleeping position to get himself to sleep again. When his parents are nearby and respond to these cries and the activity, they quickly become a necessary part of his pattern of getting himself back to sleep. It seems an important role for us as parents to "condition" them to use their own resources for sleep as early as we can. This is an important part of acculturation.

As Daniel stopped his crying periods and began to become more sociable in the evening, Mr. Kay got more and more interested. He and Mark would sit together on the couch and draw Daniel out into the sociable activity he was learning so quickly. The picture of the three males together was a warming one for Mrs. Kay. She was beginning to see the blue skies ahead.

This is an example of what Mr. Kay might miss if he allows his work to take him away right now. Certainly the workplace is demanding and can become an alternative to family life—for working fathers or for working mothers. The real trick is to learn to compartmentalize the energy for both. Otherwise, one half of one's own development will suffer. Competition in the job market is likely to press for its pound of flesh. What worries me about parents who must be away from their small infants is that they may fail to develop a feeling of importance to the baby. As they feel less and less involved and important, they may transfer the feeling of responsibility to a secondary care-giver. They may miss the point of learning about being a nurturer—that it is quality *of time rather than* quantity *of time to which one must devote oneself. If a father or mother allows working to interfere with the opportunity to develop this side of him or herself, it could be a rather tragic way to dilute one's potential importance to the child's development. Unfortunately, in the past it was more or less accepted that fathers needn't be this involved with their infants. By the time they wanted to get to know the older child, it was much more difficult. I saw this when fathers returned from the Korean and Vietnam wars. If a baby had been born and had already grown into a child while he was away, it became much more difficult for him to relate to and "make it" with that child. Infancy is a period in which learning about each other and about oneself in this role of nurturer is a real and invaluable opportunity, not to be missed because of other demands. As the workplace demands young mothers, too, it is critical that both parents consider the role each can play as the "emotional heads of the family" for the baby.*

CHAPTER VI

The Fourth Month

AVERAGE BABY

Louis was now a picture-book baby. His body was rounded, his elbows and knees had dimples. His skin was incredibly smooth and spotless. The lanugo had gone from his ears and back, and his rashes did not last long. His body had a sturdy strength that held itself in one piece as he was handled. Although he was well-padded, he did not seem fat; there was a solid feel to his flesh. He was fun to hold and to play with. His elbows and knees crackled when they were bent.

Crackling is simply an indication of how loosely supported the larger joints are at this time. As the muscles become stronger this will no longer happen.

The two older children were competent helpers. Three-year-old Tom could bring diapers or the baby food, and he was allowed to hold Louis for periods. These periods usually ended with his tiring of it or with Louis fussing and squirming, but he had the feeling that Louis was partly his, and that some day Louis would be big enough to play with him. Sibling rivalry is not at an end but it is under control, thanks to his being included in helping with Louis.

Five-year-old Martha was often a real help to her mother. She fed Louis, even helped with his bath at times, and was learning to change him. Mrs. Moore often gave Martha the baby when Martha was in the bathtub and let her bounce him up and down in front of her in the tub. Martha's interest in his penis grew to fascination and brought out many questions. Mrs. Moore found it necessary to consult her doctor when Martha's concern about having a penis reached a peak. She had asked, "Where has mine gone?" "Did I ever

have one?" "What is it for?" "Why don't you and I have one?" until
Mrs. Moore was exhausted. But after her mother answered her
questions honestly and satisfactorily, she seemed to become satisfied.

*This is an opportunity for a parent to explain to a little girl about
herself. It should be done in her language and at her level, but she
deserves an answer. The explanation that her genital area contains
two important structures—an outlet for urine and also a lovely place
where someday a new baby may be taken care of and be born from
—will be over a small child's head on the first explanation. But, as
questions arise, the two concepts can be elaborated upon in a way that
is appropriate to the little girl's stage of development.*

*The concern about losing or not having a penis is common at this
age and with a new little brother, it is more likely to be vocalized. This
is an important time to establish a working line of communication for
the future. Unless a mother is open and honest at this time, she may
lose a real opportunity. The questions and concerns need answers, and
a child needs the feeling that her mother will answer them.*

Mr. Moore was enlisted to feed and play with Louis all the time now.
His job was to feed him his supper. Since Louis sucked his fingers
after a bite and then played with his father's hands while he was
feeding him, it was a messy process. But he talked to Louis as he fed
him and was charmed by Louis' gurgling back. Louis could imitate
several notes of vocalizing. He could vocalize "ooh," "ah," and he
could even cough in an effort to initiate socializing. The meal lasted
for half an hour or more, while he and his father played.

Louis enjoyed this role as the prince. He ate well and ate a lot.
He gulped down as much as half a baby-food jar of two different
things at each meal, and then was eager for the breast. He sucked
for short bursts on the breast, turning away to see what the rest of
the family was doing. He often stopped during a feeding and looked
up at his mother to coo and vocalize, as milk drooled down his
cheeks. When she could and would talk back to him, this could
continue for as much as thirty minutes before he would go back to
the breast to finish. He often chewed on his fist and acted as if he
were teething.

*This leads mothers to feel that these interrupted feedings are due to
teething pains. I am convinced that they are more often interrupted
by the infant's interest in looking around. If it is necessary to shorten*

a feeding, or if he won't eat enough any other way, one can feed an infant successfully in a dark, quiet room.

Since she had little time for a peaceful feeding during her busy day, she kept on awakening him for a late evening feeding after the two older children were in bed. She thought of this as her "playtime with Louis," and she enjoyed it as much as he. She felt at this time that she really had the baby to herself. He continued to take four nursings, although his mother felt he would have dropped the fourth without too much difficulty.

To adjust a baby to three meals and three breast-feedings, a mother can help him make the transition by a schedule such as:
  7 A.M.—*breast-feeding*
  8:30 A.M.–9 A.M.—*(after others fed) cereal and fruit*
  12–1 P.M.—*breast-feeding, meat, vegetables*
  5 P.M.—*cereal and fruit*
  6:30 P.M.—*a third breast-feeding*
By stretching out the two ends of the day, a baby can be "taught" to span the periods that are longer than four hours apart. As he becomes accustomed to it, the two ends can be pulled together again.

For a working mother, it is even more important to set up a schedule aimed at seeing to it that she has time to see and play with and also to feed her baby. I have seen many many mothers who went back to work at this time but who continued to breast-feed their babies. The danger is that of cutting down on the number of feedings too suddenly and causing the breasts to produce too little milk. Before she has to leave, a mother should see to it that she has readjusted her schedule of feedings so that she has at least three opportunities for feeding from the breast. If she must be away for an eight-hour stretch, she can breast-feed once in the morning before she leaves, a second time in the afternoon when she returns, and a third time in the evening. It is worth waking the baby, if necessary, in order to work in a fourth feeding (a third breast-feeding). The bottle can be given in the middle of the day, and solid foods can supplement all three feedings in the day if the baby is ready for them. Long naps in the afternoon can help the baby to be awake and alert for the working parents at the end of their day.

Louis began to drool all the time and was constantly wet around his face and neck. Rashes appeared unless Mrs. Moore protected his face with Vaseline and powdered the creases of his neck with corn-starch. He developed a severe rash in his neck at one time from the plastic backing of his bib; this did not disappear until she changed to terry cloth bibs.

Plastic bibs, detergent soaps, and wool are common sensitizers. Corn-starch, incidentally, is a handy and inexpensive substitute for baby powder.

Drooling was accompanied by a lot of finger-sucking and exploring in his mouth with his hands. He seemed to have his hands to his mouth a large part of each day.

A study of extra-nutritional sucking with charts kept by mother-observers shows that as much as four hours a day is often spent in sucking activity.

Mrs. Moore wondered whether this combination of salivation, finger-sucking, and shortened interest in the breast was an indication of early teething.

This may be a teething syndrome, but these activities occur in the fourth month anyway. The more agile use of his hands and widening interest in things around him contribute to all of this exploration, which also shortens feedings.

The lower front incisors come in first. A tooth, as it comes, acts like a foreign body (e.g., a splinter) and causes swelling and irritation of the gums around itself. By rubbing this swelling with a clean finger or ice in a handkerchief, one rubs out the swelling and relieves the aching for a time. When the baby sucks, blood rushes into his gums. This extra blood adds engorgement to the swelling that is already present. Sucking then hurts an already swollen gum. A baby rubs at his own gums as if to reduce the pain. As he finds chewing and rubbing on his own gums reduces pain, he begins to rub around them and on his face. The same nerves to the teeth branch out to the face, cheek, and outer ear. He finds it helps pain to rub on any part of his face. So a teething infant may rub his jaw and pull on his ear as if he has an earache. It thus may be difficult for a mother to differentiate an earache from a toothache. Obviously, she can rub the baby's gum and find out whether it is sore. When one starts rubbing on a teething gum, the infant lets out a yowl that will be the tip-off that it is the source of discomfort. Continue the rubbing, and he will settle down. Using a temporary painkiller such as aspirin by mouth, or paregoric on the gums, may help also.

Louis played for as much as three quarters of an hour at a time on his back. He watched his hands, brought them up together, played with his fingers, and took an interest in each hand in front of him. He would look back and forth from one hand to the other, bring them together, smiling as he did so, and he grinned as he grabbed one with the other. He would hold on to each hand, pull his arms apart, and fairly snap them away from each other. He giggled as they snapped.

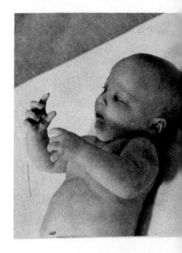

This is a rather complex exploration and use of the hands—which can be put to many uses already, including making toys of them.

He reached repeatedly for toys on his cradle-gym, grabbing hold of one, pulling it toward him, and letting it bounce away as he let go. He seemed to be able to do this with each hand and, by the end of the fourth month, took some pleasure in alternating hands to grab the objects. It seemed to his mother as if he were making a distinction between one hand and the other.

If so, this is the beginning of awareness of two separate parts of himself. It is important in his increasing awareness of spatial relationships that he realize their distinctness from each other.

He loved to be handled and played with. He chortled out loud as he was pulled to sit. He now held his head steady as he sat, and he could look around in a supported sitting position. He could turn his head in sitting and look ahead in all directions.

He had been free to look around in a reclining, supported position before, but now he could combine sitting and arching efforts with head-turning and a gaze paralleling the surface on which he sat. One by one he combines these achievements as one new awareness is piled on top of another. Now he has a three-dimensional space that he can produce or give up at will.

When he played for very long, he tired easily, indicating how much he put into it.

On his belly, he made swimming motions with his arms and legs. After he had "swum" for a period, he began to stiffen in frustration and bang on the bed with his outstretched arms.

The swimming is made up of reflex activity that we inherit from our amphibian ancestors.

As he stiffened out his legs and body, he began to rock like a seesaw, up and down. This airplane-like rocking became a new way to play, and he rocked himself back and forth, chortling. After a while, however, he tired of these activities and fussed to be turned onto his back. When one of the children would get down in the playpen with him and would play with him at his level, he could double the time that he was willing to play.

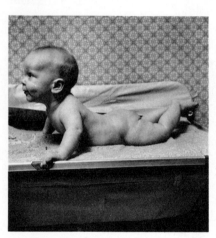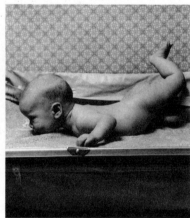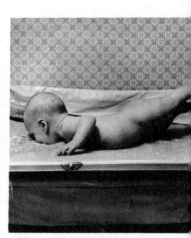

This is an index of how much elasticity there is in the amount of energy an infant can invest in a play period.

By the time Louis was three and a half months, Mrs. Moore was certain that he had learned how to make her respond to him whenever she was in sight. He would arch forward as he looked at her when he wanted her to pick him up. She saw him search the room for her when she was quietly sewing across the way. As he found her with his eyes, he cooed and gurgled until she looked toward him.

Then he began to fuss for her to come to him. He might be in his father's lap having a good time when she entered the room. He would startle, look puzzled, began to stiffen and whimper to come to her. As soon as he came to her, he'd look back to his father, whimper, then want to go back to him again. He could play this game of being passed back and forth as long as his parents could stand it. He softened all over before he smiled at his mother, then crinkled his eyes and face with an appealing grin. In contrast, the smile he gave his father and siblings was different—less appealing, and it had more muscular activity of his entire body accompanying it. He already differentiated between them and seemed to sense which activity was more appropriate and appealing to each member of the family.

QUIET BABY

The world was unfolding more gradually for Laura. She seemed to let it in at her own, slow, determined pace. Happiest when she was lying on her back in the crib or on the floor, she continued to explore the room or her hands from this safe vantage point. She continued to play with her hands, intertwining her fingers at times. When her mother held a toy over her, her arms waved in circles at her sides at the sight of it. Together they gradually tried to come up to meet it, grasp it, and hold on to it. She bounced it up and down, held tightly with both hands. Finally, she dropped it. As she did, she startled slightly at the loss. She explored each of the toys strung across her crib. She seemed to develop a definite preference for one of them. She would twist herself around with dogged determination so that she could more easily reach and play with a soft red ball. The shiny yellow block, the green ring that could be held on to easily, and the brown fur animal were ignored as she returned over and over to this preferred red ball.

This early attachment to one object as opposed to the others is evidence of sensitive discrimination. Most infants do not settle down yet to one toy over the others. It is also a sign that an infant is beginning to take a real interest in something outside of herself. This is good and is a testimony to her normal emotional development. An autistic child rarely forms such an attachment for an outside object as early as this. I am always gratified when children form attachments to objects—even though they become "loveys" and are obviously a substitute for their mothers. It certainly gives them one more advantage in coping with the rigors of growing up, with all of its frustrations and necessary separations from mother.

As she played, Laura began to coo to herself. She gurgled and vocalized with vowel sounds in a widening scale of notes. She developed an increasing range, and she seemed to listen to herself as she practiced. When her parents stood over her, her vocalizing decreased.

This is not the usual reaction. Ordinarily a baby increases her responses in number and appeal.

She watched their faces in her characteristic intent manner and seemed silenced by their appearance. She seemed to study each feature and watch their movements. They both attempted to draw her out by cooing to her. Not until the end of the fourth month did Laura begin to "speak back," quietly and gingerly, as her mother cooed to her. At last she seemed able to cope with the appearance of a parent over her. Perhaps she was increasing her capacity to integrate the several simultaneous and important stimuli that a parent represents. Instead of taking them in one at a time, savoring each independently, she began to put them all together. This freed her to absorb them more quickly as a whole gestalt.

Mrs. King held her up to a mirror to see herself. Laura examined the faces in the mirror. She seemed to be most interested in her own image. Finally, she smiled at her face. As it smiled back at her, she became active and vocalized as she smiled. She carried on this interplay for several minutes. She looked hard at her mother's image, looking back at her mother, as if she were perplexed by this duplication. When she was looking at her mother's image, Mrs. King spoke softly to Laura. Laura jumped, looked startled and worried, and turned quickly back to her mother's real face. She seemed confused by the two faces of her mother.

This confusion demonstrates the fact that she is already very sensitive to similarities. A child who knows her mother's face so well cannot accept two of them that are "almost" alike. The sudden spoken voice from behind adds to the confusion. This preference for the mother "in the flesh" over the mirror image shows keen discrimination.

Laura enjoyed the activity that accompanied her bath. She now loved to be undressed and became much more active. Mrs. King enjoyed it, too. She bathed her after her breakfast since Laura seemed to enjoy it so much more after her meal.

I can see no reason for the old custom of "never putting a baby in the tub after a meal." The old argument that one might draw her blood away from her stomach is absurd. There will be plenty of blood to go around, and, as far as I know, no baby has ever gotten cramps from being bathed after a meal. The only argument against it may be that she may spit up more if she is handled too much after a meal. This is a calculated risk, and she may. But so many babies enjoy their baths then and hate them before meals that it seems like an obvious time to bathe them.

She put Laura in her big tub with two inches of water in it and supported her head in one hand while she soaped and rinsed her with the other. As she did, Laura gurgled, laughed out loud, and kicked up and down, throwing her arms out to each side. She splashed water all around. When it splashed in her face, it made her stop with surprise. She puckered, spit, burbled, and blinked away the water. Then she caught sight of her mother's smiling face over her, took the cue from this, and began to splash again.

In bed, Laura was more active on her back. She hated being on her belly. She showed her displeasure by digging her face into the bed whenever she was turned over. She would then lie motionless, sucking her fingers, until someone moved her.

Many children show this kind of displeasure at being turned over on their abdomens when they want to play. It happens when they have been having fun on their backs or, in my office, where they want to watch what is going on—"to keep an eye on me."

She would rarely become active on her belly, even when her parents played with her in this position.

To condition a baby to like lying on her belly, one must get down on her level and play with her. Gradually, she may begin to be willing to play on it for a period. Most of her earlier conditioning for play has been on her back, and it is no wonder many infants refuse to stay on their bellies.

When she was pulled to sit, she demonstrated resistance by arching her back and throwing back her head. Placed in a sitting position, she stared with a disgruntled look at the person who placed her there, which invariably made that person feel uncomfortable. Laura has certainly learned to use her expressive face to hit her parents between the eyes.

The feeding periods were more and more fun. Mrs. King enjoyed the breast-feeding. It filled all of her desire to be needed by Laura, and Laura seemed cooperative and interested in the feeding. Their pleasure at these times increased constantly. Laura had finally eliminated the night feeding herself, and Mrs. King found she probably could have given up the 10 P.M. one also. But she enjoyed the chance to be close to Laura, and she looked forward to it all evening. Mr. King participated in this delightful "family" time. He watched the two of them, as they talked to each other. He found himself jealous and occasionally asked his wife whether she "had enough milk," "when she planned to stop," or "whether this wasn't adding to Laura's quiet, introspective behavior."

This is common for fathers at about this stage particularly when the mother is breast-feeding. They begin to feel jealous of their wives, jealous of the baby, and left out of the close unit of mother and child. Many eat snacks at feeding times. Others make plans to take their wives away from the baby for a weekend. This may be unconscious, but it is obviously in the direction of breaking up this unity.

Most women whom a young nursing mother meets will take unconscious digs at her, too. "Are you still nursing?" "The baby's too fat" or "too thin." "Haven't you started solids yet?"—all of these reflect their competitive feelings. Even a contemporary or a grandmother who has nursed her own children and enjoyed it will show herself jealous of this delightful unity. Mothers who are nursing should be aware of the envy that prompts these undermining remarks.

Mr. King fed Laura her solids in the evening. He could get her to squeal with delight as he tinkled the spoon on the baby-food jar when he started to feed her. He insisted that she could recognize her jars from other jars of the same size, and he always showed her the baby on the jar before he started to feed her. She ate readily now, licking her lips and her fingers from time to time. She inserted her whole fist after a bite. Then she smeared her face with her sticky hand. Mr. King was delighted by all these antics and described her as a fat Elizabethan dowager who could not get her food in fast enough. She smeared her hair and it needed washing each night. Since her hair was falling out rapidly, Mrs. King worried about washing it so often.

The hair will come out anyway, and more will grow in whatever her mother does. Infants' first hair usually begins to fall out earlier and will continue to come out until the fifth or sixth month. Since the second hair is growing in all along, the transition cannot always be noted.

Hair color can change dramatically in this process. Hence it is dangerous to predict future coloring from a baby's hair at birth. The tone color of the skin is a better way of predicting, although a look at the parents' coloring is by far the best prediction. One can predict a brunette when "Mongolian spots" are present. These are dark flat spots around the base of the spine. They are collections of dark pigment—called "Mongolian" because the Mongol and Negro races have them characteristically. However, even Caucasian babies who will be dark brunettes have them at birth. The pigment spreads out in time and the "spots" disappear. They are of no other significance.

Eye color is another source of interest to parents. Usually a baby is born with "blue" eyes, although I have seen a few brown-eyed newborns. In dark brunettes, the muddying of the cornea takes place in the first few weeks. This can also occur at any time in the first year. Usually by six months, one can predict brown eyes by the muddy look. Blue eyes remain china blue in the first six months.

After meals, Laura dozed in her baby chair, her head lolling to the side, and her stomach protruding in a round soft pot. When she was put to bed on her fat belly, she dropped her head onto her right cheek, sucked her left thumb, and was off to sleep. After these cozy, peaceful family times, the Kings were able to look at each other with amazement at their shared feeling of peace and contentment.

ACTIVE BABY

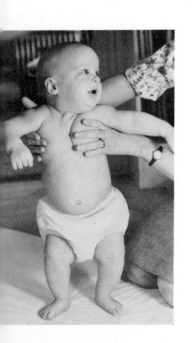

Daniel's vigor was devoted equally to activity and to maintaining contact with people. He was often caught by indecision in the midst of performing some motor act by his father's face appearing over his playpen. He would stop his bouncing, look up at his father, grin, and gurgle. Then he alternated between bouncing and talking. His bouncing and vocalizing became more and more feverish as he performed for his audience. His father called him a "ham." Unless he was picked up, this activity could continue for as long as the observer could tolerate it. Rarely did Daniel give out first. When he did, he whimpered for a change of pace, which he seemed unable to initiate. He knew already that he could not change pace as well by himself as he could when someone else helped him.

He loved to be pulled to stand and chortled as he came up holding on to his father's two fingers. He maintained his weight briefly in standing, looking down at his father's hands, which supported him. When he was pulled to sit, he quickly learned to by-pass that position and come on up to stand. In order to sit him, one had to bend him in the middle.

This is somewhat precocious at his age. It is indicative of a drive to perform, to "get going." The standing a baby is doing now is no more than a responsive or reflex stiffening of his body, but as he learns he can do it, he becomes delighted with the act and repeats it over and over. The question of what motivates an infant to stand has not been answered satisfactorily. They certainly are in a hurry to do it, and the pleasure that accompanies this simple reflex standing is a testimony to the drive to get there.

While prone, he pushed up on his straight arms and brought his head up to a ninety-degree angle, looking in all directions. He watched Mark for long periods from his playpen in this position. When he tired, he dropped to the pad, briefly arched his back, and spread his arms out, rocking back and forth in an airplane position. Then he brought his hands up by his face and scratched on the playpen pad. He giggled with delight at the loud scratching sounds, apparently aware that he was producing them. The noise brought his mother to his side quickly, even from a room away. It grated on her ears. When she came to him, he squealed.

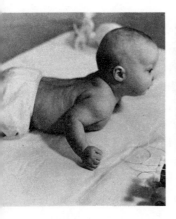 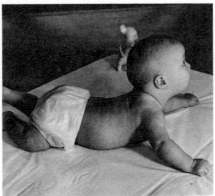 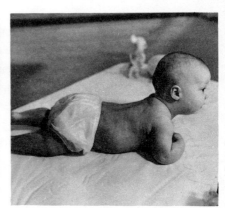

Daniel shows many more resources in each position than do the others. These resources are a testimony to a bright, quick motor aptitude, as well as pleasure in adding new areas of exploration on to the simple motor acts.

As his mother picked him up, Daniel gave out a belly laugh and arched backward in her arms to see her face. She nearly dropped him when he arched suddenly. In her arms, he wriggled, talked to her, looked up at her, and practically crawled up her chest in his eager activity. She likened holding him to trying to hold on to a sack of eels.

Daniel's parents took him to see his grandparents for a day's visit. They were utterly charmed with his cheerful responsiveness and his activity. His grandfather played with him all day. Two-year-old Mark sat huddled in his mother's lap, watching all this with quiet envy. Mrs. Kay did her best to comfort Mark and make up to him, but Daniel was able to keep the center of the stage for hours on end. Daniel took one short nap in the afternoon but maintained a constant level of activity and interaction the rest of the seven-hour visit, responding to the new audience and all the stimulation.

On the way home, he began to fall apart and had to be held by his mother. He screamed through his supper, refused all of the solids, and drank only half his bottle.

Anna Freud speaks of the "disintegration" of a baby's or child's ego that goes on at the end of a day. This is an example of it. It appears to me that the mother's ego disintegrates simultaneously with his at the end of a long day.

When he was put in his bed, he screamed briefly but then fell immediately to sleep. Within two hours, he was awake again, crying. When his father went to him, Daniel had turned himself over on his back and was kicking and crying. He refused to be patted back to sleep. Mr. Kay ended by taking him out into the living room to rock him in the big rocking chair. Here he became charming and sociable. After half an hour, Mrs. Kay tried the rest of his bottle to quiet him. He refused it. She put him in his bed and turned off the light. Three more times before midnight, Mr. or Mrs. Kay went in to turn Daniel over on his stomach to sleep. Each time he became alert as they entered his room, and each time he had to cry himself to sleep after they left. At midnight, they got into bed congratulating themselves on having solved the problem at last. At two and at four, he awakened in the same manner. Each time he was turned back to his stomach and left to cry. By 6 A.M. Mrs. Kay got up for good with Daniel. The next three days were a mixture of his demanding fussing during the day and waking at night.

Daniel is a very sensitive and even fragile baby to be upset to such an extent by a visit to the grandparents at this age. However, I hear similar troubles of this later in far less fragile babies. I suspect that the parents' distress compounds and makes a cyclic issue out of a simple upset. Thus it lasts for several days.

Mrs. Kay felt pulled apart by his constant demands. When she came to him, he broke into a broad grin, and she realized he knew he had her. She finally resolved to let him cry more during the day and steeled herself to it. Mark became upset when Daniel cried, so she had two to cope with. But after a day of studied neglect, Daniel settled into his old pattern of active resourcefulness. The Kays wondered whether they ever dared leave the house with Daniel again.

This extreme sensitivity to excitement and to new sources of stimulation is hard to handle. One solution might be to "condition" a baby to people more gradually. If a baby is not taken out enough, he cannot assimilate the experience without such a buildup and such a storing of tension.

Daniel's reaction was certainly based upon his susceptibility to receive and react to all stimuli around him. He added a dimension of his own—magnifying them into more excitement and activity. The Kays felt they had to react in the rigid unyielding way that they did, otherwise it seemed obvious that Daniel could not pull himself out of the cyclone he was creating and get back down to his routine.

Daniel's bathtime was improving. Mrs. Kay hit on the idea of bathing him in the tub with Mark. He was so delighted with his older brother that he began to enjoy being undressed as if he anticipated the bath. In the tub, he splashed and Mark splashed. Mark splashed water on Daniel and sprayed his face. Daniel loved it. By the time they were through with a bath, the bathroom was awash, but Mrs. Kay preferred that to the former days of Daniel's screams.

Daniel performed at the doctor's office as he had for his grandparents. He lay on the table, laughing and vocalizing while he was examined. He grabbed the stethoscope with both hands and clung to it. When he was turned on his abdomen, his head came up and he turned on his side to watch the doctor. On the scales, he kicked so hard that it took twice as long as usual to come to an accurate balance. When he was given his shot, he looked surprised, puckered his mouth, and looked around at the doctor who had just given it. He caught his eye, smiled, and began to perform again. The doctor sighed and said, "That baby is so resourceful that even pain doesn't faze him."

CHAPTER VII

The Fifth Month

AVERAGE BABY

Experimentation absorbed Louis' day. Since he could be propped up in a bounce chair for long periods, he had a three-dimensional world to learn about.

The infant chair is not adequate any longer. Too many active children clamber out of it. A next step can be a bounce chair or a swing in which the baby can sit for many hours a day. However, any of these should still be kept at a reclining angle. The baby will not stay in the reclining position for long, but as he arches himself forward, the lower half of his back remains supported by the angle of the seat.

He found learning an exciting job. His span of attention had increased, and with minor help from his family, he could lie on his back, or sit in his chair playing for an hour and a half to two hours. He was no longer happy with a mobile or a cradle-gym that was out of reach. He wanted it close enough to feel and examine. He needed to touch, to hold, to turn, to examine, to rattle, to mouth each toy. He was no longer satisfied with just watching—with a two-dimensional approach to a toy. His concepts were now three dimensional, and he screamed with frustration when he could not reach an object. His eyes, fingers, and mouth were integrated as he learned.

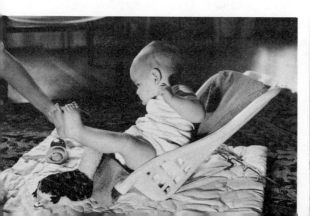

The force behind this integration can be aroused in a baby this age by leaving him with a toy that he cannot pull into him. He is left with vision and fingers. He will play happily this way for a period. Then, as if he suddenly realizes this is not enough, his frustration builds up as he strains to get his mouth on it. He ends up by screaming furiously when he cannot examine it all over with his mouth and hands, as well as his eyes.

Louis showed excitement about everything. Although he slept all night and had been doing so for a month, he roused himself in the early morning to "get going."

The four-hour cycles in sleep at night that we talked about in Daniel's third month bring about an alerting period around 6 A.M. At this time in the morning, the baby has slept enough, and he rouses and begins to make demanding noises. In more tranquil periods of development, an infant does not build himself up to wakefulness as quickly as he does at four to five months. This need to "get going" is a reflection of the incremental speed-up in awareness and frustration that precedes a new step in motor development.

Instead of being willing to lie quietly sucking on his fist, Louis came quickly awake to engage in large-muscle activity. This is comparable to Daniel in the earlier periods—now Louis was demonstrating the same urge to perform. Louis' urges came and went in spurts; Daniel's were a constant and inherent part of his makeup.

Louis airplaned, rocked, and finally turned himself over in persistent activity. When he was over on his back, he could amuse himself for a short while. The early morning light reminded him that he should be "busy with his day." He began to squeal and call for his parents. As he cried, each of the children responded, and soon the house was in a fever of excitement. After 6 A.M., no one was allowed to sleep.

None of the maneuvers that parents try seem to interfere with this pattern. Keeping a baby up later in the evening will not make him tired in the early morning. Feeding him at night does not help. Black shades to keep out the light are worth a try. Strapping him to the bed in a harness may be an answer for the desperate. It probably works. I am not an advocate of such strong-arm tactics. The baby's practicing and maneuvering are too important as integral parts of this spurt of his development. What happens when one suppresses this by harnessing the forces in a baby as strongly oriented toward learning as Louis is? This early waking is not just the morning light coming in, or teeth, or hunger—it is a real drive to learn how to perform. How can a parent appreciate it, but not allow it to dominate the household in the early morning? I would prefer to put the baby farther away from everyone so that he must build up longer and cry harder to awaken them. This not only gives them more sleep, but forces him back on his own resources for a longer time. This treatment seems to be more conducive to learning and development than active suppression of his motor skills by such a restraint as a harness.

This pattern of waking is a very difficult one for working parents (as well as for a single parent). If a mother must be away all day, it is much harder for her not to rush in to the baby at each whimper. Each cycle of coming to semi-awakeness and crying out, or talking, or playing becomes a signal to her that she is needed. And her own need to be with her baby pushes her to want to respond. A working mother is likely to perpetuate night waking by becoming the crutch by which the baby finds his way from light sleep down to deep sleep every three to four hours. My own feeling is that learning to sleep through the night is as much a learning process as any other developmental step. It must be achieved by the baby. He must "learn" to get himself from light sleep back down to deep sleep. For some it is more difficult than for others. Some will need more help from the environment to learn it. But ultimately it is the child's job. Parents who are finding it difficult to leave the child to learn how to sleep will do well to curtail their role to allow the learning process to take place in the child. It isn't easy, but autonomy or independence in the area of sleeping is one of our culture's expectations.

A single parent finds it even more difficult to separate from the baby at night. The parent's loneliness and need for the baby outweigh any other consideration at night. It can become a real problem at each of these developmental crises, when waking from sleep becomes an outlet for the motor and learning energy left over from the daytime. A single parent will do well to discuss this issue with a concerned third party who can help her (or him) to weigh all of the separation issues that are involved and that must be balanced with the baby's need to learn about autonomy or independence at night.

Louis could interact at length with anyone who was available. He watched their mouths and faces as they made sounds to him. He experimented with his own sounds after them. Since he could use a few consonants, such as "d" and "b," he began to combine them with vowels. He occasionally hit on "dada" or "baba." As he did, the family reacted. "Dada" brought his father to him. "Baba" got squeals of delight from Martha. Louis certainly sensed that they were responding to his babbling.

This is called "positive" reinforcement, i.e., a rewarding response from the environment that repeatedly follows an act that was originally a segment of random trial and error. As the reward is repeated several times, an infant begins to associate the act with the result of it. He learns to repeat it over and over to call forth the expected response. He cannot associate the specific sound with its meaning yet.

The children imitated the sounds which Louis made as he experimented.

This feedback of his own sounds may be one of the most important reinforcers to early learning of speech. In one child whose parents were both deaf, I saw this experimental vocalizing come out at this age, but after a rather short period of a month, it lost its vigor. The infant seemed to lose his interest in vocalizing without any reinforcement. Later in the year, he tried again—this time he imitated the nasal flat sounds that his deaf parents used in their speech. In normal environments, a parent imitates the baby, he realizes it, imitates himself, finds delight in the repetition, and the cycle is reinforced.

As the family imitated Louis, he brightened. Very soon they found he was trying to imitate their inflections. The pattern was set. When he made a sound, they reproduced it. He would grin and try to make a sound again. This pattern could go on for several minutes. As they added a variation, he would look surprised as if he heard a difference. The effort he put into this interaction usually wore him out, and he suddenly disintegrated into frantic activity or crying. Tom found this hard to understand, but Martha soon began to realize when Louis was getting "too tired to talk any longer."

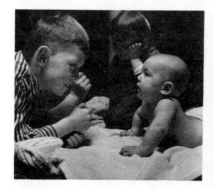

Louis tried to imitate his mother's facial movements in the same way. As she grimaced and smacked her lips, he watched her face intensely. When she was talking to him, and turned to talk to another person, Louis cried or began to call her back in some way. When Mrs. Moore went out on business and held him in her lap as she talked, Louis began to talk louder. He would start by smiling and vocalizing to the friend. When this did not stop them, he would twist to look up at his mother, trying to divert her attention. As this failed to interfere, he began to vocalize in louder and louder trills of sound. Mrs. Moore often had to put him down or in another room to continue her conversation.

This is an interesting use of the newly found vocalizing: an attempt to intrude upon his mother's conversation with another and to call back her attention to him.

The increase in his demands on her may have played a role in Mrs. Moore's decision to wean Louis from the breast. She found she was getting increasingly tired as he woke her in the early morning. He called her all day with his vocalizing and his demands to be picked up.

One of the ways a baby handles some of the frustration attendant upon these spurts of development is to "take them out" on those around him. Many are happy only when they are in motion, i.e., carried or played with actively.

Louis now held out his arms toward her as she appeared over him. Even when she did not respond to these appeals from him, she felt guilty and drained just the same. She need not have. The frustration he felt when she did not respond could be a very important force for learning how to do things for himself.

She rationalized weaning him in many ways—all justifiable.

After the initial start on the breast, which gives the infant a source of early immunity and an entirely digestible, non-allergic food, there is less and less reason from the infant's standpoint to push a mother to breast-feed him. Surely, as long as she does, he is being offered assets of extra immunity and an ideal source of milk, but these are not necessary to his survival in our culture. Many primitive tribes nurse children for years in order to provide them with the extra immunity, calcium, protein, and vitamins that they wouldn't get otherwise. In Mexico, I have seen a mother, while nursing her infant on one breast, call up two older children (two and four) to get a token suck on the other breast. In this way, she protects them as well as she can from the 40 percent mortality in children with which some mal-nourished primitive tribes are faced. It is obviously a mark of the strength of the maternal instinct and the mother's awareness that breast milk increases their chances of survival.

Mrs. Moore could now give Louis an unprepared, unsweetened, and unsterilized milk. She chose to give him evaporated milk out of a can, which she could leave open and covered in the icebox. When she needed a bottle, she mixed it with hot tap water, which warmed up the bottle as she mixed it.

She felt and I feel that warm milk is more natural. Nature gives a baby warm milk—and unless one can improve on nature, why not follow her? It is easy enough to produce warm milk to feed a baby. Cold milk seems just that to me—"cold."

The advantage in using canned milk and not regular milk out of a dairy bottle is that a mother can always be sure that she has some. Older children and adults drink the regular milk when it is there.

Canned milk can be kept in stock. Canned milk is just as nutritious as whole, since we do not depend on vitamins in it, which are destroyed by heat in the canning process.

He was eating enough solids so that he needed only three feedings anyway, and with a bottle, other members of her family could feed him for her if she was particularly busy. She felt correctly that she might not be as tired when she gave up this extra physical drain.

Nursing unfortunately can be an additive factor to a mother's fatigue and can drain her physically.

She weaned Louis slowly, dropping the noon feeding first, the evening one second, and the early morning one last. She found it harder to give up that feeding. She had found that she could take Louis to bed with her in the early morning, nurse and cuddle him, then put him back in his crib for another hour or more. In this way, she could get another treasured hour of sleep. Her milk decreased as the demands to make it decreased, and she could have weaned him in a week's time. However, she hung on to the early morning feeding for two more weeks. She also found it important to her as a last tie to Louis.

Weaning turns out to be more of a wrench than most women anticipate. It is a final giving up of an important tie, and one often experiences with weaning a mild form of the depression that occurs in the postpartum period. A physiological adjustment based on hormonal changes accompanies this depression, too—as it does in postpartum blues. This is not usually as intense or long-lasting as the earlier blues. A slow weaning gives both mother and infant an opportunity to make this adjustment slowly.

The feeling of many women that it is "time to wean" comes as coincident with the baby's rapidly increasing development. The new motor skills and the rapidly widening interest in the world are major developmental trends. They both represent the first spurts of the baby's developing his own independence. The mother may find it difficult to give up the lovely closeness that has developed over the first few months. A working mother may feel that the baby is rejecting her because she is leaving him to work. Not so. It is not necessarily a time to give up the closeness that cements them back together at the end of the day.

A single parent may feel the premonition of the baby's growing away. This is likely to result in holding on to the baby more tightly —often at an entirely unconscious level. The hardest job in being a single parent is to recognize and allow for the tiny, subtle spurts toward independence that are critical to the infant's development of autonomy. A single mother at this stage might either wean or hover more closely. Neither is necessary if she can recognize the reason for the spurt toward independence in the baby. In my own practice, I find it helps to discuss and try to understand the baby's "pulling away" behavior.

Louis became constipated as he was weaned. His movements became less frequent and hard, and he had some bright red blood on them several times.

Bright blood accompanying a hard stool, as distinguished from darker, digested blood, which could be coming from higher up in the intestinal tract (and is a sign of difficulty), most often comes from a crack around the anus—a fissure. To treat this fissure, a mother needs (1) to soften the bowel movement with either prune juice, or a brown sugar such as molasses, or a laxative food such as prunes; and (2) to protect the fissure with a coat of Vaseline spread around the anus two or three times a day. If it doesn't heal rapidly, the anus should be dilated with the little finger and kept greased so that it can heal. If it does not heal in a few days, it should be checked by a physician.

Once he was weaned, Louis adjusted to the new milk and seemed contented. He sucked his fingers more, and Mrs. Moore slowed the nipples of his bottles to assure him of twenty minutes' sucking on a bottle. She felt guilty whenever she saw him suck on his fingers, as she felt she no longer "was doing all she could for him." This was a reflection of her own ambivalent feelings about the weaning. He might have been upset by the weaning and demonstrated it by sucking more on his fingers. But he might also have sucked more at this time anyway. His own need for sucking is increased at this time as a reflection of the inner turmoil and the frustration attendant upon the spurt in motor development that is occurring.

QUIET BABY

Laura's contentment continued. This contrasted with the buildup in activity in Louis. She handled her developing awareness in an entirely different way. Her sucking on fingers and toys was increasing in intensity, as she lay looking around with wide, knowing eyes. She had learned to bring her feet to her mouth and even sucked on her toes. She also chewed now as she sucked on her thumb. With a toy, she mouthed and chewed on every available edge. As she did, she seemed to savor each separate facet of it. No longer was the soft, red ball her favorite toy. She liked harder objects with corners that were cool to her gums.

Investigation is spurred by application of these objects to swollen gums. Chewing on a cold object has the effect of reducing swelling, as does rubbing the gums. The relief afforded in chewing activity heightens the value of mouthing.

She transferred a toy easily from one hand to the other and seemed to get pleasure from this. As she took a toy with her right hand, she waved it. Next, she transferred it to the left and repeated the same waving gesture—back and forth in repetitious play—one hand imitating the other.

This might be a digesting of the awareness that she can do the same thing with each arm. It may be an example of the excitement in imitating that Louis demonstrates with his siblings. In Laura's case, it may have added value to her since this is an imitation of her own action.

As she brought the toy up to her mouth, she put her thumb in her mouth first, then thoughtfully replaced the thumb with the toy, alternating one and the other as if she were savoring the relative merits of toy and thumb.

Comparison of part of herself with an object is now evident. This kind of comparison becomes a part of the process of differentiation of self from the outer world.

Noises she produced in her play took on more significance. She experimented and digested the tinkle of a bell-toy for long periods. She even learned how to turn it so that she produced different bell sounds. The variations made by a music box were less interesting than the slight changes in sounds she could produce herself. She seemed to withdraw from the music box's drawn-out tunes and was relieved to have them end. This was a sign of Laura's characteristic sensitivity to very slight variations. She was digesting and exploring auditory sounds. The music box assaulted her and even interfered with auditory exploration, which she preferred because she could control it. She combined the exploration of listening with an appreciation of her own ability to produce the sounds.

Mastery becomes a part of incentive and an outlet as well. This same use of auditory sensitivity, coupled with active production, is what reinforces practice sessions for musicians. The combination makes it tolerable for them to practice one phrase of music over and over to achieve perfection. An idle listener feels he may go mad as he listens.

This kind of sensitive exploration is typical of Laura's special makeup. It is a real talent in her and will contribute to a kind of exploratory talent and investment in objects and people around her. The pleasure she gets from exploring and digesting each sensory aspect of a situation undoubtedly contributes to her less active investment in motor development. But who could see this complexity in Laura and not value it as an exciting way to develop?

Vocalizing was used in a similar fashion. Laura lay for long periods trilling to herself or her mother. She used few consonants except "l," saying, "ley" or "lee." She could carry an "ah" or an "ooh" up and down the octave in beautiful trails of musical tone. Her mother would reproduce Laura's sounds. Laura listened, seemed to try to imitate her. They both enjoyed it, but Mrs. King could not stand this play for long. She always tried to add a "new" consonant or "new" note to Laura's repertoire. But when she did so it cut off the session as abruptly as if she had shouted at the baby. Laura's attempts would end, her face stare, her eyes cloud over, as she closed her mouth. One could imagine that the nictitating membrane that one sees in cats' eyes came over her eyes in negative response to this unexpected new stimulus from her mother. Mrs. King did not appreciate the extent to which her "teaching" efforts were an assault on Laura's sensitivity and desire to learn for herself.

Laura smacked her lips, clicked her tongue, and learned to cough over and over. She even learned that with a series of coughs one of her parents would rush to her bedside.

The coughing may first be triggered by the increased salivation that goes with teething. An infant masters the cough, and she repeats it over and over. The cough is a dry hack that sounds like a smoker's cough. It can be told from a significant cough by the way it can be produced at will.

Nursing periods were shorter these days. Laura took what she wanted from the breasts in the first five minutes. Then she preferred to talk to her mother or play with her clothes, hair, or face.

This ability to take four to six ounces from a breast in five minutes always amazes me. One could hardly do it from a bottle or a cup. It is another tribute to the efficiency of nursing. The danger, of course, is that stimulation to the breasts may be cut down abruptly when a baby cuts down on nursing time. The mother's breasts may respond by a sudden decrease in supply. If this happens, more frequent nursing will bring back the supply. Another trick to increase stimulation and supply is that of giving morning and evening feedings in a dark room with no distracting stimuli around. Then a baby will suck for the usual length of time, and the mother's milk will come back.

Mr. and Mrs. King had been taking Laura out more. They took her to the grandparents, and they took her out with them at night. At a friend's house, they parked her in the bedroom while they played bridge in the living room.

This is a time to avoid the need for sitters. Never again will going out be as easy. Until she begins to need the same place for sleeping, it is a shame not to utilize her mobility.

Mrs. King thought these excursions were important to Laura in diluting some of her sensitivity to strange persons and places.

And they are—this may be one of the values of carriage rides—that of exposing and conditioning a baby to the world around her.

Laura continued to show increasing powers of differentiating her parents from other people. She could recognize her father in a roomful of other men, and she would wriggle and vocalize when she found his face. She showed an increased sensitivity to strange women. She broke into crying when a lady poked at her in her carriage or tried to pick her up. Some of this had been seen earlier with the sitter. Now it took less of an approach from a stranger to call forth a reaction.

The resentment of strange women, often greater than that felt for strange men, seems to me to be associated with the relative importance of their mothers and the cues associated with them. A man does not call up such poignant associations as does a woman—particularly one that may remind her of her mother.

Laura knew her name now. She would turn to her mother when she called it from another room. When her father talked along in the same room, she heard her name spoken in the stream of conversation. As she heard it and recognized it, she stopped and turned to him.

  She still got pleasure from mirrors. She stopped crying to look at herself. She could be put off before a feeding with the mirror game, so intense was its pleasure.

Is this an added dimension to learning about herself and her movements? Preference for her own face is characteristic of the self-involvement of a baby like Laura, but all infants have the same interest in their mirror images. Parents worry about rearing a self-centered adult, but this need not bother them so much, as self-involvement in an infant need not be correlated with adult self-concern. In fact, there is reason to believe that if an infant explores and understands herself early, she may be better fitted to look outside of herself as she grows.

Mr. and Mrs. King had no reason to feel that Laura had a weak personality. Even Daniel might be more fragile as a person underneath all his powerful drive.

ACTIVE BABY

Days were not long enough for Daniel. He rushed through them headlong. On his back, he was freest to perform. He rolled and rolled, twisting half his body to pull the upper half over. He rolled to his belly and arched up on his arms to look around. As he looked around from this vantage point, he seemed to digest what he had done, make a decision, and roll back again. There he bent himself forward as if he wanted to come to sit. This continuous activity took up most of Daniel's day. It also spilled over into the night. Whenever he came to semi-consciousness in the night, Daniel rolled himself over in his crib. This activity woke him, and he tried to soothe himself with more activity.

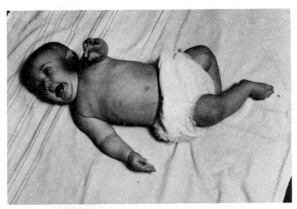
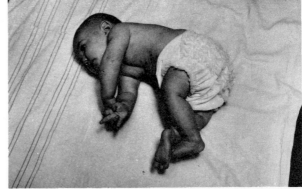
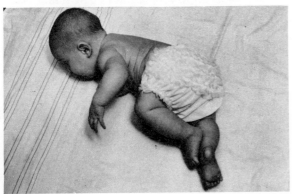
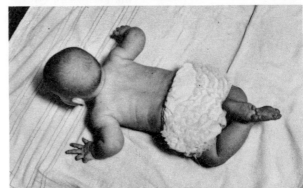

Since activity was such an important outlet for him, it was no wonder that he used it as Laura might use her looking or Louis might suck on his fingers, as a way of trying to get himself back to sleep. Unfortunately, activity usually built up to a peak from which he could not calm himself. As a result, he woke several times at night. When his mother found him, he was always on his back, and she thought turning over had wakened him. As we know, he had been turning himself over for several weeks. It was the added excitement he was getting plus the frustration of not being able to satisfy himself that woke him. She tried to pin his bedclothes down with a tight sheet, and she tilted his mattress with a blanket rolled under one side so he could not roll himself uphill. This made him mad, and he fought even harder whenever he woke up.

Eventually she did help him with her maneuvers. She woke him at 10 P.M. for a feeding and a period of play with her. This gave him a chance to let off steam. He stopped waking after she instituted this routine. Later (two weeks) she was able to drop this nighttime play period without his waking again. Another way she helped him work out some of this frustration was to practice with him during the day. She showed him how to roll both ways, how to get back. She pushed him to calm himself down as he built up to peaks of rolling activity. She flattened him out on his abdomen in a sleep position and brought his thumb to his mouth. Then she held him in this position. At first he was furious with her active interference during the day, then he began to settle as if he were learning what she meant.

He had learned to kick like a motorboat on his back—and struck the playpen pad with a rapid beat. As he kicked he propelled himself across the pad to a corner where he wedged himself. He looked chagrined, but seemed to accept his "stuck position" with a certain sense of humor—and went on kicking. But soon he tired and demanded help. On his belly, he managed to propel himself by scrabbling and scratching with his arms and legs, rocking up and down on his abdomen in an arch, as he scrabbled. This too pushed him across the playpen pad.

He could cough, and he learned how to yell and screech experimentally in much the same way that Laura vocalized.

The difference in experimentation is obvious. A child like Daniel yells

purely for the pleasure of using vocal apparatus in a loud explosion.
None of the range, the trills, or the quiet self-stimulation that we have
seen in Laura goes into these loud noises.

At feeding times, he was learning to become a horror. He tried to
hold his own bottle, putting both hands up on it to hold it. At times,
he literally wrenched it away from his mother. He could pull out the
nipple with a snap and look up at her to grin. She was inclined at
this point to leave it with him. She felt that he would eat better and
more quickly if she were not around to interact with.

This probably is true. But this kind of infant needs the soothing touch
of his mother to calm him down to a state where he can receive and
appreciate the important gratifications around a feeding. Since he is
so active and busy, he has fewer opportunities for the experience of
getting gratification from the outside world. He can be easy to push
to independence—but an empty one it would be. Such a baby needs
his mother more than Louis does, for his learning can easily lead to
a kind of precocity that is sterilized of cues from the outside world.

When she fed him solids, he grabbed the spoon and slung the food
around the room. His father wore a raincoat to feed him. The cup
was started, and Daniel loved it. He dived into it head first. He got
his entire face into it and choked as he breathed milk up into his
nose. This did not daunt him, and he took on the cup as a new
venture and grunted in anticipation as he saw it coming. He cried
as he lost it.

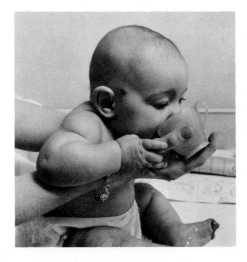 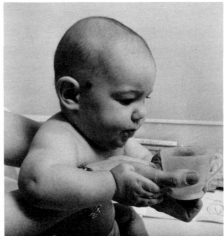

At this stage a baby can be given a spoon and a cup or a piece of teething biscuit—one object for each hand—to keep his hands full with objects appropriate to the feeding. He rarely drops them to grab his mother's spoon. Sooner or later, he may even begin to imitate her feeding gestures with his own utensils.

In his chair, he blew bubbles with the carrots and sprayed the wall with blown-out spinach. He kept a bite in his mouth for long periods as he teased his mother during feedings. Very little food managed to get into Daniel. The play with it had become more important than eating.

He gained little weight as a result. Mrs. Kay worried about his poor intake in the face of his high output of energy.

An infant maintains himself on a surprisingly low caloric intake. We are an overfed people in America, and our sights for our children are far too high. From time to time a child stops gaining weight rapidly as he develops. Development in any area—physical, mental, or emotional—rarely proceeds in a straight line upward. Instead, it is made of spurts and periods of leveling off before another spurt. At times, there even seems to be a regression before a spurt gathers enough steam. I think of these periods such as Daniel's as a kind of conservation in one area in order to grow in another. He has almost stopped growing physically in order to put his all into the motor spurt of learning to sit and crawl.

We see similar conservation at other times in a child's life. For example, when a child is ill and drawing on his resources to recover physically, we are aware of the lack of energy he has for complicated emotional adjustments. An illness is not a time to push him to learn new mental tricks. This represents a kind of economy among other parameters in order to allow extra energy for physical recovery.

In Daniel's case, his intake may well have been sufficient for usual growth, but he was placing an extra burden on his caloric resources by the kind of driving intensity with which he filled his day (and night).

Whether an infant gains weight is usually of relatively little importance—except to his mother.

Daniel explored himself constantly. He poked his ears and nose, and when he was undiapered, he quickly found his penis. He began to play with it and to pull on it, until he caused an erection. His mother was shaken.

This is the common result of the investigating activity that babies go through as they find out about themselves. The pleasure that is generated as a boy finds his penis or a girl her vagina for the first time points to the fact that it is a sensitive area for excitation. Even though the genital area may already be a "heightened zone" for pleasure, our practices heighten it. We keep this area covered and out of exploratory reach all the time. A baby can find his ears and explore them over and over until he is satisfied. And he does. But he has little opportunity to find out about his genitals. When he begins to explore, someone pushes his hand away,. diverts him, or covers him up with a diaper. As a result, he may develop an interest in this novel area. Also, the lack of conditioning of the skin of the area to stimulation may make it more easily stimulated. The rest of our bodies are more exposed to change in temperature, pressure, and the touch of moving clothes on them. The genital area is so well protected by diapers that little of this conditioning takes place except with urination and a stool. This zone must react differently from the rest of the body by the time an infant can explore himself.

One mother was so offended by the determination and vigorous manipulation that her infant son displayed in the middle of the night, that she called me at midnight to ask whether he might hurt himself or "pull it off." I assured her that little boys had always pulled on their penises and poked their testicles and none had ever pulled one off. It is a normal and important kind of exploration at all ages. Little girls poke their fingers up inside their vaginas and find this as exciting. To overreact to this by prohibiting it would not only be a mistake, but would also only heighten the excitement in such experimentation. Adults have a tendency to make it "wicked" for them by their own inhibitions.

After this episode, Daniel developed an ulcer on the tip of his penis and cried when he urinated. Mrs. Kay associated this with his investigating play.

She is wrong. These reddened ulcers on the head of the penis are part of an ammonia burn or diaper irritation and may be the only evidence of diaper rash. They should be treated as such, and treated vigorously. The ulceration can invade the canal of the penis (or the urethral meatus) and could result in scar tissue as the ulcer heals if the ulcer is allowed to persist for several weeks. This scar tissue can decrease the size of the opening of the canal of the penis and make it harder for a boy to urinate as he gets older. This can be a complication for his future genito-urinary tract, and a mother should use every method to prevent this scarring. Some of the methods that help are: frequent diaper changes (as well as a change in the middle of the night), no rubber pants, no detergents as diaper washes, using a powder (such as cornstarch) that will absorb the ammonia, using an anti-ammonia rinse for the diapers before they are dried, exposure of the inflamed penis to air and sunshine and applying protective ointment (e.g., Vaseline) frequently to the tip of the penis. This salve will give the area a chance to heal before it can be burned by the next urine. If the ulceration persists, it is worth calling your doctor.

One episode reminded Mrs. Kay that she had escaped another tragedy with Daniel. As she had him propped in his chair at the table, he reached out of it to grab her cup and saucer, which contained freshly poured hot coffee. He splashed it over his clothes and screamed. She had the presence of mind to take him out of the hot clothes immediately.

Clothes hold the heat and keep the liquid against the skin so that it continues to burn. Cold water applied immediately is the best first aid for a burn.

She applied cold water and sterile Vaseline to the reddened area. Since it was a relatively small area (three inches by two inches), she kept it greased and did not call his doctor. This reminded her to take inventory of other traps into which Daniel might fall. She moved his chair away from the cord leading to the toaster; she got him a strap for his stroller, and she began to baby-proof the house.

With an infant as active and searching as Daniel, this is none too soon. He will dream up things a mother never thought of anyway. But she can certainly start taking precautions. By this age one should have a bottle of ipecac on hand (an emetic that can be used to make a baby vomit an ingested poison—the dose is one tablespoonful every fifteen minutes for three times with strong salt water poured down between each dose until vomiting is induced) and a poison book to advise how to handle ingestions (see Bibliography). In a city where there is a poison control center, it is wise to copy the phone number onto the phone for just such an emergency. At the time, a parent is likely to be too frantic to be able to look it up successfully. It is never too early to check out the entire house for substances a baby can reach and swallow. (See Children's Hospital Medical Center in Bibliography.)

CHAPTER VIII

The Sixth Month

AVERAGE BABY

Louis had worked out many uses for his bounce chair. He had begun to sit so well that his father had untied it, and now he sat for most of the morning in it. In his chair, he sat and played with toys tied to the tray. As he tired of them, he dropped them over the side. When they were gone, he cried for Tom or his mother. They retrieved them for him. He repeated this game daily and several times before his mother caught on or Tom lost interest. He leaned forward over the tray to reach his feet. He leaned over each side to explore around him on the ground.

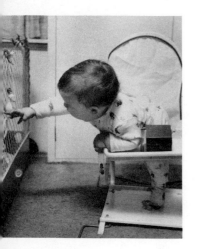

The chair should be weighted so that it will not topple with him. A heavy baby can topple the chair over unless the bottom is weighted.

He could bounce it and work his way in it over to a nearby table. He reached for whatever was in sight.

Louis was fed solids in his bouncer, which was a good feeding seat for him at this age, as the tray held his play spoon and cup, and his mother could sit near him feeding him between bounces. When he was placed at the table near the older children, he spent his time watching and attracting them. The bounce chair could be moved around and into the kitchen for meals. On more than one occasion, Mr. Moore moved it into the bathroom so that Louis could scatter his food where it could be cleaned up more readily.

In the chair, he had learned to stand with very little support. At first he practiced holding on to the tray. As he became more adept, he let go and supported himself by one hand alone. As he stood, he held up the other hand, chattering away as if he were making a speech.

When he was stood up out of the chair, he looked around for his accustomed support, looked worried, and then collapsed in sitting.

This is evidence of the "crutch" value that these gadgets take on.

Mrs. Moore varied his activity in the mornings by putting him on the floor or in the playpen. But Tom was always a threat to Louis when they were left alone. Louis in the playpen was relatively safe —except from flying objects and Tom's climbing in with him. He was safer and better amused in his chair in the middle of the playpen. This arrangement gave her time to get to him when she heard Tom begin to clamber in.

After some practice with his father or mother, Louis gathered necessary courage and pulled up to stand with very little support from them. As he did, he let out a chortle and a squeal. Even when he was crying, he could be stood, and the delight in standing would stop his crying.

This is proof of the meaning to an infant of being upright. How does he get the feeling of its importance so early? Does a baby place this value on it because he wants to imitate those around him, or is it an inborn drive to be upright? If he shows this much eagerness to be stood in the early months, there must be an inborn urge that this upright position satisfies.

Most of the afternoon when he was home, he was out on the floor with Martha and Tom. Martha was an added safeguard against Tom's ebullience with the baby, as she protected Louis and diverted Tom. They treated him like a rag doll, romping around the house with him. Martha could carry him on a hip. He was now solidly able to maintain himself in one piece. Mrs. Moore correctly felt that the play with them and all it meant to Louis, as well as to Martha and Tom in working out their relationship, was worth any minor chance of his getting hurt. Martha had learned what might hurt him, and she handled him dextrously and carefully. He adored it and could be counted on to last for two hours of play with her. Martha played "mother" and she pushed Tom to be "daddy," with Louis as the baby. He was stood, put to bed, fed, and diapered as if he were a doll. As he cooperated in sitting or standing, or as he gurgled at them, they rewarded him with more encouragement. Occasionally he was spilled off a chair, or dropped onto his head, but these were rare accidents. The family unity that this play engendered made up for it.

Louis, of course, learned more than one can estimate. He had opportunities for watching, imitating, and was given constant, encouraging reinforcement.

Tom had learned a new way to get his mother's goat. Instead of trying to bother his mother at Louis' feedings, he concentrated on distracting the baby. When she was trying to feed Louis his solids or his bottle, Tom would jump up and down on the floor, run past Louis to make him turn his head, or steal the implements that Louis used while his mother fed him. He knew how distractable Louis was at mealtime and knew how much it upset his mother for him to manipulate him like this.

Dressing him was a wrestling match. Mrs. Moore tried occupying him with one new toy after another. Each worked a short time, but he was too interested in everything around him. He was bored when he had to be held down for a diaper change. He twisted and turned in all directions. He loved to arch on his back, look backward over his head and upside down at everything behind him. In fact, one of the ways to keep him busy had become setting pictures upside down at the end of his changing table for him to look at.

This interest in looking at things upside down also carries over to the period when a baby is walking and begins to look back between his legs. It is reminiscent of his usual way of looking at the world from a lying position and back over his head. This is also a way of changing the visual world oneself—as such, it becomes a way of testing and exploring its boundaries.

The best source of distraction at changing times was the older

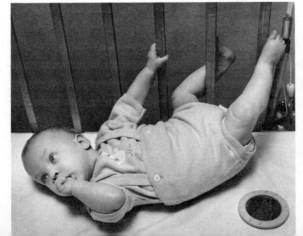

children. They amused him with their antics while his mother changed a diaper—cutting the procedure time in half.

On the floor or in his bed, he was constantly active. He could move forward or backward. Although he attempted to get himself forward to a toy in front of him, he could not count on which direction he might go. He went backward more often than forward, and it was quite a while before he began to be able to push himself ahead without an equal number of backward moves. When he aimed for a toy, he worked for long periods grunting and pushing, in order to get to it. Occasionally he landed on top of the toy, with it hidden securely under his belly. He looked around in amazement—his goal no longer visible.

He was able to twist over and over. By twisting and rolling, he could move from one end of a room to another. Since this wedged him under pieces of furniture, it meant constant running after to extract him. In rolling over, he found he occasionally rolled himself to a near-sitting position on his side by bending as he rolled. Although he was not yet trying to sit, he practiced this over and over.

Long before an entire act is achieved, each bit and piece of it is practiced and readied like bits of a puzzle—to be put together in a thoroughly worked out act when the appropriate time arrives.

His vocalizations were less frequent as he worked at motor tasks. He spent most of his time grunting or complaining when he got into a tight spot—however, he seemed to have associated certain words with their meanings. He now said "dada," and his father's response was a certain one. When he was in trouble, he called "mamamama" in a long string of vowels connected by a complaining "m" sound. His mother responded dutifully, and the cycle for associating "mama" with her was set in motion.

It is no surprise that the names have taken the meaning they have. "dada" is one of the first vocalizations an infant seems equipped to make. It is quickly associated with play and pleasurable learning. On the other hand, "mama" comes out first as a complaint. Since she relieves the reason for the complaint, it is easy to see how this gets stuck to her.

He soon learned to call to his mother from another room. She would hurry to him expecting him to be in trouble. Instead he might be lying on his back, grinning as he realized that his call had summoned her.

To associate the act with its result is quite clever. A budding sense of humor becomes apparent. Fortunately mothers sometimes have one, too.

QUIET BABY

There was little evidence of Louis' large motor development in Laura. She was limp to pick up. Until she was in her parents' arms, she had little body tone. Then she nestled in warmly as if she had what she wanted. When she was sat up, she sagged forward until her chin touched the floor. There seemed to be little effort on her part to hold up her head or her body. Her legs stiffened out in front, and she made no effort to form a triangular brace with them to balance in a sitting position. If one held her up under the arms, she leaned over one's hands.

There is more than lack of practice, there is active resistance in this. Some babies like Laura will not be pushed to perform and even being sat is a form of being pushed. They will do these things when they are ready, and not an hour before. This stubborn determination is a kind of strength.

When her father tried to pull her to stand, she gave way in his hands. She would not stiffen her body as her legs and trunk sagged. If he held her up under the shoulders, she bent her legs up at the hips so that they were stretched out in front of her. This effort took as much vigor as it would have taken to stand—but it was a negating effort, characteristic of Laura. Propped in her bounce chair, she flopped over to one side or the other. When she was interested in a new toy or her cup, however, she could sit and play with it. She could manipulate a toy over and over, turning it back and forth, holding it between thumb and several fingers as she manipulated it. She took two similar blocks, one in each hand, compared them, held them together as if this helped her see the likeness and changed each from one hand to the other as if she wanted to be sure this simple act wouldn't change them.

Such comparing is complex for this age and may be new evidence of the ability to sort out likenesses, as well as differences. The complicated maneuver to try them out on different sides of the body shows that a baby is becoming aware of the two sides as different, also.

As she sat in her chair and played with a teething biscuit that her mother gave her between feedings, she looked at it and manipulated it. Finally, after many minutes of postponing and savoring the pleasure, she brought the bread to her mouth. Then she licked it all over before she began to chew on it. When she finished one, she licked her fingers delicately.

One of her favorite toys was a piece of paper. She could hold it up, look at it, work it around from one corner to the other, rattle it, bend it to make it crackle, roll it up, and finally chew on it. She made delicious soggy balls, which she swallowed. Occasionally she choked on a ball, and her mother had to dig it out.

There are two ways of extracting a lump caught in a baby's throat. One is to whack her on the back, head down. The other is to dig a finger in and extract it manually. There is always a possibility that you may shove it in farther this way, but in desperation, any method goes.

A last resort is the Heimlich maneuver. In this one lines the baby up against one's own body, facing her out. Sudden pressure is applied around the base of the rib cage, in order to get positive pressure from the lungs to blow the object out. One can hurt a baby with too much pressure.

Paper may not be the safest food. Newsprint in large quantities is certainly not a good idea, and small bits of paper can be aspirated into the infant's windpipe. Nothing from which she can bite off pieces should be given her while she lies on her back. Only in sitting should she have a biscuit or cookie that will dissolve quickly as it comes away in bites, and only when she is near an adult to help her if necessary.

Laura loved music now. After she had learned to make different sounds herself, her appreciation for music seemed to increase. She could sit in her chair and sway or bounce gently in time with the radio. She occasionally hummed as she rocked. Her timing seemed rhythmic even though it was not necessarily the rhythm of the music. When her mother turned the radio off or turned it up too loud, she indicated by fussing that she did not approve. She seemed to associate the music with her mother's going to the particular place to produce or change it. She also could associate the sound and the place it came from. On one occasion, a baby cried on the radio. To her mother's surprise, Laura puckered and began to cry, too. Mrs. King had seen this happen to Laura at a friend's house. She was sensitive to the moods of other babies and had imitated the other infant's laughter as well as his crying.

On some days in my office, one baby will pick up another's cry and this crying will spread itself around the office like a contagious disease.

Laura could now express herself in many ways. She used her voice to show her pleasure, gurgling in lovely trills. She growled with displeasure, and fussed at her mother with long unintelligible sentences when she did not come on command. When her father arrived at night, she could batter him with all uses of "ah-ah-ah-ah," increasing in volume and insistence, until he came to her.

They played games of peekaboo. He covered his face. As he took his hands away, she squealed with pleasure. She reached out to pull his hands away when he hid for too long. When he took them away abruptly, she jumped, as if she were caught up in the game completely. After several games, her excitement built up with squeals, laughing out loud, and bouncing her body. This was one of the first areas in which Laura had responded with activity.

On her stomach, she banged the floor with her arms. She made no attempt to move. Mrs. King compared her and the other babies of her age and still found her behind. She certainly was not interested in the sort of activity that Louis and Daniel were already involved with.

Large motor milestones are the commonest measure for estimating developmental progress, and, as such, a baby like Laura may seem dull when in reality she is perfecting much more complicated skills.

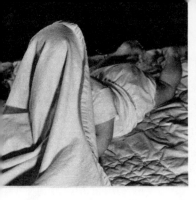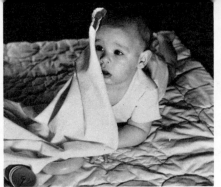

Mrs. King blamed this sluggishness on Laura's weight. At six months she weighed nineteen pounds and was a big baby.

Big children do have a problem. Their weight may immobilize them. Then they stop using their musculature as much. This inactivity results in more fat being laid down. As they become frustrated with their inability to move, they eat more, or they must be fed more to keep them quiet. In our culture, moreover, many mothers use teething biscuits or cookies in a conscious way to "plug" their children's protests.

Laura was not being "shut up," but perhaps Mrs. King fed her because she herself felt unhappy that she was not stimulating her "to keep up with the next door neighbors." As Laura became more active, the fat would then be utilized and incorporated into more solid flesh.

Laura's mother tended to dress her in dainty clothes when she took her out in the carriage. She brought her expensive shoes and felt that they were important to support her feet "in case she wanted to stand or walk."

This is a sad example of the way a mother can worry about her baby's motor development. Of course it is too early for expensive shoes. At best, at this age, shoes serve the purpose of covering an infant's feet, and the cheapest shoes serve that purpose.

Mrs. King seemed to be proving to the world that Laura needed them and that she was ready to provide whatever she needed. Underneath, she was denying both of these, i.e., she seemed to be afraid that Laura might never use them to walk. She resented Laura's lack of interest in motor activity. The shoes were symbolic of this concern.

Laura's taste in foods was difficult. Her mother continued to nurse her—even though Laura had bitten her several times. She was really trying to do well by Laura. Indeed, she tried too hard.

There is no reason for a mother to be willing to be bitten. An infant does bite as part of her exploration of her world and of her learning to bite—but no one likes to be bitten in such a sensitive area, and no mother needs to be. In primitive cultures, where breast-feeding must go on, mothers react by startling and pulling away, or by reprimanding their infants and using a finger as a biting object, or by letting them know in certain terms that this is not acceptable. There is no reason for women in our culture to accept this exploratory biting except that we are "afraid" of our children. We feel we must enforce their reactions—not value our own. Perhaps they need honest reactions to help them see reality. A mother who accepts this biting may be showing ambivalent feelings about her child.

Laura was definite in her likes and dislikes. She refused spinach. She loved all fruits and sweets. She disliked jello but she liked junket. She still disliked the taste of the meats in jars and preferred her meat mixed with other foods.

Some children prefer the meat-and-vegetable mixtures in jars—but I advise against them for several reasons: (1) there is little meat in them, and meat contains the iron and protein that becomes more and more important as the infant grows; (2) the mixtures contain many foods —all potential sensitizing agents; these make it difficult, if a child shows an allergy, to single out which one is the sensitizing food; (3) they are filled with inexpensive cereals that supplant more valuable meats and vegetables, which means that a parent gets little food for his or her investment.

ACTIVE BABY

When Daniel found that he could get himself off the floor, he practiced for hours at push-ups. He straightened his legs and arms, his body high like a daddy-long-legs. For the first weeks of this, he was immobile, teetering on four wavering pins. Then he sensed that by moving one an inch or so, his trunk went with it. Gingerly testing each move, he inched a leg to one side. On the first tries, the second hitch threw him off balance, and he rolled angrily onto his side. But

Daniel was learning to master his own frustration now, and he (unlike Louis) rolled back and pushed himself up, to try again. After a few more tries, he learned that one hitch with a foot could be followed by a hitch with an arm—the two supports making a better balance. As he learned to integrate the leg and arm on the same side again and again, he found at last that he must bring the opposite leg and arm along. He flopped on his face many times before this occurred to him.

The wonder is that this complicated piece of understanding can take root as quickly as it does. With the number of repeated trials, it is not a wonder that a baby hits on it sooner or later, but it is marvelous that he recognizes right away that it works. His ability to store this recognition for repetition is another interesting aspect. I am sure there are inborn connections between motor acts that feel "right" when they are made by chance in exploration. When they are integrated, the infant must receive a rewarding signal. This helps him sort out that part of his experimentation, and he gives it a higher priority for the next attempt.

The practice sessions lasted an hour at a time. When his mother tried to interrupt them, Daniel was clear in his determination to continue. He fussed and protested until she replaced him on his belly on the floor where he could continue.

The strong orientation in one direction is an important asset in a child's learning powers. This same determination and unwillingness to be distracted is an asset to an athlete who is perfecting a skill. The remarkable store of energy that must go into hours of practice such as Daniel's can hardly be reproduced by an adult. Jim Thorpe, the famous four-star athlete, is said to have imitated each move in a baby's active day. He gave out, exhausted, after four hours. The infant continued for eight or more.

Daniel was able to creep by pushing with his feet as he steered himself with outstretched arms.

Creeping is distinguished from crawling by the fact that the infant's abdomen is on the ground. A crawl results when a baby gets up on his elbows and bent knees.

Daniel (like Louis) had learned to go backward first—and he looked like a crab as he disappeared backward under a table. Daniel was getting the concept of escaping from a pursuer, and he soon found that he could push forward harder and faster to get away than he was able to do in crab style by pulling himself backward.

Sorting out the relative values of going backward and forward must depend on more than this kind of awareness. It must be more satisfying to our inherent value system when we go forward. Certainly in the newly found game of running away, it is more effective to turn one's back and run. When the pursuer is constantly in sight, one tends to give up more easily—particularly when the pursuer is one's parent.

The push of the legs is more powerful than their pull at this age. The arms can be used more effectively in guiding and pulling—a baby sorts this out very early and against odds—since nature usually sends him backward first. This is another instance of Daniel's ability to compare, evaluate, and choose.

The game he liked best was the come-and-get-me game. Whenever he saw a parent starting toward him, he squealed happily, scrabbled, and began to push himself away as fast as he could. He liked to play this game over and over. If he were abducted to his meal or the changing table on the first sprint, he was furious. Given two or three runs, he was much more likely to sink resignedly into the slot the parent had ready for him.

On the changing table, he was a whirling dervish. Mrs. Kay had long ago resorted to strapping him to the table. She had nearly lost him overboard too many times. She had learned with Mark never to turn away without her hand firmly on him. But Daniel could slither away from under a hand. Now she found she could immobilize him best by strapping him on his belly to the table. Even then, he was able to wave his buttocks at such a rate that she felt she was pinning the diapers on a whirligig. If she had to leave him alone now, the floor was a much safer place than either bed or table.

He sat well by himself for a half hour at a time. His back was straight, and his hands free. He came to sit by pulling his legs under him as he was crawling. He was free to survey the world in this position now.

The hands and arms are used for balance in sitting at first. Even after an infant can sit alone, an observer can estimate how new the skill is by watching his hands. When he no longer keeps them ready to catch himself, but frees them to manipulate objects, he has become sure of his prowess in sitting.

He had been able to use his hands to hold and manipulate a cup in his chair for a month. But now he no longer needed the steadying support of the chair. He could sit in the middle of the floor, pick up the cup with one hand, bring the other hand to it, and bring it up to his mouth.

 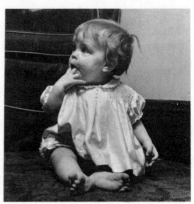

This is quite a combination of skills: sitting, balancing, reaching and using one hand skillfully, then two together, and finally imitating a complex action such as bringing the cup up to his mouth.

On his father's shoulder, Daniel sat balancing well, grinning as he was jostled. As part of his balancing, he had learned to grab his father's hair to support himself. He was so firm there that Mr. Kay hardly needed to hold on to his legs. As he sat, he learned to bounce himself, as he had in his bouncing chair. He loved this game.

Heights do not bother infants yet, and this balancing is part of the learning to balance that a baby must also do on the floor. But the hair is an easy and available saddle pommel.

He loved being stood. As in Louis' case, this was one way to stop him when he was crying. But Daniel was no longer content to stand in one place. He grunted "uh uh uh" until his supporting parent allowed him to go somewhere, holding on to his hands. Then, stiff-legged, he would step out with one leg, then the other. The rest of his body was rigid as all energy focused on this new activity. His face puckered intently as he walked himself around holding his parent's hands. He could keep this up as long as anyone would support him. In fact, when the parent tired, he gave up reluctantly. Daniel had little ability to give up—particularly when he was learning an exciting new skill.

Feedings were better than they had been. He still preferred to hold and manipulate his own bottle, but he had resigned himself to being held. In fact, he seemed to want it now. On several occasions, when Mrs. Kay had had to park him to tend to Mark, she found that he held his own bottle high with both hands but stopped sucking and waited until she returned. When she gathered him up, he began his sucking again, smiling up at her with his eyes. He had begun to appreciate the coziness of the feeding situation himself now.

Mrs. Kay had wondered whether Daniel was not ready to be weaned from the bottle, but now as she appreciated this response to her holding him, she felt he needed the bottle longer.

I certainly agree. Even though a precocious baby such as Daniel can probably master drinking milk from the cup, and might even prefer it at certain stages in his development, he needs to have ways of regressing to a more tranquil "infantile" state than he will find for himself. One probably should push an infant like this back, rather than follow him at his rollercoaster speed.

He had learned to drop his spoon and cup overboard when his mother fed him solids. He dropped them and leaned over to look after them, avoiding the proffered spoon. When Mrs. Kay retrieved them, she found she was soon playing a game with him of picking up his spoon over and over.

He became more interested in teething biscuits, and she found he was scooping up bits of food from his tray. He studied the small pieces, brought his hand to them, closed it around them with his whole palm, brought his full hand up to his face, and tried to smear the bits into his mouth. She found it successful at his feeding to give him little pieces of toast or banana, which he could manipulate himself while she fed him his baby food from a spoon. His interest in manipulating bits of food left him free for her feedings. The new interest in his hands was the beginning of control of the smaller muscles of his body. In Daniel's case, they were to become a concern *after* he had mastered the large movements (compare to Laura in whom they were first and large motor development second). But already his interest in experimentation was enough to divert him from his resistance to being fed. Daniel loved to clown with Mark. He and his brother sat on the floor or across the supper table making faces at each other. Each broke into giggles as he made a silly face. Daniel tried out his own repertoire, and then seemed to try to

imitate new faces that came from his brother. Spitting food and blowing bubbles were the inevitable degeneration of such games. Mrs. Kay intervened wearily at such times, but she was glad to see the boys play with each other. Daniel was much less interested in Mark than Louis was in his siblings.

The reason for this may lie in the way they learn. In Daniel we see learning that is more oriented toward self-stimulation and fulfillment in his own way. A child like Louis learns by watching, digesting what he watches, and then by imitation. Such learning results in an act with more potential facets, more color, more choices. Daniel's is linear and may produce a more stereotyped performance as its end result.

Up to now, Daniel's poor feedback to Mark had not made for a mellow relationship, like Louis' with his siblings.

Mrs. Kay had begun to consider her return to teaching. She had felt needed by Daniel in the first five months. Now, unconsciously, she was beginning to feel shoved out.

Many mothers express this feeling to me at just this time. As the infant's demands decrease, and his motor independence begins to come to the surface, they may see the end of their need as a mother in sight. In spite of the reality that this end is still quite far away, it is the beginning of their preparation for giving up this delightful, rewarding intimacy.

Her old discontent with the "simple" role of mothering—of having just children to communicate with all day, of doing chores just as well done by someone else, of not feeling as rewarded by being just a mother as many of her friends said they did—all these were rumbling around in her head.

Many women like Mrs. Kay have too many other interests for this role to satisfy them completely. Gratification in performance and in intellectual pursuits is geared to a more immediate kind of reward than is afforded by childrearing alone. Even with a child as exciting as Daniel (and maybe at desperate times, he would push a mother back to her own interests more quickly), they feel the old urge to get out of the house and do something for themselves. Although women do feel guilty about their own inability to be satisfied at home, they realize that all the family is better off when they respect their own needs. My bias is that a woman's most important role is being at home to mother her small children, but I have learned that there is a time when a mother's awareness of her needs is critical to her and to their adjustment. Besides, many women have no choice but to work. We need to know how early it is possible for them to leave a baby without losing too much for either themselves or the baby. Then we need to make it a natural and institutionally backed possibility. At present, women are penalized in the job market if they don't return to work as early as possible. As a pediatrician, my role is to push a mother in the direction of finding a good motherly substitute, rather than to press her to stay at home. Her best adjustment may be that of satisfying her intellectual needs in a way that leaves her able to give the best of herself to her children at the end of the day. When she does bring in a substitute, she must introduce her to the children ahead of time, let them get to know her. The warmth, understanding, and competence of this substitute, be it sitter, grandmother, nurse, or housekeeper, are of course all-important, as we shall see in the chapters that follow. Any decisions about working or not working must be based in part upon the availability of such a qualified person or nurturant day-care center.

One of the great dangers in this double life is that the woman feels guilty about it herself. When my own critical attitude as a pediatrician reinforces her unconscious guilty feelings, she cannot turn to me for help in this adjustment. If she will still consult me, there will be times when I can see pitfalls of guilty reactions to her children and can help her out of them by being able to point them out.

I should like to urge a mother who is on the point of making this decision to consider the balance between meeting her own needs and her infant's still present needs for dependency on a consistently dependable mothering figure. It is important for an infant to have constant figures to relate to, to understand, to absorb as he sorts out his own reactions to the world. As he gets older and more independent, he can certainly be freer to manage multiple sets of cues from his environment. One motherly person as a substitute could certainly be a good solution. The problem for most working mothers is to find that kind of person and to keep her as a consistent figure for the baby. If his father can be available to share the time, that is ideal. If not, the mother of another baby may be available, and each parent can take the babies for part of the time.

For a full-time working parent, the best solution may well be a good day-care center. As we give up some of our prejudices against such centers, we are improving the kind of day care that is available to the enormous number of working parents for their babies. I see certain basic criteria that must be met by such a center for infants:

1) The ratio of one consistent adult to three (or at most four) infants is critical. That person should be warm and motherly and trained to understand and value the developmental processes in babies. She must be able to accept strong individual differences in each of them. We found that the best day-care centers could be selected by observing their sensitivity to each baby's need for cycles of play, sleep, feeding, etc. If they were able to be sensitive to the cycles of these basic needs in each baby, it was likely that they would build a rewarding day for each infant. The opportunities for play, for learning, and for interaction with an adult are a critical part of each day for an infant, and the quality of these should be observed by a parent who is attempting to choose such a center.

2) Equally important is the feeling on the part of the parents of being included as important to their baby's progress. Many day-care centers have not recognized their critical role in keeping families together. The grieving that parents are likely to feel about sharing a small baby can cause them to pull away in order to "leave the baby's care to the more expert day-care people." This reaction is often reinforced by the competitive feelings of the day-care personnel. The resulting distance is a tragic and unnecessary result of parents' working. Parents should be included in planning for their baby's day as they leave them off each morning. They should (and must) have an opportunity to discuss the day's events as they come to get the baby in the evening. And they must be prepared to understand that of course any infant cries at the end of the day, having saved up all his important feelings for his parents' arrival. This should be understood by them as a chance for recementing, rather than as a reproach. For it is likely that after this outburst there will be a wonderful time when the baby is alert and available to communicate with them. I would urge parents to look for a center that is nurturing for them as well.

3) Safety, good nutrition, and health standards are a critical part of good care for babies, and they should be assured in such a center.

The question of dividing oneself into at least two parts as a working parent is the critical issue. One must learn how to save enough energy to be available to parent the infant at the end of a long day. The quality of the time spent with the infant is more critical than the quantity. Hence, saving special times for each child and each baby becomes a critical part of the day and the week for a working mother and father.

Mrs. Kay, and others like her, deserve real backup for their work in adjusting to a job as well as mothering. An understanding of the importance of their role as mothers, as well as a realization of its potential in their developing families, should help them to see mothering as a goal that is as important as anything they can achieve in their professional life. This is a goal for the future education of women. Mothering calls up experiences from a woman's own past, and it demands a constant adjustment to the conflicts these memories bring with them. It is likely to be the most demanding challenge a woman faces except that of no longer being a mother.

CHAPTER IX

The Seventh Month

AVERAGE BABY

Now that Louis could sit easily by himself, his hands were freed, and he discovered all sorts of new uses for them. The new sitting widened his world by freeing him to wheel around, lean over to pick up objects, and drop them in order to retrieve them himself. He relished these independent additions to his repertoire.

The fact that babies are often propped in chairs to look around all through infancy takes away some of the discovery of sitting as a new achievement. But new freedom is found in the free movement of the trunk and the increased scope of arms and hands.

Louis used each hand independently and seemed to have little preference.

Although most infants alternate between one- and two-handedness all through the first year, some, like Laura, do demonstrate a dominance of one side of their body. But at this period, both hands are likely to be used with the same importance.

He held toys in each hand and banged them together with glee. First he banged one toy on the floor, then he banged the other in the same way.

This is reminiscent of the mirrored, alternating activity in the newborn as he wheels his arms and legs. At this stage, mirroring is put to work to sort out one side's potential versus the other. In this way, a baby works out the use of each hand.

He picked up the big block with his right hand, the smaller one with his left, compared them, and placed them on the tray in front of him next to each other. As if he were digesting the difference in size, he took the large one with his left, the small with his right, mouthed each one, and put them on the table again in reversed order.

Louis was rarely without a toy in his hand now. As he manipulated one toy, he held on to the table with the other hand. He crept around the room dangling a toy in one hand or the other, often in both. The dragged object frequently was a piece of clothing, a blanket, or a diaper.

This can be evidence of his attachment to one particular thing that is becoming his "baby" or "lovey." How easy it is when one can carry one's own symbol of comfort to feel or look at whenever one needs it.

The sucking on two fingers was diminishing rapidly. Not only were Louis' hands too busy now, but life was more constantly rewarding.

The period of frustration preceding the developmental steps of sitting and creeping is over.

His mother could tell when he was tired, or hungry, by the sudden return to his fingers.

He loved to feed himself bits of food. As she fed him solids, Mrs. Moore gave him soft bits to finger, examine, and pick up for himself. She gave him a few bits at a time since he was likely to stuff them all in at once and choke. Also, giving him a few at a time avoided a mess, for when he had had enough, he smeared them or swept them all off onto the floor in a *grand geste* of satiety. As he ate, he held something in one hand while using the other to play with food.

The grasped object seems almost forgotten. Perhaps it is necessary to block off one hand by keeping it full in order to free the other to more activity. In a period of bimanual orientation, this makes sense. When a baby's hands are full, his parents can feed him more easily.

He tried to use his thumb and the first two fingers to pick up a piece of food. Sometimes it landed in an inaccessible part of his closed fist. He would then work to extract it from his closed hand, ending by smashing it against his mouth, palm flattened out. The deliberation that went into the exploration of the use of his hand and fingers gave Mrs. Moore time to feed him. Had she not allowed him to amuse himself, he could have prolonged each meal interminably.

The determination to participate in his own feeding will soon take the form of flinging his head, shutting his mouth tight, and grabbing for the dish and spoon. A baby can find innumerable ways to thwart a determined mother who does not take this independent drive into account. How much easier to let him participate in simple ways—like finger bits or a spoon and cup—one for each hand.

He teased his mother in many ways at feeding times. He spluttered out her food. When she fed him lumpy food he turned it around in his mouth, then oozed out each lump delicately. This was after he had been picking up and feeding lumps to himself.

The fact that he chews and swallows larger lumps that he feeds to himself but will not accept smaller ones from his mother is a sign of the difference in incentive. He will master new lumps of food if he picks them up himself, but he resents any change in the texture of the food offered by his mother.

As he spit out her proffered food, he laughed. When she became angry with this teasing, he sensed it and quieted.

Since Mrs. Moore rarely gets exasperated with Louis, he is sensitive to such a change in her mood.

Creeping improved daily. He maneuvered well and could go forward each time now. He pushed up on his arms and could turn himself to one side or the other as he moved. He maneuvered over to a sofa, pulled his knees under him and pulled up with his arms as he pushed with his legs. He finally got himself to standing. As he did, he began to prattle in a loud voice, as if he were calling his family to admire him. Standing, he teetered precariously and had to be helped down. This new experiment in standing shook Louis' self-confidence. He had been standing whenever the children pulled him up by the arms. Now, as if he had learned some of the dangers of standing by performing it himself, he refused to be pulled up by them any longer. Only his parents were able to entice him into a standing position at their knees.

The realization of the dimensions of an act comes with the awareness that one can perform it oneself. He wisely turns to the adults for their reassurance and limits—not to his siblings.

As he crept around in the days following this experiment, he became irritable and fussy whenever he came near the sofa.

The sofa seems to call up the memory of standing and, with it, the indecision.

He did not try to stand again for several weeks.

Louis' new freedom to creep brought with it a more acute awareness of his mother's location. When she left the room, he cried and tried to follow her. He no longer liked to be left in his playpen to play while she worked around the house. As long as she was in the room or where he could see her, he played contentedly. She was determined to keep him in his pen, so she had to let him cry when he needed to be put in it. But she was conscious of doing more around him to satisfy his new dependence. When she went into another room, she turned to tell him she would be back and called to him from the distance. He called her from time to time to check on her whereabouts and usually managed to get himself into a predicament where he needed her, in order to get her back.

His increased dependence accompanies an awareness that he can get away from her now. As with Daniel, it precedes the real mastery of getting away. At first this awareness is frightening. But an infant's inner drive to progress and independence presses him onward.

His brother and sister distracted him from his problems. They could amuse him with games of peekaboo. He imitated their gestures and gurgled with delight as they jumped at him from behind a chair. Tom took great pleasure in leaping at him with a loud roar. Louis was enchanted with this game and stopped crying when Tom burst at him. Nothing Tom could do was frightening to Louis. He watched his brother whenever he was nearby, as if he were waiting for some fun. When Tom ignored him, Louis called "um—um" and seemed to be giving Tom a name. On one occasion, as he sat in the middle of the playpen, Mrs. Moore was pleased to hear them both laughing out loud. She crept around the corner to look. Tom was pounding on Louis' head with a plastic baseball bat, making loud cracks. At each whack, Louis winced but roared with laughter, as did Tom. Mrs. Moore was horrified and she stopped Tom—to both children's great disappointment.

A baby can be rewarded by play with an older sibling in a way that outweighs any pain or fear. He will gladly overcome these feelings in order to please the sibling and keep him nearby.

Louis was now a great "poker." He poked at his ears, nose, mouth, and navel although without the intensity that Daniel showed. He seemed to investigate each orifice and part of his body. He would allow his mother to change him without a wiggle if Martha hung over him. He poked at her eyes, nose, ears, and mouth. As she let him investigate, he compared the sensation of poking her nose with poking his own; he poked at her mouth, then his own. When she sucked on his finger, he looked surprised, then giggled. He tried it himself, then he returned his finger to her mouth to be sucked. After a few times of this, he dreamily put his middle two fingers in his mouth in the accustomed sucking position. This exploration of the difference in sensation between her mouth and his own was too reminiscent of the old pleasurable situation. Martha imitated him by sucking hers.

This demonstrates that he can already make the visual association between her act and his own.

The poking took a frightening turn. He began to poke at objects as he pulled himself around the room. His mother found him poking his finger into an electrical outlet in the wall.

These are real hazards. If his finger is wet, a baby can burn himself badly. A little girl in my practice poked her tongue into an outlet and burned a portion of it off. An electrical burn does not heal without scarring. Plastic covers that fill up these outlets should be used at this age. Anything to do with electricity should already be designated as definite "No's" (see Active Baby, below).

Someone had to be near him all the time now whenever he was "at large." Of course, Louis loved this, and it added incentive to his exploration.

QUIET BABY

In her own leisurely manner, Laura began to move. She could inch along on her back by hoisting her buttocks in the air and flopping down so that her body followed. As she found that this moved her in the direction of her head, she seemed to realize that she could move to a new place. She preferred to lie on her back and investigate the new vistas overhead. She also seemed to enjoy the splatting sound that she made as her buttocks flopped to the ground. In her crib, she lay for long periods, arching and flopping. She maneuvered herself off the playpen pad and under a chair, where she played with the fringe of its cover. She was found under the table, toying with the edge of the tablecloth. Louis or Daniel might have pulled it off on them. Laura was not so vigorous in her new games.

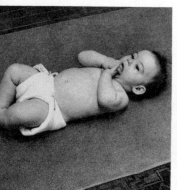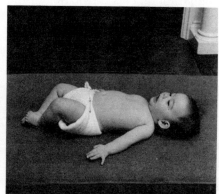

On her back she babbled constantly. She now had a series of consonants and could produce most vowels. She had mastered "sh." She used "sh" as she imitated her father and was delighted to be able to do so. He taught her several others; one such sound was "boo," as they played peekaboo. She said "buh" as he took his hands off his face. She called for both parents by appropriate sounds. Her mother spent the first day rushing to her side until she realized that Laura was practicing her skill at saying "mama." Like Louis, she used this to check on her mother's whereabouts. Vocal contact with her mother was still gratifying enough for Laura. Soon she was content enough to have her mother call back to her from the other room.

Laura spent a lot of time chewing on her fingers and sucking her thumb. She rolled her head in bed, rocking it back and forth. This rolling activity stirred up Mrs. King's old fears. Laura's expression looked vacant as she lolled back and forth. She wore away some of the hair on the back of her head. She poked at her ears a lot and scratched them so that her mother found blood on the sheet.

Playing with an ear or rubbing it is a common accompaniment of teething. Blood in the ear canal may be from a scratch, but it should always be investigated to be sure the drum has not ruptured and the ear is not draining. Place a wad of cotton in the canal. Drainage will continue to wet the cotton. A simple scratch in the canal will not.

She was teething, and when she sprouted two new teeth at once, some of this chewing and rubbing decreased.

The first two teeth are usually the two lower incisors, and they are followed by the two upper incisors. The first tooth is usually the worst. Perhaps a baby becomes conditioned to her discomfort with later teeth, or else has other resources to turn to by then. Most infants do not mind any but the first incisors and the molars that come at around a year.

Teething patterns are inherited, and whenever there are unusual patterns in their order or timing of appearance, one parent or the other has usually had the same pattern.

Once she finished getting her teeth, she seemed to take a spurt in activity. Her thumb-sucking decreased and the head-rolling stopped. She learned to twist herself over onto her stomach. She also began to bend herself forward on her back, as if she wanted to sit. Now she took a more active role in sitting when helped. Although she still needed support, she could sit alone by hunching forward and supporting herself on both arms.

A baby should not be left sitting this way too long, for she can tire the rather sparse musculature of her lower back in an effort to maintain her sagging position.

Her arms were not free in this sitting position, and she tired of it quickly.

While prone, she was less mobile than the other two babies. She lay in one spot looking around. She reached for bits of fuzz off the floor or blanket. She saw minute collections of dust that her mother could not see—poked at them, gathered them up in a thumb and forefinger to bring them to her mouth. She usually used her right hand to perform these acts.

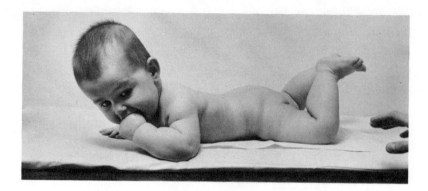

This is comparable to her earlier dominant right-sided head position.

She could amuse herself on her stomach for thirty minutes, fingering a string of small beads of different shapes and textures. She loved to play with a cluster of keys, handling them, rattling them, mouthing each one lovingly.

Small motor manipulation is advanced in her as compared to Louis. One baby can use this as an outlet in much the same way that another baby such as Louis uses large motor achievements.

Laura learned to push a toy just out of reach and cry for it. Her mother realized her trick and began to let her cry. As soon as Laura realized that she had to manage for herself, she reluctantly began to hump forward on her stomach in much the same way that she had learned to hump on her back.

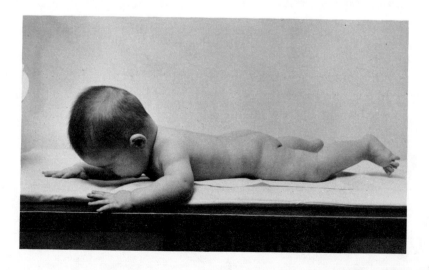

Frustration is a force for learning. One of the difficulties of a baby like Laura is that there are few motor areas that she cares enough about to realize any frustration. A mother does well to realize that frustration is necessary to a baby's learning. A baby like Laura is undemanding, and it would be easy to feel that one should meet the few demands she places on her mother.

Laura's associations were keen. When she heard the sound of the front door opening or closing, she called out to greet her father. Most of the calling was babble, but she usually included something like "dada" in it somewhere. When he hurried to her, she wriggled all over in anticipation of play with him. She knew that sounds of the refrigerator door meant food and began to squeal in her pen as mealtime arrived and her mother made preparations.

She associated elderly ladies on the street with her grandmother, whom she adored. She gurgled happily as a lady leaned over her carriage. But as soon as Laura heard the strange voice, unfulfilled expectation made her stiffen and cry.

Disappointment in cues a baby relies on occurs frequently as a fore-runner to the more direct stranger anxiety so familiar in eight-month-old babies.

She was developing a sense of humor. When she was singing to herself, her mother joined in. She smiled and resumed her humming. As her mother enlarged on the song, Laura began to keep time with her, waving her arms and bouncing her trunk. As her mother came to a sudden "Pop goes the weasel!" Laura bounced once more, stopped, and laughed out loud. When her mother dropped a piece of butter on the floor, and said "damn" as she leaned over to pick it up, Laura laughed at the suddenness and the unusual posture of her mother. Mrs. King could call up a laugh with a swearword thereafter.

Humor often starts in response to a surprise situation. Then a segment of the total situation can be the trigger for remembering it. Such a repeatable response with laughing is part of an ability to remember segments as representing whole situations. This laughing at one cue to the total incident is precocious at this age.

ACTIVE BABY

Sitting and creeping were old hat to Daniel. He could start on his stomach, turn himself over halfway, and push up with his arms on one side to a sitting position. He tried one way, flopped back onto the floor and, cracking his head, turned to the other side to perform the same maneuver. After he had tried one side, then the other, he seemed to choose between them and settled into the stereotype of coming up from his left side.

Many babies need not try out both sides and fall more quickly into a pattern. But a baby such as Daniel gets too much pleasure from each of these steps to miss an opportunity to explore each one fully.

He sat and bounced on the floor. At times, he bounced himself across the floor on his buttocks.

This is a mode of locomotion for some babies who use it in place of creeping. Since we reinforce the sitting position with infant seats and bounce chairs as they grow, this substitute for creeping may be the result of a lack of experience on their stomachs.

He crawled on his knees and elbows. After a number of tumbles, he learned that he was steadier on bent arms and legs. He could soon speed across a room. Mark played a go-and-get-it game with Daniel. He threw a toy across the room and waited for Daniel to go after it. Then he ran across and snatched it out of Daniel's hand to throw it again. Daniel was delighted with this game and outlasted Mark at it.

This could have been ruined by a parent's interference. Had Mrs. Kay rushed to protect Daniel's right to the retrieved toy, and made Mark feel guilty for snatching it away, she could have placed the game in a different light for each participant. As it was, it satisfied Daniel's love for action and Mark's struggle with his feelings about his brother. Mark could tease Daniel without being scolded for it. Daniel had Mark to play with. Since Mrs. Kay had returned to work, they played more with each other anyway. When their mother left, they turned to each other. The sitter was not as important an intermediary in their relationship with each other.

Without their parents present, children are more likely to make a direct relationship. This is one beneficial side effect of a parent's being away.

Daniel and Mark looked at books together. Mark was interested in magazines and books. He loved to turn the pages, mumbling long sentences in imitation of his parents' reading to him. He "read" them to Daniel, who would grab at pages and tear them as he tried to turn them. For this Mark spanked his hands. Nothing Mark did bothered Daniel. Mark pointed out pictures to him and, like their father, he bow-wowed at the dogs, meeowed for the cats. When they reached the picture of a baby, Daniel looked at it and crowed before Mark could comment.

Is he aware that the baby is like him? A baby's awareness that the picture is like him can come from play at a mirror. But there must be more to it than that. An infant like Daniel shows a preference for another infant in a crowded room, watches and imitates him. This preference must be based on a recognition that need not always be founded in past experience with other babies. The cues must be so familiar that the observing infant recognizes them as part of his own repertoire.

Mark played tea party with Daniel. As he poured a cup of make-believe tea, Daniel held his hands in readiness for the soon-to-be-offered cup. Daniel's agile use of the cup was fostered in this game. The sitter, Mrs. Corcoran, gave them chocolate milk in their cups at teatime. Daniel was successful in handling small bits of it in his own cup by himself.

"No" came first from Mark. As Daniel began to get into his toys, Mark began to cry for help. When his mother was at home, she came to remove Daniel. After she left and Mrs. Corcoran was not as speedy in removing the baby, Mark learned to handle this for himself. He pulled Daniel away from the toy box by the legs. This triggered a game. He pulled, Daniel waited until he was dumped across the room, and scrambled back to the toy box. Until Mark learned that pulling him away only meant more fun to Daniel, he spent hours in frustrated complaint. He found that slapping the infant's hand and shouting "No" was slightly better. The most

effective way to change Daniel's course was to entice him away with
another toy. He called from another room, or he dragged a toy in
front of Daniel's nose into another room, then he quickly slammed
the door on his toy chest.

*At two-and-one-half this child has learned what it takes parents
months to learn—simple removal from a goal without a change of
interest for the infant is nothing but a challenge to repeat the original
investigation with renewed vigor.*

Daniel practiced standing at furniture by the hour. He moved easily
along a sofa, sidestepping as he went along.

*An infant's ability to sidestep with speed is lost when he learns to walk
forward.*

He could reach out from the sofa, teeter for a period, lunge, and grab
hold of a nearby table leg, thus moving from one piece of furniture
to another. He fell forward on his face many times in these lunges,
but he made a surprising number of them successfully. The judgment and bravado that went into them improved in time. The
bravado never seemed daunted by failure. As Mark dashed by him

in the practice of these maneuvers, Daniel seemed shaken in his balance. He fell forward as he grabbed the chair more firmly. Here he remained clinging until his brother was out of the way.

Feedings seemed to deteriorate. He ate poorly and seemed to lose interest in his bottle and the baby foods. Mrs. Kay blamed this on herself and her new job. Mrs. Corcoran claimed that Daniel ate well when Mrs. Kay was out of the house.

A child is less involved with a sitter and responds to pressure from her to eat in a more submissive way. Children always eat better for people other than their parents.

Mrs. Kay's reaction to this was to push Daniel even harder. She sat with him at supper, playing games to tease him into accepting the food she offered. She turned on the television in front of him, hoping this would distract him so that she could push more food into him. She laughed about how she could get a bite in, when he was startled by something on the TV and opened his mouth in surprise. It is no wonder that Daniel reacted to these maneuvers with resistance. Feedings became prolonged and a nightmare. As her tension built up, Daniel's negative reactions became entrenched. At last she hit on an obvious solution. She let him feed himself. In this way, she got her tension out of the situation, leaving it to Daniel to solve his own conflict.

Since dexterity with a fork or spoon comes at about sixteen months, it is not practical to turn the infant loose with utensils and liquid baby food. But many babies show an interest in using their fingers to pick up bits of food. Now this can be utilized to allow them to take over. There are plenty of soft finger foods that a baby can gum up in his mouth or swallow whole, if they are in an appropriate diced size. They should be fed to him in small quantities at a time. He can manage by himself bits of dry cereal (one of my patients calls this the "Cheerio phase"), scrambled eggs, bits of soft toast, french toast, diced, cooked carrot or potato, peas with skins broken, bits of soft ground meat, bits of soft cheese, diced sandwiches—made with baby beef or a spread. As he learns to gum up or chew up the first bits, he gets more—but always two at a time. Meanwhile, the parent can be busy about the kitchen. If the parent sits there, she or he may add pressure to the situation. A baby might start teasing them by throwing the bits of food around. If he does, the parent should stop the feeding and put him down. He will learn the reprimand in this, provided the parent does not "plug" him with food between meals.

Parents tell me that they offer a little bit of food off and on between meals because they are so worried about how little their children eat at meals. This is a not-too-subtle form of pressure to eat, and they end up with what they deserve—children who nibble all day, but who are basically feeding problems.

Feeding is an area that is often difficult for working parents—and for single parents as well. The feelings of not having done enough come back when a parent who is away a lot sees a child beginning to refuse to eat. Fathers are likely to have a difficult time around feeding issues. Being a good parent is instinctively equated to seeing to it that a child eats well. For parents who find such feelings conflicting, it is hard to recognize this "new" experimentation with food for what it is—the baby is exploring his new independence in the feeding area. Finger-feeding himself is a critical step and one that must be recognized and encouraged.

No one needs to create a feeding problem today. We have too many substitutes for food that a child needs. The substitutes make it possible for parents to stay out of their child's feeding conflicts. His nutritional needs are completely met by (1) a pint of milk or its equivalent in cheese, ice cream, or a calcium substitute (one teaspoon is equivalent to eight ounces of milk); (2) an ounce of fresh fruit juice or one piece of fruit; (3) two ounces of iron-containing protein, such as one egg or two ounces of meat (one-half jar of baby food meat or a small hamburger); and (4) a multi-vitamin preparation. (This last may even be unnecessary, but it makes me feel one can forget whether a child has eaten green, yellow, or any vegetables.) With these four requirements in a day, a child will grow and gain weight normally. No more is necessary. It would be hard not to meet these four requirements in a twenty-four-hour period, unless the parents' anxiety sets up conflict in the child and his need for autonomy in this area. One can continue to press a child beyond his own interest in food for a while, but the backlash will be disproportionate to any gains made. Around a year old, he will begin to demonstrate his strong determination, and he will win.

In analyzing the need of any parent to see that his or her children eat, I am reminded of the phrase "Essen und brechen," which a Jewish grandmother explained to me. She said it meant "Eat and vomit" and was symbolic of what a good mama used to do to her child. As long as she got the food down him, she had done her part. What happened later was not her responsibility. Today we know her responsibility does not end with food but with the feeding climate. Mealtime must not become a battleground between parents and children. Allowing a baby autonomy consistent with his interest and capacity, coupled with lack of pressure, is the most likely approach from this age on to avoid later feeding problems.

CHAPTER X

The Eighth Month

AVERAGE BABY

Being awake meant being in motion. Louis seemed wound up, pro-pelled by a force over which he had little control. This force kept him going, trying new maneuvers, which he added gleefully to the old. He wanted to stand again. He remembered how, from a sitting position, to spread his feet apart, draw his knees up slightly, and tug on a table leg to pull himself up. He repeated the procedure so often that one could see that the slight variations in technique were not merely random acquisitions. As he got control of each step in his pull-up, he was freed to recognize and use these variations. At first he seemed to place his hands and feet in a stereotyped position to start his pull-up. Then he teetered to a bent, semi-standing position, still holding tightly to the table leg with both hands, his buttocks straight out and waving around. This left him with a choice: should he let go with one or both hands? When he let go with both, he flopped to sitting and had to start again. But if he let go with one hand and scaled up the leg hand over hand, he quickly got to his goal, the tabletop.

In a day or so, he learned to start up with both hands, move one as he began to rise, and achieve the heights with one hand in place at a time.

This is conscious learning. The baby must give up a two-handed grasp in favor of alternating from one hand to the other. He must add to this a flexing and straightening of other parts of his body in order to scale upward. For scaling mammals, learning to climb is instinctive and comes about simply by joining reflex behaviors that are appropri-ate and ready for this action. Although the human infant inherits some of the instinctive urge to climb, the several techniques that are needed for climbing are learned and used for other activities having nothing to do with climbing. The infant must consciously borrow a technique here and another there and put them together into one smooth climbing performance. This is obviously a method of learning we all use; we push around the "knowns" until they form the pattern we are looking for.

Louis stood at the tabletop and yelled for the others to come. He banged his hands flat on the surface and was fascinated by the thumping noise that he could produce. He soon began to know which table made the most noise. He found that a table full of china produced extra rattles. He would rush to bang on the breakfast table and seemed disappointed when the cups and saucers were removed. He learned which pieces of furniture were sturdy enough to pull up on by trial and error. One day he pulled over one of Martha's doll's tables full of china. The clatter frightened him, and she was so angry that he never tried it again. He pulled sofa pillows off on himself and fell backward covered with blankets off a bed. He learned by each of these attempts and settled down to a few favorite, sturdy spots to which he returned daily to do his pull-ups.

Freedom to explore and make one's own mistakes must speed up the assimilation of such an achievement. If a mother keeps after her baby to stop him before he makes mistakes, she diverts his exercise into something else entirely. Instead of simple trial and error it becomes a testing of her in each situation. The baby becomes more interested in drawing her into his play than he is in exploring the results of his own efforts.

After he had been standing at furniture for several days, he found he could lean against it with his stomach in such a way that both hands were free and the noises he could make were redoubled. In the excitement of banging he often threw himself backward, lost his balance, and fell back on his head with a crack.

Learning to bend as one falls backward is not easy for a baby. Extension of the neck and arching of the body is a part of the earlier Moro reflex (see Chapter II). This reflex is set off as the child falls backward, and it may reinforce an infant's inclination to fall straight back with

his head and body extended. It is a wonder more infants do not hurt themselves in such falls, for they certainly hit their heads with a resounding crack. Fortunately, as has been pointed out before (see Quiet Baby, Chapter III), their skulls, made flexible by open fontanelles, protect the brain and cushion it so that each fall does not result in a concussion as it might with an adult. Parents will be well advised to see that there is a rug under each large piece of furniture from which the baby can fall. A cement floor or slippery hardwood would add to the danger of his hurting himself.

Louis took several painful weeks to learn to get himself down from standing. His recourse after he had stood long enough was to start banging louder and crying until someone came to help him. He tried falling backward but realized how painful this was. In the daytime his siblings came rushing to help him. As a result, the Moores had not realized how little he was learning about getting himself down, until he began to pull up on the sides of his crib when he was first put down for his nap or at night. He pulled up on the crib sides, then clung there screaming for help. After he had repeated this a few times each evening, his parents became angry and flopped him hard on his belly, pinning him down with his bedclothes.

This is a game that many babies use to call everyone back to them when they do not want to go to sleep. It is fostered by the excitement that is engendered whenever a baby learns a new skill. This excitement interferes with the ability to give up naturally and break off into sleep. Unless a mother is firm, he can keep this up for an indefinite period. Fatigue adds frenzy to this activity. When he senses or suspects any ambivalence in the parent, a baby at this age is unwilling to make the decision to give up. This is another instance in which the parent must be firm and determined that he or she is right in settling the issue for him. Otherwise the parent deserts him at time when he is not really equipped (and is hindered by his frenzy) to make the break into sleep for himself. Nothing is as sad to me as seeing parents wait for a child to exhaust himself enough to ask for bed. As the child builds up hysterically and they cajole him, trying to settle their own indecision, they show how little strength they have to offer him. Bedtime is largely a parent's decision. It should be handled firmly and with an understanding of the fact that few children ever want to give up at night.

As a baby comes to his light-sleep state periodically during the night (described in Active Baby, Chapter V), he will relive the latest developmental task. This is leftover energy from the daytime, which is so determinedly channeled during the day that it flows into the same channel at night and surfaces when his state of consciousness allows for it. Automatically, and still not awake, he reproduces what he has been working on all day in very much the same way. (Is this evidence of how thoroughly he is internalizing this behavior?) When he gets up but cannot get back down, he wakes himself up further as he calls for help.

Since he called for them as many as two or three times during the night, the Moores had two alternatives—either to strap him to his bed, or to teach him to get himself back down and then leave him to get himself back to sleep. They had never harnessed or strapped their children. So they spent an hour a day for several days teaching Louis to bend in the middle when he wanted to get down. He enjoyed this teaching and giggled as one of his parents bent him to sitting, but he did not learn it as fast as he would have on his own. Finally they thought of standing him at their knees, getting him bent slightly, and then shoving him down, so that he half fell into a sitting position. This seemed to give him more of a feeling for having done it himself, and he picked it up more easily and quickly. After three days he was able and eager to get down by himself. They could hear him (from another room) as he practiced this new task.

How much better it is to add to his repertoire and give him a feeling of mastery than it might have been to strap him down—cutting off any chance of learning (see Chapter VII).

After they knew he could get himself down, they let him cry at night for fifteen or twenty minutes each time before they went to him. When they went, they bent him in the middle and pushed him into a sitting position, leaving him to find his own way back to sleep. In two more nights he had stopped crying for them. Once he was able to get himself back to sleep during the night they all found themselves happier and more rested during the day. Louis seemed as relieved as they were.

Although it may seem cruel for a parent to push a child to master his own sleep pattern in this way, I feel it is necessary. If the parent allows the child to remain dependent upon him or her at night, tension will build up between them. No parent can really tolerate night demands over a long period, especially with other children who need them. But even more important than this, they lose the opportunity to push the baby to an acceptance of independence at night. I am sure that children, too, in some way, understand and appreciate the need for independence at night. They may not like it, but in our culture we expect them to develop such independence.

When he was in his playpen, Louis was miserable. He crawled over to the side, pulled up on it, and stood at the side banging away, screaming loudly for "out." Mrs. Moore wanted to be able to leave him in it for short periods when she could not be nearby, but it was an agonizing period for each of them. She finally asked Martha to get in with him when she wanted to leave Louis in the playpen. Martha could interest him in playing a game with her. This softened the transition for him. However, as soon as she came out, he wanted to, too.

Unless parents hang on to structured use of the pen right now— keeping the baby in there at regular intervals that he can expect and will continue to accept—they will not be able to depend on using the playpen again. He will be too upset by being penned up at unexpected intervals. If it is not necessary to keep the baby in his pen, it certainly is easier to give it up at this stage when locomotion is becoming so important. But when it is important as a safety measure because the parents cannot be nearby, it had better be held to rigidly. They can offer him special toys, or a cracker or a sibling, as they put him in, to make it more attractive to him. But to let him know that he might get out by engaging in battle with them would serve to defeat any chance they might have of using it without a battle.

In the playpen, Louis spent most of his time pulling up and sitting down or pivoting on his bottom as he sat. He could go round and round sitting until he got dizzy and fell over. He went round in one direction only and rarely practiced at reversing.

Experimenting with reversing or changing direction might be expected if a baby is experimenting with standing in many different ways. But sitting is more limited and is not as exciting as standing.

As he played in his pen, he experimented with putting small objects in a large beaker. He put a small block in, then took it out with his thumb and forefinger, exploring it delicately as he turned his hand over and over. The "pincer" grasp was so new that he was testing out his ability to hold on to the object when his hand was turned in various positions. Over and over he sat watching his hand as he approximated his thumb and forefinger and as he picked up a block with these two fingers. In mid-air he dropped the block on purpose, watching the process, picked it up, dropped it—digesting the new use of his hands with his eyes. He began to put several objects in the beaker, one after another, and seemed to be playing with the concept of "more than one." He shook the beaker with one object in it to make a rattling noise. Then he shook it with several as if he "heard" the difference. He could pick up objects in each hand, brought one to his mouth, then another, then both, as if he were establishing the difference between "each" and "both" with his mouth. With finger food he seemed to develop rituals, such as picking up Cheerios with one hand and banana bits with the other, as if he were sorting out differences by relegating each to a different hand.

Although Louis hated being left in a room when his mother went to another and scrambled to follow her, he was satisfied when Martha or Tom was in the room. He could play with either of them at their speed and for as long as they would allow him their play. But he needed to be an active participant. He had been willing to sit and watch them before, gurgling when they gurgled, smiling when they smiled, but now he had to be part of the give and take. When they ignored this and turned away from him, he either crept into their midst and broke into what they were doing or crept out of the room to find his mother. He loved "ball" games and chortled as a ball rolled up to him. He tried unsuccessfully to roll it back. But he could grasp it with one and then two hands, then push it out and drop it, as if he understood the process.

He loved to be fed by his siblings—who fed him all their own unwanted leftovers. At a time when he would shake his head violently if his mother tried to feed him, he would sit quietly allowing Martha to feed him a whole bowl of cereal. Mrs. Moore capitalized on this on a particularly bad day—and Martha often fed him his supper.

He is willing to hang on to Martha in any way. When she pays attention to him he submits to anything—even a passive role. He realizes that he must "play" a role in order to hold her. This further demonstrates how important siblings are in the environment of a third child, whose parents must spread their parenting time over the other two as well.

Mrs. Moore became aware that Tom was feeding Louis, too—everything from earthworms to baby aspirin, which he knew better than to eat himself. Mrs. Moore found the earthworm in Louis' stool, and she caught Tom feeding Louis aspirin. She fortunately caught him in time and prevented him from giving Louis an overdose.

Baby aspirin is still the highest scorer in poisonings in the United States. It must be stored away in an unreachable place, preferably a locked one. I saw a most striking example of a three-year-old's ability to overcome all of the precautions parents can take. A boy in my practice pushed a chair up to the medicine closet, unhooked the hook on the door, unscrewed the aspirin bottle top, ate all the aspirin, screwed the top back on the bottle and returned it to the shelf, closed and latched the door, and finally pulled the chair away. Not until his mother went to get him an aspirin four hours later when he was acting "queer" did she realize that he had eaten all fifty aspirin in the new bottle. Ingestion of ten or more one-and-one-quarter-grain aspirins should be reported immediately and dealt with. When there is any reasonable doubt, an emetic (such as ipecac) should be administered promptly (within fifteen minutes) to induce vomiting (see Active Baby, Chapter VII, and Bibliography under Children's Hospital Medical Center). Hence, ipecac should always be kept on hand, for the fifteen minutes necessary to fetch it from a drugstore makes it too late to administer at home. With your physician's advice, the child should be taken to a hospital for stomach pumping and treatment. The resourceful three-year-old survived, but we all felt it was a miracle.

When Tom gave Louis the aspirin that he wanted himself but did not dare eat, he was acting upon a combination of unconscious and conscious jealous feelings. Consciously, he probably wanted to see what his mother would do to Louis, and to enjoy the punishment; unconsciously, he may well have hoped to hurt Louis with the aspirin. Just as he could not be trusted earlier with his complex feelings about Louis, now he demonstrates even more resourceful methods of torture.

When his mother was nearby, Louis spent most of his time teasing her. When she sat down to rest or read the paper, Louis clambered up to her to pull up at her skirt, untie her shoes, or bang on her paper. When she attempted to ignore him, he got himself in spots where he needed to call for her help. She found herself going to him over and over without realizing it. When she tried to pull out, she saw him go for a "No" such as an electric outlet or the stove. She realized that he was already beginning to use danger zones as a way of attracting her attention. Distracting him was of no avail. She had to say "No" to him in a forceful way, to expect him to change his course. When she did say "No" he stopped, startled, turned to look at her, to see if she meant it, puckered up as if to cry, then finally pivoted and went on to something else.

When a baby begins to tease for attention and also begins to understand "No," it is time for parents to begin to think about their role in setting limits. An experienced mother like Mrs. Moore can be comfortable in a disciplinary role, not worried that the baby's feelings may be hurt by her sudden sharpness. A new mother and father can feel very guilty when their baby looks at them with a hurt expression after they have taken such a stand. This does not negate the importance of taking the stand. Many times, parents will see a look of gratitude on the baby's face after a disciplinary action. Then they know they were right.

QUIET BABY

Laura's relative immobility was strikingly different from Louis' and Daniel's activity. She was content to sit with a rounded back, falling forward over her fat stomach, which pushed itself up into her chest and made her pant. Her face red, her arms circling in the air beside her, she sat looking helpless until her mother readjusted her. She often seemed to assume a more helpless, puffy look when one of her parents loomed into sight (compare her "helplessness" in Chapter IX).

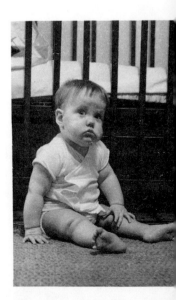

On a weekend when her mother was ill in bed and her father was too preoccupied with taking care of Mrs. King to pay the usual attention to Laura, she began to move. He left Laura in the living room on her back with a toy to play with and went off to help Mrs. King. Half an hour later, forgotten, she suddenly appeared in Mrs. King's bedroom inching herself along on her belly. Since this was the first time she had gone from one room to another by herself, they decided to leave her alone more often to see whether she would learn how to get around. Mr. King left her sitting in her typical position, slumped forward, with several toys just out of her reach. Feeling like a cruel father, he left the room but peeped around the corner. Laura searched the room for help, then straightened herself up, put one arm in front and one leg bent at the knee behind and began to inch toward the toys.

When she reached them, still sitting, she pulled the leg back and began to play with them. But when Mr. King reappeared, Laura looked surprised and promptly dropped the toys, resuming her customary attitude of helplessness. She knows how to play her role as an only child whose parents hover about her.

Parents who notice such a clue might try a little more studied neglect to feed their child's progress. This "act" of dependence is an indication of how perceptive a child like Laura can be and how stubbornly locked to her parents she might become. Instead of finding excitement in motor achievements on her own (the way Daniel and Louis do), a child like Laura seems to get more pleasure out of manipulating the environment to help her. Are they parallel mechanisms in very different children? If a child can give up such an approach as soon as she is forced to, it is nothing to become concerned about.

The new means of locomotion replaced the slower belly flops, and she was soon able to move more quickly in a sitting position, using one arm for pulling and one leg for pushing. She could approach her father while he was reading in his armchair and pull on his trouser leg for attention, before he knew she was around.

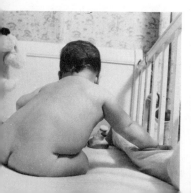
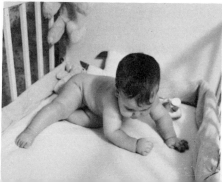

There are many fascinating ways in which different children first learn to locomote. Often they seem to reflect the character of the child. Laura's semi-crablike sitting position, moving with silent grimness, could be almost a symbol of her unwillingness to conform to the usual crawling that other children use. Upright, a baby can keep her "feelers" freer—her eyes and ears, all of her antennae are far above ground catching every nuance of change in the atmosphere and in the important adults around her. Laura by now is doing as much visually as most children do by motor exploration. Her senses are so keen and are working so hard that she is practicing visually what other children must do with motor activity. Her musculature will not be as well developed and her joints will be floppier when she is "ready" to crawl or walk, but if she is motivated, she will overcome that. It may well take her longer to achieve such acts as standing and walking, but she will have learned about the world in other ways by that time.

Sitting, Laura babbled constantly—calling her parents with "da-da-da," "ga-ga-ga," "ba-ba-ba" in long strings. When a parent left the room, she called out with strings of these syllables. She was content when they called back the same sounds and maintained contact from several rooms away. When they returned, she clapped her hands in joy. She played "bye-bye" with her father, waving as he left the room, laughing and clapping when he came back. Mr. King and Laura played this over and over. Her gaiety was a delight to them both. She would laugh out loud at her father when Mr. King sat down on the floor beside her and imitated Laura's postures and movements after her. She seemed to be aware of the correlation of her father's body and movements with her own. Watching her father imitate her added a new consciousness of her own movements, and she loved it.

When Mrs. King put on her overcoat, Laura began to ask for her own. When it was not forthcoming, her mother realized that she made the association between the overcoat and a sitter coming. She had been left with the same sitter on Mrs. King's days off for some time, and Laura had always gotten along well with her. But Laura did not want to be left all of a sudden. She cried as if her heart would break when Mrs. King left the house. The sitter reported that this crying continued only until Laura realized Mrs. King was really gone, then she accepted the inevitable and resumed her play. When she heard her mother's footsteps returning, she began to wail all over again. Mrs. King was torn between wanting to stay to avoid all of this, and the knowledge that Laura was not as upset as she put on. The sitter assured her that they had had a nice time while she was away.

Indeed it is a stage, and the sitter is right. The increase in dependency at this age is a mixture of things (see Average Baby, Chapter IX). Now that a baby can move and separate from her mother, it becomes more frightening when the separation is against her will. Also, many new cues and ways of doing things are coming all at once. One defense against this onslaught is to want to cling to one's parents and to keep strangers with their new and poorly understood cues out of this too-rapidly changing universe. In my office, babies are fine at this age as long as they are in their parents' laps, or as long as they approach me—but if I come to them quickly or produce the new cues, we are lost. Hence, I urge a mother to hold her baby for an examination at this time, and I try to stay behind her as I examine the infant. I never look a baby in the eye at this time. When I do, I can expect a wall of screaming as a protective response. Being looked at too closely is obviously piercing to an eight-month-old's armor. (Compare a chimpanzee who fights when eye-to-eye contact is established by a fellow chimp.)

When the Kings took Laura to a strange place at this time, they could expect anything from desperate clinging to loud wailing. Her protest could last throughout a whole visit. Mr. King began to realize that she seemed to carry on too long and that she was effectively shutting out everyone else by means of her crying. He decided that he would try to stop Laura. As they left home, he spoke to her in a warm, calm voice. Once they arrived he told her repeatedly, in a few simple words, not to cry, and held on to her tightly. Whether because she understood or was comforted by his voice and firm grasp, she was much better. She was able to maintain her composure, although with frantic clinging to her father, throughout a visit. Now and then, she sobbed deeply as if she were crying inside. However, she maintained a stony, anxious silence for whole visits to friends and grocery stores. But if a well-meaning adult came up to chuck her on the chin, she broke down in open sobs and had to be taken home.

When she was successful, her father praised her. He was determined to help her overcome her fear of strange places and strange people. Gradually she gathered courage and, by the end of the month, she was able to sit in her grandmother's lap with only an occasional racking sob.

Preparation for an ordeal works even at this age, perhaps because it helps both parties involved. Preparation of grandparents or of those about to be visited helps, too. Then, if they produce one of these wailing shut-outs by too aggressive an approach, they will not feel quite so guilty. I suggest that they be warned not to approach or look at the infant for a little while after arrival and until the infant approaches them. Though of course this is hard for an eager grandparent to remember or to understand.

Laura showed new idiosyncrasies in her feeding situation. She loved to pick up food bits, examine them, mouth them, spit them back out, reexamine them with her fingers and eyes, put them on her feeding table, pick them up again, and reinsert them in her mouth. This kind of play with each bit of food could go on many times before she swallowed a bite. Mrs. King was ready to scream when she watched her. So she put a few bits on Laura's tray and went off to do her own work in another part of the kitchen. In this way Laura could prolong a single meal for up to an hour.

It seems sad to me that many mothers feel so compulsive about getting food into their babies that they miss out on the obvious value of this

kind of exploratory behavior with food. To be able and allowed to look at, touch, turn over, and taste bits of food (the same exploring with mouth and fingers that begins earlier with inedibles) obviously can make mealtimes one of the choice satisfactions in the day. The combination of touching, looking, tasting, exploring with her mouth and fingers the many qualities of a piece of food before she finally swallows it, enhances the entire experience of eating for a sensitive baby such as Laura.

Laura was varied in her approach to different foods. She did not like to play with slippery foods and ate a banana very quickly without any fingering. A piece of cookie or toast was tortured until it was unrecognizable. After she finished eating finger foods, she licked her fingers, as if she didn't want to miss a bit of the pleasure of it. Mrs. King handed Laura one towel, and she wiped the feeding table with another. Laura swiped away at the table as if she were imitating her mother's cleaning gestures. She was picking up some of her mother's rather compulsive cleanliness.

Laura would not imitate her mother with a cup or spoon. She accepted them as objects to play with when Mrs. King handed them to her at mealtime, but when Mrs. King tried to get her to put the cup up to her mouth, Laura looked blank. She was able to drink out of a cup when Mrs. King held it for her, but she made no effort to hold it herself. When Mrs. King tried to put Laura's hands up around the one she was holding, Laura withdrew them violently and let them hang limply behind her. She refused to carry a spoon to her mouth although Mrs. King felt she could do it if she wished. She seemed to feel that the cup and spoon were her mother's job, and she was not going to take over.

Some babies who are perfectly competent to hold their own bottles, to manipulate their cups or feeding utensils, refuse to do it. It seems to me that they are aware of how nice it is to be dependent in the feeding situation. I agree. As long as they want to be fed, they should be. Infancy is all too short anyway, and we as a culture are all in too much of a hurry to make our babies grow up. The feeding situation should be an intimate one in which the mother is the giver and the baby the receiver. Any baby is likely to sense that as soon as she shows that she can hold her own bottle, she may be left alone with it. The same goes for the cup and for the spoon. Babies are often willing to be independent with their fingers and their new grasp, but not with old familiar objects like the cup and spoon.

Laura seemed to play with her ability to change the visual world. She sat in the middle of the floor looking at a distant object. She cocked her head to one side, as if to see it in one way, then to the other, savoring the change. She shook her head from side to side as she kept her eyes fixed on the object, changing the speed of her head's motion, and the direction. As she recovered her equilibrium, she laughed as if she appreciated the differences she could make in her world.

In front of a mirror, she became mesmerized. She watched herself for a long time as if comprehending what she saw. When she smiled at herself, she laughed to see the image smile. She patted the image with her hand and tried to kiss it. She put her forehead up against the mirror and blinked hard as she did in games with her parents, as if she were trying to make sure whether or not this image was a person. She caught sight of her own hand in the mirror and compared the real hand with the mirrored hand, watching each intently as it changed shape. She was intrigued by this play for long periods, and her parents felt that she was digesting the fact that this was an image of herself.

 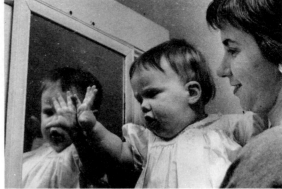

I feel it is more likely that she is intrigued by seeing portrayed out in front of her her own body's movement. This enhances the visual-motor perception that goes on as a baby learns to master each new

movement. To see herself out in front provides a more conscious awareness of herself and her body. This may be as exciting to a baby as it is to us when we gain some new insight about ourselves.

ACTIVE BABY

Nothing in the house was sacred any longer. Daniel could move so fast on his hands and knees that he could follow his mother or father wherever they went. He was closed in the bathroom door more than once. It became necessary before opening a door to call first to see where Daniel was. He enjoyed sitting or standing at doors that were likely to open and screamed lustily when he was thrown down by them. When he wanted to get anywhere quickly he crawled. But his playtime was spent exploring the intricacies of being upright. As soon as he entered a room, he checked it to be sure Mark or the adults were settled there for a time. Having assured himself that he could afford some "practice time" before he would have to move on, he began his second evaluation of the room. He seemed to look it over for exploration possibilities. If a chair had been moved, or a table contained a new object, he headed straight for it.

The marvelous memory of the "gestalt," or whole, as he last knew it frees a baby to pick out a novel stimulus in a very economical fashion. And of course, it needs exploration.

Since Mark had never been as persistent or as alert to detail, the Kays were caught off guard. The demitasse left in the living room from the night before often went down before Daniel's assault. A burning cigarette in an ashtray was a fascinating object until he burnt himself. After that, he respected both cigarettes and ashtrays.

Although this method of teaching babies not to play with burning objects cannot be entirely recommended, it does work. In the highlands of southern Mexico where the Indians live in huts built around a central fire that is always going, no one ever stops a baby as he crawls up to it. They say, "He will learn." He does, and he must. Perhaps we expect too much of our children when we stop them and expect them to learn the meaning of "hot" without having experienced it. One mother tells me she always allows her baby to try things out before she imposes a "No," because this will help her baby to be the exploring kind. She feels that shutting her off too soon will replace curiosity with fear.

The family mealtime was a nightmare. Daniel spent the time going hand over hand around the edge of the table, chinning himself to see what was available, pulling the tablecloth to him to get at whatever would come with it, or begging at his parents' knees for handouts. Since he often ate very little at his own feeding table, Mrs. Kay resorted to feeding him bits off her plate "to get it into him." When she tried to sit him at the table, he ruined dinner for all of them. He stood in his chair to show off, ignored his food, begged for pieces of theirs, ignoring his own, and as soon as they gave it to him, smashed it onto the table or dropped it provocatively over the side of his chair. Mr. Kay felt his ulcer returning after three meals like this, and Daniel's mother decided it was no solution. So she continued to feed him from her plate and tried to put him in his room when she could. Since her job kept her away from him during the day, she liked to keep him up in the evening, and rarely could she get him to bed before they ate.

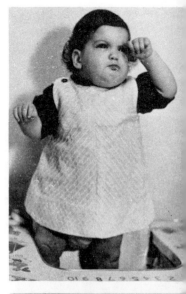

A mother who is less involved in how much her baby eats (see Chapter IX) could handle this more definitely and effectively. There is no reason for a baby to be included at meals if he uses it as a provoking situation that achieves nothing except a heightening of tension between everyone. If he is not treated so permissively and like a begging puppy, he will learn quickly that mealtime is sacred. He can even be expected to play nearby, or eat a few bits at his own feeding table. If a mother is definite about such expectations, a baby can learn some of the social importance of mealtime, which may heighten the value of meals for him later when he can partake better of the social interaction.

Daniel could now feed himself entirely with finger foods and could handle his own cup. Rarely was he allowed to do this, however, as his mother and the sitter could not restrain themselves from attempting to push food into him. As a result, he used feeding times

to tease adults. He refused food from a spoon—by shaking his head violently or by accepting it, then blowing it across the room. When he had an audience, he drank a little out of his own cup and demonstrated that he could manipulate it amazingly well. At the end of such a performance he carefully dropped the cup over his tray to the floor. As he dropped it, he blinked his eyes in anticipation of the noise as it hit the floor.

This demonstrates a memory of timing. A baby becomes aware of the time interval before the cup hits the ground and then begins to anticipate it.

Life with Daniel was not all torture. He was so agile and bright that it was fun to watch him as he played. He preferred his parents' things to any toys of his own. He loved to play with a box of spools, or his father's chessmen, putting them away in the box, taking them out one by one. He used one hand, then the other to pick them out. He had the concept of putting down one object before trying to pick up another. Although he liked to crawl with one hand filled (see Average Baby, Chapter IX) while he explored with the free hand, he freed both hands when he was sitting and playing. He picked up one block with his right hand, another with the left, then banged them together noisily. After this was done, he tried to reach for a third with his mouth. Then he seemed to hit upon the concept of putting one of those in his hand into his mouth, picking up the third with his empty hand. He banged away with each hand at the block in his mouth. This play came to an end when he whacked himself in the face.

He loved paper—magazines, newspapers, and even books. He learned to tear them noisily, and Mark imitated him gingerly in these destructive games. Mrs. Kay was at a loss as to how to stop this kind of destruction. When she tried to snatch a book or magazine away from Daniel, he gripped it so tightly that he tore it as she pulled. She found she could offer him an unimportant one in order to take away a treasured one. She gave him some magazines of his own to play with, so that he would leave theirs alone. This was only partly successful. Mr. Kay covered the bookcases containing his valuable books with chickenwire so that Daniel could not get to them and tear them up while he was gone.

He could open drawers, and one of his favorite games was to pull everything out onto the floor. Then he climbed into the empty drawer and cried for help to get out again. Mrs. Kay found it worked to insert a broomstick through the loop handles of bureau drawers, to keep him from opening and emptying them. Mark's toy chest was a favorite for his forays. Poor Mark could only fuss and fume. He tried to teach Daniel that putting everything back in was as much fun as taking it out—and it *was* as long as Mark participated. But as soon as he tired, so did Daniel. Once Mrs. Corcoran heard a muffled screaming from Mark's room. When she followed the sound, she found that Daniel had emptied Mark's toy chest, climbed in, and closed the lid.

This is all too reminiscent of the ice chest tragedies to which little children are prone. Less agile babies will do these things later than Daniel, but for the same innocent, exploratory reasons. During these months a mother should constantly reevaluate the traps into which her baby might manipulate himself.

He now crawled to the front door when he heard it open—and in the evening he was often at the front door to greet each parent before the door even made a noise.

The sense of timing that children develop around an important regular event leads them to know when to wait for Daddy at the window.

When the telephone rang, he beat Mrs. Corcoran to it and would be caught sitting quietly holding the telephone when she arrived. The person at the other end of the line was either furious or had given up when there was no response. One of Daniel's favorite sports was to take the telephone off the hook and to listen to the series of sounds that developed.

The telephone company has offered little help in "baby-proofing." This should have been an area for research by now. One of our children at under a year reached the Jordan Marsh shopping service by random dialing and was enjoying the ranting of the service personnel as they scolded him for not declaring what he wanted to order.

A firetruck or a noisy truck in the street brought Daniel and Mark on the run. Daniel learned to say "wa wa" for trucks in his own imitation of the sounds they made.

The noise is a part of the fascination that children have for cars and trucks. Noisy, aggressively moving trucks seem to be exciting, especially at a distance.

He learned to play "so big" with his father. When Mr. Kay said, "How big is Daniel," he elevated his arms to shoulder height if he were standing, up over his head if sitting.

This is not entirely based on a difference in his concept of how high he is in the two positions. It is also a recognition of the necessity of keeping his arms in readiness to balance or grab for furniture as he teetered in standing.

Sleeping was again a problem for Daniel and the Kays (see Chapter VII). He found it difficult to give up exciting exploration in order to go down at his nap or night. The Kays had never been definite enough in their approach to putting the children to bed, and with Mark it had not mattered. He had been easy to direct and had been ready for bed when an appropriate time came.

Quiet children, like Mark and Laura, expend a great deal of energy sorting out stimuli around them. They are not active physically, but the sensory and intellectual activity that is necessary to sort out daily stimuli exhausts them. They are ready for a chance to get away from the family commotion, which is more expensive for them than it is for a more motoric, direct child like Daniel.

Since Mrs. Kay had gone back to work, she felt torn by wanting to see the children at the end of the day and by her guilty feelings about their needs that she was no longer meeting as fully as she felt she should. When Daniel wanted to keep going, she hoped he would stop himself (see Average Baby, Chapter X). As he became giddier, he carried Mark along with him, so the two built each other up to a real frenzy. Then, as they collapsed in tantrums or disintegration, Mr. and Mrs. Kay could see that it was time to force them to give up. Getting Daniel and Mark into their separate beds seemed to be a real relief to each child, and they were often sound asleep before Mark's bedtime story and Daniel's bottle were finished.

This is evidence to me of the relief that children show when a parent takes a definite stand and thus lets them off the hook.

Naps were short; Mrs. Corcoran found it easier to put Daniel in for his naps on her days than did Mrs. Kay on weekends. She found she had to let Daniel give up a morning nap and concentrate on the single afternoon one. Daniel was more excited when his parents were home and more interested in staying up. But Mrs. Corcoran was also more definite in her structuring of the boys' day, and they knew this.

Daniel awakened in the night and cried out for his mother. She went to him and found herself giving him an extra bottle to get him to sleep as she had when he was five months old (see Chapter VII). She enjoyed this intimate period with him alone. As she gave him his bottle, she thought of all the things she had not done for him during the day, of all the things she had done wrong with him, and she was caught by her guilty feelings about her double job—working, from which she received so much pleasure, and mothering the boys, which she felt she might be neglecting.

This is not so. She is gratifying an important part of herself and is a better mother as a result. The danger is that a working mother will let her guilty feelings cloud her judgment. At such a time she must keep her baby's need for firmness as well as tenderness clearly in mind. If she gets caught up in her own feelings, she can break down the discipline and schedule that are necessary to him. It is hard to remember this.

Daniel became even more demanding at night, and she began to realize that she should not go to him repeatedly. Again, as at five months, she solved the conflict by going in to him at ten or eleven before she went to bed. She roused him, changed him, cuddled and talked to him, and gave him extra milk when he wanted it. Then during the rest of the night she ignored him. She was surprised at how easy it was for both of them. Daniel woke only a few more nights and was content when his mother told him firmly that she had already been in, and it was time for him to go back to sleep. Settling her own ambivalence plus giving him the extra time with her (which was symbolic to her and important to both of them) settled the nighttime issue for them both. After a week, Daniel seemed to need only a pat and a change at ten o'clock, and the waking crisis had been solved.

CHAPTER XI

The Ninth Month

AVERAGE BABY

Louis' ninth month was a month in which he seemed to slow down and consolidate some of the gains he had made. He was not as driven to learn new tricks as he had been in previous months. He did find out how to get himself from his back to a sitting position—all in one lovely rotary movement. He curled up on his back on the floor, turned over on one side, and imperceptibly shifted balance so that he rolled up to sit with little apparent effort.

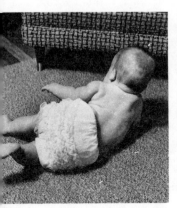  

Many children come to sitting by bringing their legs up under themselves in a crawling position. Then they flop the legs out, landing adroitly on their bottoms. As in other developmental steps, each baby has his own method.

Standing was more of an effort, but he practiced letting go of supports in midair to teeter from one leg to the other. As he grabbed hold of a chair or table again, he let himself down smoothly to a sitting position by reversing the hand over hand he had learned the month before.

Sitting in the middle of the floor, he learned new games. He piled two blocks on top of each other. The concept of one on top of the other came from Martha, who taught him how to do this. With further pushing from her, he attempted a third block, but this was beyond his capacity, and he lost interest. As soon as she let him, he splattered the tower apart with his wide-open hand. The control that was necessary to grasp a block with a two-finger grasp, pick it up, and convey it to another similar block, and to approximate the two so that they stood as a tower, was demanding, and Louis' power of concentration could last under pressure from Martha longer than it could for anyone else—but there was a limit.

One forgets what an achievement is the separation of thumb and forefinger from the rest of man's "paw." It enables him to achieve delicacy in sorting of objects, in piling up objects on top of each other, in poking, in squeezing with reinforced power between thumb and forefinger—it makes the refined use of tools a uniquely human accomplishment.

Louis loved to throw objects, and with Tom he was learning ball games of give and take. When he threw (or dropped) a ball, Tom threw it back. Although Louis' aim was hardly an asset, Tom's incentive to throw back at Louis led him to run and pick up the ball. As Louis played with Tom he chuckled with delight. He began to foresee the return of the object he had thrown, and he looked disappointed when Tom did not return it. He often instituted the game himself, crawling over to the ball, picking it up, taking it to Tom.

Games like this are instrumental in bringing about an awareness of a child's ability to let go of a toy and anticipate getting it back. In Louis' case, they are fueled by his desire to keep Tom interested in him, but they come at a time when babies are able to learn other, similar concepts—such as leaving mother and being able to come back to her at will, allowing her to leave him with an anticipation of her return.

He carried out simple commands and found pleasure in understanding them, completing them, and coming in for the reward of approval at the end. His father said, "Go get my slippers, Tom," and was delighted to see Louis scramble off toward the bedroom after Tom. The next night he directed the request to Louis, and everyone enjoyed seeing him crawl out to return with a slipper for his father. This became an evening ritual, and Louis loved it.

A third baby learns so much from his siblings by imitation and competition that a reader may wonder how a poor first child can ever learn to compete in the games of life. The hunks of behavior that Louis learns from imitating Tom and Martha are cheaper at the time, but they may not teach him as much about the process of learning as the same achievement teaches Laura or any other first child.

The children adored to roughhouse with Mr. Moore at the end of the day. One of their favorite games was to crawl all over him as he lay on the floor. Louis chose to land on his face and plopped on his belly right across his father's nose. Another game was to be thrown up in the air, to be caught by his father. Louis loved this before, but now he took in a deep breath when he was thrown up, clung to his father's hands desperately, and refused to be thrown a second time.

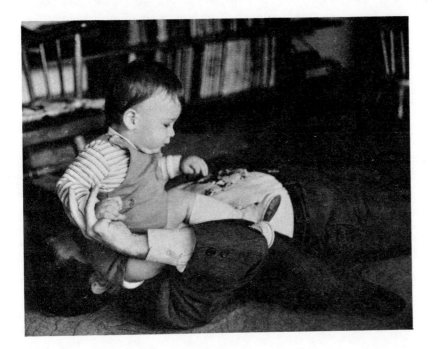

An increased awareness of heights comes at a time when a baby is learning about vertical space himself, e.g., getting up and down from standing. Being thrown up and down bothered him less before he had learned to climb or rise to a height by himself.

Exploration of space was demonstrated by Louis after these periods of play when he got himself to standing, then fell down to his knees or buttocks on purpose. He repeated this kind of falling "on purpose" over and over as if he were trying to overcome the fear he had just been made aware of. After this he whimpered whenever he found himself up in a chair. Although he had been climbing up and down into chairs before, he was afraid to come down—as though struck by this new awareness.

He began to be afraid of the big bathtub. He had been used to playing in it with Martha and Tom—all three bathing together— ever since he had been sitting alone. He screamed now when he was put in with them. Even in a tub alone, he cried pitifully and clung to the tub sides. His mother respected his new fear and bathed him on his old bathinette. She took him in the tub with her, holding him tightly to her as she lowered him into the water. Slowly, he began to regain his old confidence about baths. After another month, he was equal to a bath alone. He could not rejoin his siblings in the tub for several months—their quick, unsettling movements and noises were too much to tolerate when he was conquering new fears.

The price of new awareness is great. With it comes fear, insecurity, and a need to reevaluate an old skill that has taken on a new meaning.

Louis played out some of his fears with his favorite toy dog. He put him in the armchair and dropped him out onto the floor. Then he sat down beside him to comfort him.

Bits of play that portray a child's fears, wishes, and goals are not uncommon if we watch for them. Even at this age I have seen babies demonstrate what they are experiencing by "playing it out." To be able to see for oneself what it is that is disturbing, to play it out, using play as a way of surfacing one's anxieties to consciousness where one can control them better, is the essence of therapy. This process is at the root of psychotherapy with children, as it is with adults. Even after

*a traumatic experience such as a hospitalization, an older child will
be able to work out the scars and the anxiety produced by the trauma
he has experienced in a play situation. Such a situation can be set up
by parents after a traumatic experience.*

Louis began to be concerned whenever his mother started the vacuum cleaner. He cried pitifully in a corner until his mother stopped
the machine and went over to comfort him. Since this came along
with all the other fears, she saw it as part of the whole scene and
tried to figure out how to help him. She closed the door when she
had to vacuum, but leaving him out made him miserable. He obviously was both fascinated and frightened. She held him tight with
one hand while she vacuumed with the other. She took him to the
silent vacuum cleaner to touch and explore. Gradually he overcame
this fear also, and he was content to play while she cleaned.

*Louis' sudden period of fearfulness is earlier than I hear about it in
most children—except when they live in a noisy, aggressive environment, such as that created by Tom and Martha. It is as if the younger
sibling can master the noise and excitement level most of the time,
but the delicate balance becomes apparent when a new increase in
sensitivity to noise throws him over. Then one realizes that he has
been constantly working to master all that happens around him. The
fact that a child like Louis consistently wants to and continues to
master the onslaughts of his world is evidence enough that a stimulating environment such as his is a wonderful way to grow up!*

Because of these signs of increased fearfulness, Mrs. Moore began
to feel that she was not pushing Louis hard enough to grow up.

*It is easy from where we sit to see that this is no time to push him.
These fears reflect a need for more dependency. Fears are a precursor
to spurts of independence and aggression. They seem to be a baby's
attempt to pull in his horns and gather security from the environment
—before he has to try out new wings.*

She tried to get him to drink from a cup, but he refused it. He loved
his bottle and was content to hold it himself. In the past month Mrs.
Moore had been using it to quiet him at the end of the day. She put

him in the middle of the kitchen floor with a bottle in his mouth. He lay there, sucking away, jerking it out of his mouth with a snap, exploring it lovingly with hands and eyes, then sucking it back in with fervor. All of a sudden she resented his attachment to the bottle. She could not see why he was so clumsy when she offered him the cup. A sip of milk out of the cup rolled down each side of his mouth. Ginger ale or soft drinks went down beautifully out of the same cup. She finally realized that he was resisting her efforts to wean him from his beloved bottle. As she realized this, she became more determined to wean him. She discussed it with her friends. Some of them appeared to agree with her that he should be pushed onto the cup.

This is an example of the subtle ways American parents compete with each other. Each is ready to help another feel inadequate as a parent, to see the other's baby's behavior as inadequate. Few are willing or perhaps even able to point out the marvelous strength a baby shows in clinging to an important symbol such as a bottle. The speed with which each child takes steps to grow up seems to be equated with success in parenting. I hope the next generation will understand that a better goal is to see that each step is a solid one, taken for good reasons, however long that step may take.

Her friends' criticism reinforced her determination to push Louis off his bottle. The more she pressed him, the more determined he became. She added flavoring to the milk in his cup and then he took it, but when she stopped the flavoring, he refused it again. She thought of stopping all his bottles and starving him until he gave in, but other household struggles took precedence, and she finally relaxed on that one.

Mrs. Moore is doing what many parents with more than one child do. They suddenly become aware of something that they think needs their attention. Guilty that they have neglected it before, they pour themselves into it. There is no need for this. A skill such as using a cup will come. I have seen children in primitive societies, who have never practiced with a cup before, watch their elders use one, and then at the age which is appropriate, they pick theirs up and drink from it as if they had been practicing for months. In these societies the emphasis is on learning by imitation rather than by teaching, and it becomes apparent that there are many ways to achieve the same end. A baby like Louis will learn to use a cup when he is ready.

Parents also reinforce the value of the bottle by giving it to the baby to explore and master by himself. One reward in holding a baby (through the first year) while he has his bottle is that he will give it up more easily when he wants to get away from his parents in the beginning of the second year. I may seem to join the group who feel it matters when a baby gives up his bottle. I do not.

QUIET BABY

On the surface, Laura appeared to have made little progress toward her parents' goal for her of more motor activity.

Unconsciously, parents are driven by their foreknowledge of what their friends' children are doing; what babies "should be" up to in our society—information gleaned from baby magazines and other parents' talk. Even at the office fathers and mothers compare their babies' achievements. Motor milestones are the basis for these comparisons.

Laura's day was spent sitting. She experimented quietly with all aspects of sitting. She propelled herself in sitting—using her characteristic leg push and arm pull to get herself around. The speed with which she could get around increased slowly. Now and then, she followed her mother or father from room to room in their apartment. However, their apartment was not large, and she could see and hear them from any one room. There was not the incentive to keep up that there might have been in a larger house.

She rocked as she sat, backward and forward. She swayed from side to side in rhythmic time with music. She played with her fingers, examined each one as if it were new—placed them in various positions, seemed particularly interested in approximating her thumb and forefinger. She was interested anew in her feet. As she sat with her shoes off, she watched her toes move as performers. She grabbed hold of them one by one as if remaking old acquaintances. That's exactly what they were. Laura had played with and even sucked on her toes at the age of five months. Also, she could be remembering her father's game of "This little piggy," which they played.

When she was in shoes, she played with the laces, pulling on them, trying to poke the end of the lace in the holes that she saw her mother use. The shoes became friends. She cuddled them when they were off, and she carried one with her by the laces when she moved around to play.

A baby's shoes become so important to her that I find I can use them to show her each step that I will use to examine her in my office. I put the stethoscope on the shoe first, and as if this breaks the ice, she is then able to allow me to put it on her. When I flash a light into the shoe, she is not so worried about having it flashed at her. This is another example of a baby's ability to identify herself with an object —particularly one that she wears or carries.

Laura loved her toys. She sat on the floor for several hours exploring each toy in new ways—every surface was fondled, banged, poked with her tongue and forefinger. A toy with a string on it was held in her left hand while she delicately fingered the string with the thumb and forefinger of her right hand. Occasionally she switched hands, as if to try out the pincer grasp of her left hand. Finding it not as perfect, she gave up quickly and returned to her right thumb and forefinger.

Other parts of her body became sources of interest. She had never been able to see her navel or her genital area before. She poked at them repeatedly after she discovered them. At one point, Mrs. King became embarrassed and concerned that Laura was "learning to masturbate." Laura poked into her vagina with her forefinger when she was undressed and seemed to struggle to get her hand into her diaper after she was dressed again.

Discovery and exploration of the nether regions is normal. Since babies do not really have an opportunity to see this part of their body until they begin to sit and can bend forward, is there any wonder that they then explore it? Whether at this age there are heightened eroto- genic zones around the navel and vagina or not, exploration would be rewarding. If there are (and indeed there seem to be), this is a naturally important part of an infant's learning about herself. Our puritanical backgrounds make us self-conscious and lead us to feel that there is something wicked about this. By reinforcement, our prohibition can quickly change a baby's natural need for exploration and self-stimulation into a use of these zones as outlets for tension-release or masturbation. I see many, many babies go through this kind of exploratory self-stimulating behavior, but I am sure that they do not get "stuck" in it unless the environment reinforces it in some way— either by trying to prohibit it or because the baby has too little else in the way of stimulation. Institutional babies are often "stuck" in self-stimulating behavior—but because of environmental deprivation —a negative kind of environmental reinforcement (compare Active Baby, Chapter VII).

Laura's navel protruded as she sat. Her full belly made the scar tissue beneath the umbilicus more prominent, and there was a real button of tissue on her watermelon-like stomach. Mrs. King worried about whether this was a hernia.

Hernias of the umbilicus are common in smaller infants. The muscles that go vertically down the abdominal wall from the ribs to the pubis do not seal together at first. As these muscles strengthen they pull together and most babies no longer have a muscle separation. The hernia goes when the muscle wall becomes firm. About 5 percent do not disappear with time, and a simple operation is necessary to pull the muscles together. An umbilical hernia is almost completely without danger and can usually be ignored. Strapping them, putting coins over them with tape to hold the coin down, maneuvers aimed at keeping a baby from crying so it will not get worse—all these are unnecessary and useless. The hernia either goes or it does not. The scar-tissue button such as Laura has will disappear and become a deep indentation when she is about four and her abdomen is flat. Meanwhile, it is a source of pleasure to explore and manipulate.

In her stroller, when she went for walks with her mother, she was content to sit for long periods. When her mother stopped to talk or to buy groceries, Laura played with sensory changes she produced for herself—covering her eyes with her hands or bending her head over backward. She covered her eyes or closed them tightly to shut

out what she did not want to see—a stranger who was too intrusive, loud noisy places, other babies who were crying. She was very sensitive to other children and jumped when they made sudden movements as she watched them. She stared silently as they played around her, withdrew if they came up to her stroller, and covered her face when they looked directly at her. Another baby's crying was painful to her. She puckered up, whimpered to herself and, closing her eyes, seemed to shrink into the protection of her stroller. Laura needed more contact with other children so that she could learn about them —and about herself. Her increased sensitivity to them was evidence of her increasing interest in them (compare this with Louis' increasing fears as his awareness of his surroundings increased).

Her father was the consuming interest in her day. In the morning, she smiled at her mother, but she giggled and wriggled coyly when her father came to get her up. When he left in the morning, she humped herself over to the window. She screeched for her mother to come. Mrs. King would pick her up to wave at her father as he disappeared down the street. "Bye-bye" had become her father's signature, and whenever he put on his hat, she began to wave. She knew what "Here comes Daddy" meant and was waiting for him at the front door as he arrived. When he came home at night, she took on new energy. She imitated his cough, tongue clicks, learned to hiss after him, and even tried to purse her mouth the way he did when he whistled, blowing out in a noiseless blow.

He could teach her anything, and often Mrs. King felt wearily that she was an extra wheel. When she wanted Laura to learn about the cup, she turned it over to Mr. King. He gave her one cup while he used another, and soon Laura was imitating him. He gave her a cup in the bathtub, and soon she was feeding herself bath water. He poured milk into her cup while she sat in the tub. She drank part of it successfully and poured the rest down her front into the tub water. In this way, she learned to use the cup by herself, and by the time Mrs. King was ready to wean her from the breast, Laura could feed herself milk. In fact, Laura first refused a noon breast-feeding after a large dose of milk from her cup with lunch. From this cue, Mrs. King felt it was time to wean her.

There are at least three lags in interest in breast-feeding that originate in the infant. The first is at four or five months and is associated with

*the sudden widening of visual interest in her surroundings. The sec-
ond accompanies the tremendous motor spurt at seven months. The
third occurs between nine and twelve months in most babies. A few
never lose interest and probably have to be pushed away. When a baby
begins to lose interest after nine months, it seems appropriate to me
to take her up on it. She has had enough nutritional sucking, and I
do not find that many need much more extra-nutritional sucking after
they have had as much as nine months at the breast. The spurt of
motor development and independence that will be coming at around
a year is geared to a natural separation from the mother, and weaning
seems indicated by then. In our culture, mothers do well to withstand
even for this long the pressure on them to wean a baby, and I do not
feel I can urge them to go on longer with breast-feeding unless I am
aware of some unusual and pressing reason to continue. It is a wonderful thing to have given a baby nine months of this kind of closeness.
Mothers who have "given" this much of themselves should not feel
"rejected" when their babies take the first step in refusing the breast.
It is nice when it can come from the infant. But it is a unity that most
mothers find difficult to give up (see Average Baby, Chapter VII).*

In Mrs. King's case, Laura's close tie to her father made it even
harder for her mother. She felt even more rejected by Laura (see
Average Baby, Chapter VII, for how to wean). As she weaned
herself, Laura began to want her mother to put her to bed. Almost
imperceptibly, she showed that she missed the closeness she had
found at nursing times. When she looked at her mother, she put her
thumb in her mouth, as if she were reminded of the old sucking
experience. She came up to her and climbed into her lap at the end
of a play period with her father. They instituted a game in which
Laura could be called (like a puppy) back and forth from one parent
to the other, as each tried to attract her away from the other. She
could play this game many times before she tired.

In this game there was obviously a certain amount of tension and
competition between the parents for Laura. The next step would be
for Mrs. King to begin to want another baby that would be "her
own," go back to work, or get another degree.

*Many women are aware of their unconscious need to fill up their
"empty arms" when they wean a baby from the breast. But a baby*

needs mother desperately at this time, and mothers must not let any childish feelings of being shut out by the weaning or by a baby's closeness to her father interfere with their mothering. This is a time when many mothers will think about going to work again, but the baby's needs must be accounted for (see Active Baby, Chapter VIII).

ACTIVE BABY

Daniel could stand alone. He teetered precariously and stood close to a chair or table at first so that he could grab it when necessary. Anything upset his balance, which Mark soon learned. He would whirl past Daniel, close to, but not touching him. The latter would teeter and fall, or grab for furniture. Mark could yell or slam a door and accomplish the same effect. Daniel had to learn to practice when Mark was not around.

Many second or third children do not stand or walk as early as they might because of this upsetting influence of the older sibling. Often the interference is less conscious than it is with Mark. This is a common time for such a peak of it to come out in the older child (see Average Baby, Chapter XII). After the older sibling has mastered the first bout of negative feelings toward the baby, parents feel they should be over and done with it and have little patience with a resurgence. But since it is a natural state for people to be competitive and to want everything for themselves, these feelings are never under complete control.

Now Daniel was better able to get into Mark's way, and since he was more of a threat as a person now, it was an appropriate time for Mark to feel angry. It was good for Mark to be able to let himself show it.

As soon as Daniel mastered standing, he began to try to add to it. He quickly learned to sit down—at first with a crash, but soon with some grace. In another week he learned to push himself up to stand from the middle of the floor. He rolled on his abdomen, pushed up on both arms (in a crawling position), straightened out both legs to push his buttocks high in the air, then, teetering forward, he pushed with his arms and came up to standing. Looking around for praise, he often saw Mark coming toward him. Sizing up the gleam in Mark's eyes, he plopped backward quickly into a sitting position. His triumph in standing had been short-lived, and if positive reinforcement from the environment were always necessary to fuel an infant's learning, this might have stopped Daniel's attempts to stand. On the contrary, he waited until Mark was out of sight and repeated the same maneuver. Each trial (and there were many that day) became easier, and by the next day, one would have thought he had always known how to get up to stand from his stomach.

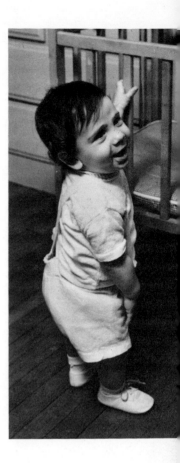

The speed with which an infant learns to put together segments of a whole piece of behavior is remarkable. The smoothing off of the act is even more so, and an athlete might take note of the process. It is obvious that each part of the whole is learned beforehand. For example, we see that Daniel has already learned how to get from his abdomen up on extended arms and straight legs. He has learned how to straighten his body from a flexed position sitting to standing. He knows how to gain his balance after leaning on a table and then standing precariously alone. He has learned each of these maneuvers separately. To put them together means that a baby has a concept of the end result and a way of planning to that end. Then, to practice until it is an easy task becomes the mark of real determination to achieve one's goal.

At first glance this exercise in standing may sound like Louis' pull to stand, which we have seen in the eighth month. There is an essential difference, however; in Daniel we see a baby with a master plan for reaching his goal; in Louis we see a baby with a spectrum of skills, trying them out until he finds the ones that work.

Daniel often lost his balance and teetered forward as he straightened out his legs and arms. This propelled him forward, and he learned a new way to crawl. Arms and legs straightened out, buttocks waving from side to side, he crawled like a spider around the room. He made a game out of looking back through his legs at whoever was behind him, and he laughed when Mark came charging up.

Climbing stairs was easy. He learned to go up with speed. Coming down was not so easy. Mrs. Corcoran found him halfway up one day, turning around and ready to launch off into space. She enlisted Mark's help, and the two of them practiced backing down on all fours, to show Daniel how to do it. Mrs. Kay came home to find her entire household on their knees at the stairs, Mrs. Corcoran and Mark trying to demonstrate how Daniel could put one leg backward to go down instead of up. Daniel seemed "stuck" with his newly learned forward progress and was not willing or able to comprehend reversing direction.

This is a dangerous time if there are stairs in the house. A gate across them at the bottom insures against a baby getting up and falling down. A stair carpet helps pad his descent. Sooner or later, he will find the gate open and try to go up or he will be upstairs and try to come down. Probably the best thing to do is just what Mrs. Corcoran was trying to do—to teach him how to master both directions.

Incidentally, this concern on Mrs. Corcoran's part for Daniel's overall progress and not merely his safety is one of the qualities a working mother should look for in a nurse or sitter. Her willingness to get down on a baby's level and not just confine him in a pen or "plug" him with food can make all the difference at this stage.

The act of standing became more and more important. Daniel refused to be put down. He wanted to eat standing at his feeding table. He screamed so hard when he had to be changed that his mother and Mrs. Corcoran found it easier to diaper him standing up. As soon as he was standing, he stopped crying and began to help with his undressing. He lifted one leg, holding on to the wall next to the dressing table. He held up his arms to have his shirt removed, and he allowed tight shirts to be pulled over his head—all without protest when he was standing. Even when he was stuck with a pin during a diaper change, he yelped but did not cry. On his back, everything made him furious.

The satisfaction of standing can take up the slack of pain or frustration. In my office after a shot, I stand a child of this age and am always amazed to see how quickly he is diverted from the pain to the pleasure he receives from this exciting new developmental step.

In his stroller, which he loved, he was a menace. He stood up in it, he leaned over the sides to grab passers-by or to reach for objects on the ground. As long as someone was nearby to keep him from falling, he was safe. But he could not be left to sit in it when his mother went to do an errand. After he fell out of it one day when Mrs. Corcoran had her arms full, on the way home from the grocery store, the Kays decided they must find a harness for him. They found one that allowed him to stand and lean over, but that kept him from falling out.

Unless the stroller is solidly built, a child at this age can pull it over on top of himself, nonetheless. The necessity for a harness' safety may only temporarily outweigh its drawbacks.

He seemed so eager to walk that Mr. Kay borrowed a walker for him. As soon as he was put in it, he became a different, wild, driven person. He lost contact with everyone around him, propelling himself forward to the right, to the left, into furniture, bouncing over door thresholds from one room to the other. No one could reach him, and he could not stop moving. When he was finally taken out, he began to scream wildly, as if he had been separated from something terribly important to him. This frantic overreaction frightened the Kays with its intensity, and they returned the walker.

I would certainly agree. I have found that the excitement that accompanies the precocious mastery of a step may lead to an unhealthy dependence on such a crutch, and it may not be a good thing in the long run. A baby can put all the energy and frustration he feels about not walking into learning how. When it is done for him, he no longer needs to learn, excitement takes over, and his efforts to do it for himself may be curbed. I saw a baby of sixteen months whirl through the house in a walker, but collapse in a frightened, inactive heap when he was taken out of it. In that baby's sad face, deprived of his crutch, I could see the effect of such unfortunate overdependence.

Daniel's nap was almost nonexistent now. He crawled away rapidly when he heard the word "nap." But a break was necessary for everyone—for him and the rest of the family. When he was put to bed, he spent the first hour talking to his beloved blanket or grinding his new teeth. As he cuddled his stuffed tiger, he used a special

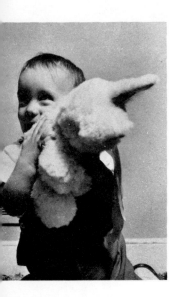

jargon of sounds that he rarely used any other time, resembling those used by his mother with him. He patted the animal to love it, threw it over the side of his bed, and called for it. As long as Mrs. Corcoran came to retrieve it, he called, but by the third time, she was angry and he knew it. He did not throw it again.

The sensitivity that children show when they recognize a parent's turning point is remarkable. Of course, the feelings of the caretaking adult are the major focus for their conscious world.

At night he no longer cried for his mother, and she had stopped the 10 P.M. "cuddle period." But he could be heard rousing to grind his teeth or croon several times during the night.

As soon as children have teeth, they learn to grind them. It makes a terrible sound, and parents worry about whether it will injure their teeth. It will not. It seems to be a mechanism for releasing tension similar to sucking their thumbs or rocking their heads in bed. As long as they outgrow it, and most of them do, I think of it as a normal mechanism.

The stuffed animal is what we called a "transitional object." This term is given to it because it represents a crutch for the transition from dependence on mother to independence. Being a difficult transition at best, one needs only to think of making this transition without a crutch to realize how important it is to a child. I have always felt that a child who has the gumption to find such an object for himself is already showing strength and resourcefulness (see Quiet Baby, Chapter VI). Growing up is not easy. In Daniel's case, it is particularly wise of Mrs. Kay not to snatch such a crutch away from him. A mother in her position might well feel guilty about it. She might consider it a reflection on her mothering, a consolation for her absence at work. It is well she does not, because a highly geared child like Daniel needs a crutch more than a Laura does. For such a child, it is hard to give up, to make the transition from doing to not doing at bedtime, to comfort himself in quiet ways. A crutch such as this may make him an easier person with himself. Without the crutch, I can easily translate him into a keyed-up executive with ulcers and hardened coronary arteries. With it, I feel he shows a core of resourcefulness. Indeed, a mother can take it as a compliment; she has provided him with the kind of warm resiliency that leads him to find a "transitional object."

Daniel was a great actor. He could make himself cry when he saw his mother begin to get ready in the morning to go to work. He forced a kind of crying that was obviously put on for its effect on her. He even worked himself up to spitting up his breakfast on two occasions. She picked him up and cuddled him instead of reproaching him, as she might have done. She talked to him about how much she would miss him, how much Mrs. Corcoran and Mark would play with him, and how much fun she and he would have at the end of the day. While the content of what she said may have passed above Daniel's head (it was more for her own reassurance), this interval of cuddling and talking seemed to satisfy Daniel. He was content to wave good-bye to her when she left. Then he turned to his active day.

He demonstrated several new developments in play. Mark could hide a toy and ask Daniel to find it. Daniel had the memory of a hidden toy that could last until he did find it. He uncovered other objects, but they were not what he wanted, and he continued to search for the one Mark had hidden.

It is evidence of the kind of memory that children can use—even in relatively unimportant things. Their memory for a doctor's office over several months' absence is evidence of more important recall. Finding a special toy also means that Daniel has a concept of looking for a particular object, discarding others, and not allowing himself to be distracted by other, equally attractive "finds."

He could crawl to a place with one toy, then go back several times to get others that were necessary to the play he wanted.

Here we see an ability to carry a series of ideas in tandem—and, again, not to allow distraction to interfere with the ultimate goal. Since a characteristic of infancy is its distractibility, this shows progress toward a more adult form of prolonged concentration.

Daniel developed a sense of space in using his hands that was demonstrated as he reached for objects. He reached for a pencil with his hand and turned it to approach the long axis of the pencil. A small object was approached with two fingers extended, the other three flexed. A large, round object was approached by both hands, as if he already knew he would need both to hold the larger object.

He began to gather toys together in his lap and hover over them when Mark came near. He learned from Mark the lessons of self-protection and of defending one's own goods against a dangerous marauder. As he began to defend himself and his toys, Mark began to be more openly aggressive, more openly teasing, and their play began to take on a much more competitive aspect. With this came more respect from Mark, and Mrs. Corcoran noticed that they began to play on each other's level. Along with the increased fighting came more real pleasure in each other to balance it.

When a parent cannot allow siblings to work out their struggles without interfering, she cuts into their total relationship (see Average Baby, Chapters VI and IX). Not only do most children enjoy the fights and squabbles, but they need a chance to express that part of the relationship in order to free the more positive side of their feelings about each other.

CHAPTER XII

The Tenth Month

AVERAGE BABY

Learning new motor steps had leveled off, but Louis' activity had not. He enjoyed keeping up with Martha and Tom and had little time for experimentation. When he did play by himself, he seemed to smooth any rough edges off the steps he had learned. Crawling had been an important step for him because it gave him the speed he needed to keep after the other children. For Louis, as for Daniel and Laura, creeping preceded crawling by several months (see Active Baby, Chapter VIII). He was creeping forward effectively at six months; Laura inched along on her belly by seven months. Daniel, of course, was navigating by half rolling, half pushing at five months. By six months, Daniel was navigating with speed. Crawling came two months later for Louis (at eight months) and for Daniel (at seven). Laura had not tried it yet, and her means of locomotion was still that of hitching around on her bottom.

A most interesting interlocking of developmental steps is that which allows creeping to be followed by standing, and before a baby crawls. Then, as if he realizes he needs more practice on the ground, he flops down again to learn an alternating pattern up on his arms and legs as he learns to crawl. After he digests this patterning of alternation, he stands up again—this time to work out all of the important steps of forward locomotion on just two points of ground contact!

As Louis crawled, he raced, getting ahead of himself and getting tangled in legs and arms, flopping forward on his face. After a few of these accidents, to which his mother responded with laughter, Louis began to produce such flops deliberately. He threw himself flat on his face and stomach and squiggled with loud laughter.

Here we see how a baby becomes aware by "accident" of his ability to achieve something new for himself. Reinforcement of it by his parents' amusement enhances its value to him as a performance. Turning an accident into a funny game is a way that a parent can help the baby turn his fears into positive experience.

He continued to be cautious about heights. He became more courageous as he practiced, and after a while, he dared climb out of a chair after he had climbed into it. Before he came down, he carefully surveyed the distance, let one leg down first to test the space, and then clung to the seat until he felt the ground below him.

I see children at this age who, their parents tell me, are careful about heights. As they try to slide off an unfamiliar changing table, they drop their legs over first to find the floor distance. When they cannot find the floor, they pull themselves back up on the table. Not trusting their visual cues in this strange situation, they try more reliable feelers. Not finding a purchase, they are clever enough to pull themselves back. This caution is not present in children like Daniel who are "hurtlers"—but more cautious babies like Louis show that they already have the capacity to understand and respect heights.

Louis tried only two or three stairs, then turned around to look at the floor below (compare Daniel's lack of caution, Active Baby, Chapter XI). Realizing he had gone far enough, he began to let himself back down. The Moores did not have to use a gate on their stairs.

He loved music. When he was sitting in the middle of the floor, a familiar tune set him in motion. He rocked back and forth and side to side in time to the music. He hummed with it and often made vocal sounds as if he were imitating a singer. When he became aware of an audience, he stopped. Even when one of the other children joined his humming, he looked at them as if he were suspicious that they were teasing him and stopped humming. Experimenting with his voice was still too new, and he was on shaky ground. His response to being joined by his siblings was similar to the way Daniel sat down when Mark whirled by as he tested his new ability to stand alone.

Soon he gained more confidence, and he performed for his father a week later, standing at his knee, rocking from foot to foot in time to the music as he hummed with it. If he looked at his father, if anyone joined in, if anyone laughed, or if they tried to get him to show off for anyone else—he refused to go on.

He played with separation from his mother. When she was sitting safely in her chair, he crawled away from her. Crawling around a corner, he turned back to check on her. As he got out of sight, he kept in touch with a steady stream of calling. If she moved or stopped calling back, he scuttled back to her. When he arrived, he demanded to be picked up and cuddled.

The cost of learning to separate is great (see Chapter IX). It demands assurance that the parent will be there when he returns and that he or she will be able to refill the gap he has made by bringing this separation about. This is a serious game all of a sudden. The future implications of separation are in sight. A baby's capacity to separate is tenuous still, and this pre-walking period is no time for an unnecessary separation from mother or father or from the familiar surroundings of home (see Quiet Baby, Chapter X).

He liked to drag a blanket in one hand as a "lovey" while he crawled. Mrs. Moore felt embarrassed to see it dragging beside him all day. She made an effort to confine it to special times—the end of the day or periods when he felt bored or sick. She told him that it would be in his bed when he needed it, and she pushed him to use other toys as carrying objects. He accepted her pressure to restrict its use and began to carry other toys in his left hand as he crawled. The right hand was free and was used for more active exploration (see Chapter IX). He found he could carry two small objects in his left hand and he experimented with this new skill. He began to carry two blocks in his left hand, across the room to their box container. He kept the assignments of each hand rigidly separated—the left for carrying, never the right.

The increasing use of the right hand to explore and to manipulate is furthered by using the left hand as a container and carrier—reinforcing the differentiation of an active side and a passive one. Keeping the left full and tied up, he facilitates the dexterity of the right hand.

He learned how to push a merry-go-round toy so it would turn around. Many attempts to force it by backward and forward shoves, his natural way of pushing, served only to stop it. Martha taught him the secrets of pushing to one side and letting go at the end.

Neither of these steps comes naturally to a baby.

His finger-feeding gathered steam. He was able to feed himself whole meals now and ate with Martha and Tom. He ate the same food they did, if it could be made into finger-bit size (see Quiet Baby, Chapter X, and Active Baby, Chapter IX). He much preferred this to being spoonfed. He picked up pieces of food and tried to feed them to Mrs. Moore or to Tom. When they accepted and swallowed them, he was delighted and watched the process of their chewing and swallowing with intense interest. He laughed when Mrs. Moore smacked her lips over a piece of his food.

Louis learned when to get out of Tom's way. Tom, now nearly four, was going through a second hump of sibling rivalry (similar to that which Mark was feeling about Daniel, in Active Baby, Chapter XI). As Louis made a play for Mrs. Moore at the end of the day when his father came home, Tom charged in. Louis called out "hi" when he heard the door open in the evening, and this delighted his father. Tom screamed to drown Louis out. When Louis crawled to get to his father, Tom rushed to beat him and to shove him over as he passed. Louis quickly learned how to dodge these assaults. He flattened to his abdomen, head down between his hands, when he heard Tom coming up behind him. When Tom was in an angry mood, Louis sensed this and spent long, quiet periods playing in a corner or in a protected spot. He was much more threatened by Tom's dark moods than he was by Martha's or his parents'.

Babies are sensitive to the kind of unrestrained lashing out that comes from a slightly older sibling and are aware that the controls older members of the family use cut down on their danger. This is a basic part of the self-protective instinct. Dogs recognize this in a family and avoid small children. They also learn which adult's anger to dodge.

QUIET BABY

Laura weaned herself. Her mother found it more difficult than she. Mrs. King hung on to the last feedings at night and in the early morning long after Laura refused the noon breast-feeding. One day Laura turned up her nose, put the flat of her hand on her mother's breast, and pushed. Mrs. King felt rejected and angry, but she recognized Laura's stubbornness, and she knew the nursing was at an end.

Laura sucked her thumb more now. When she sat playing, she put her left thumb in her mouth and played with her right hand (compare Louis' "lovey" in left hand while he explored with right). She could pivot ninety degrees while she sat, never letting go of the thumb in her mouth, as she reached around behind her to retrieve a toy. This irritated her mother, who felt Laura had asked for this weaning and should not need to resort to a substitute now. Mrs. King chided her and took her thumb out of her mouth. Laura resisted with all her strength, making it pop as it was extracted. With this, she offered her mother her wrinkled thumb to suck on—as if she were turning the mother's prohibition into a joke. This pulled Mrs. King up to a stop, and she let Laura's sucking alone after that.

The thumbsucking and sitting began to give way to a long-awaited spurt in motor activity. As if she began to be aware of her new freedom as the breast-feeding ceased, she began to show more motor independence.

This is not uncommon. Many infants seem to be in a lovely cocoon as long as the nursing continues. When it comes to an end, they take a spurt in development—and, of course, in independence. I have wondered whether the baby and mother sense this spurt coming on and whether it may not be an unconscious reason for weaning. At any rate, the increase in motor progress is more than a coincidence, and it may even seem like a slap in the face to a mother if she feels she has been holding her baby back by nursing her. On the contrary, I feel that in this cocoon the baby has stored up much fuel and many experiences that far outweigh any delay in the motor steps. In all likelihood, she will take these steps in a shortened period in the end anyway. Maturation of the nervous system goes on in a "cocoon." At a certain stage of development with very little practice, an infant can put an act "on the road" that, at an earlier stage, would have taken longer. We see children encased in body casts in the hospital who have never walked. They are able to get up and walk within a few days after the casts are removed—provided they have reached a stage of maturation of their nervous system at which walking is appropriate.

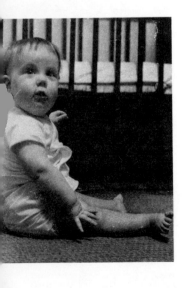

Laura now sat with a straight back to play and invariably aimed herself in her mother's direction. When Mrs. King was in another room, Laura faced the door she might enter and called to her from time to time to check on her whereabouts. When Laura called and found Mrs. King's voice coming from behind her, she turned around to face the direction of the voice.

She became feminine in her play. One of her favorite games was to take a long piece of material and put it around her neck like a scarf. She loved her mother's necklaces and draped them over her shoulders. She put her mother's hat on her head and sat in the middle of a room, cocking her head coyly.

This is an interesting stage in a little girl's development. Boys are more rarely coy or "cute." Little girls go through this. We reinforce it so quickly that one cannot be sure how it first develops. In any case, the kind of femininity that we see in Laura may be part of early identification with their mothers. No doubt it begins as simple imitation, but the environment approves and reinforces it so quickly that it gathers steam from outside as well as inside the baby.

Mrs. King taught Laura to stand by refusing to give her an object from her lap that Laura wanted. She sat steadfast while Laura pointed at it and whimpered "uh-uh." Laura crept over to her mother, pulled on her legs, finally on her skirts. As Mrs. King sat, offering only two forefingers, Laura grabbed for them and allowed herself to be pulled to standing at her mother's knee. Within a week Laura was trying it on her own, but wailed for her mother to let her down. She was now at the stage where Louis was at seven months and Daniel at six months. She was on her own timetable of sure, steady development.

With courage gained from standing, she also began to crawl. She rolled over on her stomach, banged with arms and legs, then pushed laboriously up on her knees and elbows. As if she had never moved before on her belly (she had been creeping for two months), she began to push one arm ahead, to follow it by the leg on the same side, and to push the second arm followed by the second leg. As Laura inched along, laborious though her pace might be, Mrs. King was able to see grace and rhythm in her style. She seemed less able to retrieve toys with this kind of crawling—retaining her old sitting style of locomotion for that. (This style also left her in a better position to go on playing when she got to them.) She seemed to crawl for its own sake. Her goal was usually a corner to curl into, or a couch to creep under, or a table to hide under. There she retreated, turning around to survey the room she had just left. When her father came into the room and could not find her, he called for her. He thought he heard a soft "boo" from under the table where she sat, watching him.

Now when her father called to her from another room, she used this method to get to him, slowly but surely. On one occasion, she was playing with a toy when he called. Instead of dragging it in one hand (as did Louis and Daniel), she put it in her mouth and crawled to him, the toy dangling from her mouth, like a puppy with its master's slipper.

Laura's crawling led her into places from which she needed to be extracted. She got herself behind the toilet and could not go ahead or turn around. She had not learned to crawl backward (although she had crept backward *first*), and for a few minutes she was stuck. She screamed, and Mrs. King had to drag her out by the legs.

She began to crawl up to the television set and to the stove—both of them "No's." She waited until Mrs. King was nearby and paying some attention, then she crawled up to the prohibited object, mumbling "No" to herself. If her mother did not object immediately, Laura slowed her pace, and finally turned around to see whether her mother was watching before she proceeded. When she saw her mother watching her, she smiled, said "No" aloud, and went right ahead. As she was picked up and pulled away from the object, she giggled. This game was good for several tries—until Mrs. King became angry or ignored her.

Laura is obviously using a game for trying out Mrs. King's meaning of "No." She is not really interested in the forbidden object per se, and a child shows this by rarely returning to such an object unless she has the parent's attention. Often a child will try this game even when she has understood the rationale for the "No" and has accepted the prohibition. But the use of it to tease and keep her mother involved with her makes it foolish to allow anything as potentially dangerous as the stove to be used in such a game. Although a child like Laura appears to know enough to stop herself, others can get carried away with this game and push it too far. A more definite way of saying "No" about the stove would be safer—a firmer response in which there is no question of play. A baby can understand this immediately (see Average Baby, Chapter X).

She showed many real moods now. She looked sad at times and appeared hurt after a bout with her mother. She sat daydreaming in the middle of the floor as if she had many things to think about. She was overjoyed when her father came home and clapped her hands for joy when he walked into the room. She giggled and laughed for half an hour after he arrived.

She learned many new things now. She said "No" as one of her own words and shook her head with it as she sat playing on the floor.

The most natural axis of movement of the head is from side to side. Rene Spitz points out that the "Yes" gesture is more complicated.

After she learned a new word and gesture, she spent days repeating it over and over. It became the response to every question. Soon the word lost any appropriate meaning it might have had, was used to fill in bored times, for play with toys, and to attract parents' attention when they were absorbed elsewhere. It lasted as a focal action as long as the parents responded. When they indicated boredom with this achievement, she sensed it and went on to a new one. In this way, she learned to "look sad," to "snuggle and kiss," to clap hands to music, and to say "bye-bye." All of these were performed at home, but not away from home. At her grandmother's house, Laura was silent and grim, refusing to do any of her new games. As they left her house, and after the door closed, *then* she started waving and calling "bye-bye." The more her parents pressed her to show off, the more stubbornly she refused.

She pointed to her teeth when asked, "Where are your teeth?" Hair, eyes, ears, and toes were also part of her repertoire. She learned the game via a doll that she loved. Her mother pointed first to each part of the doll and spoke its name. Laura learned to do the pointing. After a few times, Mrs. King said, "And where are Laura's eyes?" To her delight, Laura made the appropriate connection with herself.

This does not seem to be as big a jump as it is—the doll is inanimate, is out in front of her, is not as charged with interfering connections as parts of her own body are. It demonstrates how personified beloved objects are, and how identified a child becomes with them (see Laura's use of shoes in Quiet Baby, Chapter XI, as well as Louis' use of toys to work out his own fears in Average Baby, Chapter XI).

She refused to point to her father's or mother's eyes. When they asked her, she looked at the appropriate part of their faces, but turned away, apparently embarrassed. Was she not quite sure enough, or was this too big a jump in terms of what they meant to her? They were obviously different in meaning from her own and the doll's.

Since she had been weaned, she had been drinking more milk out of the cup. She entered into finger-feeding with real gusto, but still let her mother feed her mushy foods. Without her mother's milk she slowed down on her monthly weight gain. (She weighed twenty-three pounds at ten months.)

Mrs. King learned to pick Laura up from the floor by bending her knees to gather her in and then pushing herself back up to standing with the help of her leg muscles. She had hurt her back muscles when she bent over at the waist to lift Laura.

Parents of heavy babies learn this too late. The back musculature is not adequate to the strains that young parents place on it with heavy babies. Many "low back" difficulties in women start at this stage of a child's development. When she is older and will stand, clinging to a parent, monkey-like, as she is lifted, it is much less strain than at this time. At this age an infant is a "dead" and often resisting weight.

Laura had difficulty with constipation as she switched over to cow's milk. She began to have harder and harder bowel movements—small pellets at first, but later large and harder movements.

Breast milk is more laxative, and many children become constipated when they are weaned to cow's milk. This is a time to be sure to keep their bowel movements soft and to prevent their hurting themselves with hard movements. There is already sphincter control in a baby this age, and after a few painful movements, she begins to hold back to avoid the pain that she expects. Her reaction quickly becomes circular, for as she holds back, constipation increases, and each movement produces more pain. Prune juice, brown sugar, or mild laxatives under a physician's surveillance should be started before this cycle is established (see Average Baby, Chapter V).

ACTIVE BABY

Daniel spent his day on his feet. He stood next to furniture; he stood in the middle of the floor; he stood in his feeding chair; he stood in his bath; he stood to be changed; and he fell asleep standing in his crib. He learned to turn the upper part of his body to reach for something behind him or to wave to a parent. At first, he held on to something to steady himself. Then he tried it without a prop and made it. Soon he had learned to balance as he turned by holding out his arms. The next step was to pivot his whole body, and this he did by turning the upper half and, with his arms extended, staggering around to the same axis with the lower half.

These were among the first unsupported steps he took. He practiced stepping sideways along a couch and could speed along to one side, sliding one foot along after the other. But he was in close touch with the couch as he did it. He also practiced walking by holding his father's hands. Occasionally, when his father let go, Daniel took a step before he realized he was not being helped. Then, he dropped to the floor, angry at being duped and deserted. But soon he used the balance he gained with turning and spread wide his arms, rocking his forearms and hands in small flat circles to add a kind of rotating forward propulsion. When he added a wide, stiff-legged gait, he was off. In a matter of two days, he changed from a baby who looked as if he knew how but not daring, to one constantly staggering forward hour after hour. The joyful look of achievement on his face that appeared when he walked was proof of the realization that he had reached an important goal.

The thrilling excitement that a baby shows when he first starts walking is a peephole to the gratifying force that propels an infant from one stage of development to the next. The realization of having done it for himself is so openly rewarding to him that nothing we can do for him could ever really replace this. This is the best indication I know that we should aim our teaching methods to support this self-realization, not to ignore or overwhelm it. There seem to be at least two ways of teaching a child—one is by using a system in which reflexes are "taught" by positive reinforcement at such a rate that the child learns to reproduce responses in an automatic (but unexcited) way. The other method would be based on a wait until the time when a voluntary mastery from the child is added to the reflex response system, when choice and freedom of exploration are a part of his mastery. Since choice is present, an infant can negate as well as accept what he is about to incorporate. When he does incorporate it, he realizes the

kind of excitement and thrill in learning that we see in Daniel as he walks. This to me is worth the waiting and any extra effort that may be involved on the part of the teacher.

An example of the first method of teaching by reflexes might be demonstrated by a six-and-a-half-month-old baby in my practice who was able to walk alone. She had been propped in a jumper with her legs touching the floor as early as three weeks of age. For periods during each day, her mother and grandmother held her by the arms and "taught" her to walk. By five months, she could step forward in an automatic way when they held her up. At six and a half months, she took stiff-legged steps forward unsupported, her arms extended rigidly, her face a mask of tension. She looked and walked like a wound-up tin soldier. There was no pleasure in it, and not until she fell into someone's arms could she relax the fearsome tension that invested her body and face. At three and a half years of age, she still assumed masklike expressions and a stiff-legged automatic gait, arms extended, whenever she walked. She still had not learned to do anything else while she walked and fell into the same rigid frame of concentration that was "set" for her at six and a half months.

Is this the model we are using by attempting to teach two-year-olds to read and three-year-olds to write? I worry about adultomorphic methods of teaching small children that do not take into account the psychological forces that are more important than performance at each stage of their development.

When Daniel was praised by his parents, he kept walking for long stretches of up to ten steps before he fell. They were fascinated with his tireless, almost feverish devotion to this activity. Even Mark's subtle ways of interfering—such as running nearby, slamming doors in his face, littering the floor with rolling toys, could not stop Daniel. He turned from Mark or got up from a fall and started in again, his face lit with excitement and set with determination. This new activity during waking hours made naps and nighttime difficult all over again (see Chapter X). He could not give up when he was put down to sleep and woke easily at night. He rolled and banged his head when he tried to get to sleep and whenever he roused during the night. He soon found that if he rocked hard, he could make his crib squeak. Rocking on his hands and knees whenever he was trying to get to sleep, he banged his head at the end of the crib. The noises he produced with the squeaky crib as it rocked were terrible. He learned he could move the crib across the room by rocking it, and he could end up at the wall, banging against it, squeaking, and banging in alternation. Since this could recur periodically all night, the Kays were wild.

The energy that is left over in children like Daniel and must be expended in some rhythmic, self-stimulating way seems always one step below consciousness. How does the child's body stand this constant demand for energy? How can he continue to meet his demands with what appears to be a minimum of sleep? (Active babies like Daniel may sleep only one hour in the day and about eleven at night.) Mothers become very concerned about the physiological demands of such a high-powered child. A child like this does not eat any more than a Louis, and he surely does not sleep as much as most babies. Their hormonal mechanisms are geared differently from those of a Laura or a Louis, and their bodies seem more efficient (or differently so) in the use of fuel and rest.

The noises added to the rocking become an intensely important secondary goal. I have seen children come to full waking (usually they are only half awake when this activity is taking place) when the screws of the cribs are greased and tightened, and no noise results. Hence, this had better be done early in the process—before he becomes used to the noises as an accompaniment to his activity.

Rubber casters under the bedposts and thick rugs to cut out transmission of the noise to other parts of the house make this much less of an intrusion to the rest of the household. Since rocking seems to be a common accompaniment to rapid spurts in motor development for many children, I feel this can be equated to thumbsucking or other self-soothing habits. To cut out this rocking by harnesses or other restraints would seem to be going against the natural needs of the child, and unless it is absolutely necessary for the rest of the family's sake, I would be against trying to shut this off. When parents meet this rocking activity with restraints, the child rocks his head more vigorously, or turns to other ways of self-stimulation, with what appears to be renewed intensity. Intense masturbation can be set off by interfering with these natural outlets.

Mrs. Kay looked for ways to help Daniel get off to sleep more peacefully at night. She took him into his room, turned off the lights, crooned to him and rocked him, and gave him his tiger to hold while she fed him his last bottle in her arms. She felt his tight little body relax as she rocked him, but it took as much as thirty minutes. She felt it was well worth her effort, and she used it as a time to communicate with Daniel. When he roused later, she did not feel as guilty about not rushing to him, and she let him find his own way back to sleep during the night.

Mrs. Kay is demonstrating for him the value and importance of being able to break from this high activity level to a relaxed one. When a mother repeats this, the child may be able to incorporate such a pattern of relaxation into his own repertoire. When he can, he will be a better balanced person.

He played with his own toys now and was less interested in Mark's things. He sorted out one of his animals from a heap of Mark's toys. He picked it up and patted it vigorously in imitation of Mark.

Daniel is showing growing tenderness, which began with his tiger (in Chapter XI) and is spreading to other toys now. This is evidence of how healthy his environment really is. The capacity to love an object or "mother" someone else can derive only from the experience of being mothered. Hence, when we observe a baby in a diagnostic situation who cannot play affectionately with another child or who does not play at mothering, we worry about whether the child has had a good experience with it himself.

One day Daniel lost a toy behind his father's chair. Mrs. Corcoran found him trying hard to push the chair away to get it. As we saw before, Daniel has the concept of hidden objects and knows how to retrieve them. On another occasion, he remembered the game he had been playing with Mark the day before when they were interrupted for bedtime. He tried to get Mark back to it in the morning. What a prolongation of attention and of memory this represented!

Daniel became more clinging to his family and home. He began to show the same anxiety that Laura did about strange places and strange people at eight and nine months. Since he had never been like this before, his parents were surprised when they took him to his grandparents' house. He became immobilized in the strange setting, refusing to move or to play with any of the toys he had played with before. He whimpered to be allowed to sit on his mother's lap during the visit and cringed when his grandfather came to pick him up. He submitted, but never smiled or allowed his grandfather to play with him. This was entirely new for Daniel and his parents were perplexed. As soon as they returned home, he broke gaily into his old activity. (See Quiet Baby, Chapter X and XI, for some of the reasons. Daniel was less sensitive to cues from the outside, but he was becoming increasingly independent at a rapid rate.)

Daniel saw very few children besides Mark. One day Mrs. Kay took them to visit a friend with children of similar ages. Mark and his peer ran off to another room. As soon as he was gone, Daniel seemed to lose his anchor. He curled up on the floor and watched the other baby his age. He looked frightened and jumped visibly every time the other baby made a loud noise or a sudden movement. All this time he seemed engrossed in the other baby's activity. When they returned to their own home, Mrs. Kay saw Daniel imitate the baby's play as if he had learned it all. She had never seen him place rings on a spindle before. He went directly to his unused tower cone and began to take the flat blocks off the spindle and put them back on—exactly as the other baby had. He put several blocks on top of each other in the same kind of imitative behavior.

We have already talked of a baby's interest in watching children rather than adults, and even more in watching children his own age. This wonderful capacity to learn a hunk of behavior by watching someone else do it can be observed in twins. One twin is often the doer and practices doing things a large part of the time. The other twin, who is the sitter and watcher, will suddenly perform in toto the act that his brother has spent days practicing to do (compare to Quiet Baby, Chapter XII, and Average Baby, Chapter XI). In Daniel's case this is a new way of learning for him—by pure imitation.

Daniel (like Laura) liked to put pieces of clothing around his neck and walk around the house. He had a preference for his or Mark's shirts or sweaters and loved to find his father's neckties. He helped wriggle into clothes, helped pull off his shirts when he was asked, and he stuck out the proper leg for dressing or undressing. He tried to pull off his own socks by catching the toe and pulling on it. So far, he pulled backward and had very little success unless the sock was practically off his foot anyway.

Mrs. Corcoran was eager to toilet train Daniel. He was so quick to learn, and she had noticed that he could stay dry for an hour or more at a time. She also pointed out to Mrs. Kay that Daniel squatted and grunted, red in the face, when he was having a bowel movement. Although Mrs. Kay was sure that Mrs. Corcoran could achieve some sort of "catching" equivalent to training with Daniel, she refused to let Mrs. Corcoran train him. She argued that she wanted to be the one to introduce it to Daniel, and she wanted to do it when Daniel could understand what she expected of him.

I agree with Mrs. Kay. Although there is sphincter control to "train" at this age—and many children are "trained" in the first year—I feel that this is reflex training and/or training of the adult (compare this to reflex training discussed earlier). And it certainly can be fraught with dangers later on. What I have witnessed has been a kind of passive submission on the part of the child at this stage. This is often followed by rebellious breakover and by holding back feces or urine in the sixteen- to eighteen-month period, when a child realizes what has been done to him and when he learns to fight back. In our culture, we foster independent achievement in too many other areas, and perhaps this leads to a more clear-cut rebellion in our children when training is instituted under adult pressure. At least, the incidence of rebellious breakover and unsuccesses is higher in the United States when training is started in the first year than it is reported to be in Britain and in Europe, where training is expected to be successful by the end of the first year. But I have also read of a very high rate of bedwetting and chronic constipation in those countries, which could be an end result of such early training. (There were reported to be as many as 15 percent bedwetters in eighteen-year-olds inducted into the army in England.) Certainly, in a child who is driving all day to stand and walk, it would be fighting the tide to try to force him to sit for long periods at this time. A child as bright as Daniel, with a brother to learn from, hardly needs to be pushed until he is intellectually "ready" to learn such a complex process. It is so easy and so rewarding when a toddler can be shown and learn for himself in the second year.

But a mother must be as firm in her resolve as Mrs. Kay is, for the older generation still remembers how successfully its children were trained in the first year. Many grandmothers or "old school" sitters will make a young mother feel she is neglecting her child by not being ready to put enough time in to train him at Daniel's age. There are more appropriate times for this in the second year, in the lull after the big motor achievements of standing and walking have become a matter of course.

CHAPTER XIII

The Eleventh Month

AVERAGE BABY

Louis fashioned himself a walker. Standing at a small chair one day, he leaned against it and it moved. He looked startled but seemed to understand that he had been responsible for its movement. He leaned again, and it slipped more. He smiled and pushed a third time. As it moved, he giggled and staggered to keep up with it. Mrs. Moore directed him to a small chair, which she turned on its back, and showed him that he could push it. He began to spend a part of his morning each day pushing the chair ahead of him as he reeled along behind.

Many antique straight chairs show flattening wear on the backs of the posts from this kind of pushing on hard floors by learning toddlers. How much more excitement and self-realization has gone into Louis' having found his own crutch to walk with than had his parents provided him with a gadget that "takes over" (see Daniel and walker in Active Baby, Chapter XI).

He looked down at his feet as he pushed the chair. As he experimented with lifting one foot at a time, he fell forward on the chair, banging his head. He cried for his mother. She came to him and saw that he was more surprised than hurt. She placed him standing again without a great show of sympathy. He went on with his experimentation.

A parent who is too solicitous can reinforce the baby's surprise and perhaps push him into fear. There is surely a fine line between a parent's appropriate comfort and sympathy, and reinforcing a baby's natural disappointment over the failures and surprises he creates for himself. Each episode takes quick sizing up and an awareness on the parent's part that controlled support from him or her may be as comforting as sympathy, and better in the long run. Too much sympathy may be equivalent to pity in its ability to undermine a baby at a time when he is ready to return and try again. Certainly, there is some truth in the song, "You have to be taught to be afraid." (But it is not always true; see Louis' fear in Average Baby, Chapter XI.)

Standing alone followed soon. Louis was cautious (more than Daniel, less than Laura), but he gathered courage. He (like Daniel) had to learn to balance himself in the midst of activity around him. This was the most difficult test of precarious balance. He fell several times as he learned, banging his head with loud whacks, and crying out for help as he did so. When Mrs. Moore responded to his cry right away, he was content with a pat and a word. If she waited until he continued to build up crying, he collapsed in a heap of wailing self-pity.

He is aware of the tremendous implications of the next step: being upright and self-reliant in an upright, whirling world. A baby's desire to be a part of it and his awareness of how far he still has to go are reflected in his cries for extra support at this time.

Louis often clung to her now. At the end of the day he was fussy until she held him. He curled up in her arms like a much smaller baby when a new person came to visit, especially a child Martha's or Tom's age. He followed his mother like a worried puppy. When she left the room suddenly, he tried to follow her. The whole family

accused her of having spoiled him, and she wondered about it herself. Her inclination, as well as her desire, was to pick him up and
cuddle him when he pleaded for it. He had not been a particularly
dependent baby before (except in Chapter XI when he was full of
new fears and awareness). She felt he was going through a phase
now, through which he would pass to more independence again.
However, she felt shaken by her family, as she had at nine months
when she tried to wean him to a cup. But this time she followed her
own instinctive reaction—to give Louis extra support.

*Many parents are too shaken by "public" disapproval (i.e., spouses'
and parents') to follow through this way. I suspect that the reason for
the disapproval is that onlookers are a bit jealous of the child's
regression to an earlier kind of dependency on the parent. It seems
like a threat, for all of us have a wish to regress under stress. Perhaps
the other adults also wish that a Louis might turn to them. Certainly
the other children in the family are angry and jealous that the baby
can make demands on the parents that they are too proud to make.
As has been repeatedly brought out, this is a "phase." Without the
parents' refueling, the phase might well take a longer time to pass
through. With it, the baby can gather the necessary steam and plow
along to more independence.*

He was able to hold a toy in one hand while he pulled up to stand
with the other. He would drop the toy in order to lean over to pick
it up. He first squatted down, gathered it into the same hand, then
stood up. Next he tried squatting to gather it up with the other hand,
and he came back up to a standing position. Last, he learned to lean
over to pick it up with each hand while he anchored himself at the
furniture with the free hand.

*He is experimenting with his body's maneuvers around squatting and
stooping, finding out for himself what the distance to the floor means.
He is also comparing the feeling of doing it with each side of his body
—as if they were very different ways of doing the same thing.*

He moved the toy from one place in the room to another so that
he could try this out in various places.
  Watching his siblings, Louis imitated their play with push toys—

pushing a train across the room, saying "shoo-shoo." He banged on the floor with a hammer toy, delighted with the noise he could produce. When they were coloring with crayons, he watched carefully and picked up a crayon to bang with it on the paper. Martha took his arm to show him how to move it to write. He pulled away from her and refused to be shown. But he did return to try it, closer this time to the scribbling motions she had tried to show him. Balancing his dependence on his mother was an increasing independence with others—particularly with his siblings. Even though he refused to be shown by Martha, he picked up the cues that would help him follow her later—all the while apparently protesting and unaware.

He tried to imitate the children's speech. He was able to produce a few intelligible sounds, but his speech was primarily gibberish. He copied inflections, however, as well as speech rhythms, and even produced facial attitudes of theirs in comically close mimicry.

He knew the functions of many things by their names—when Tom said "airplane," Louis would point up in the air; when Martha said "doggie," Louis would try to growl. He responded with these gestures to pictures of airplanes and to pictures of dogs. The children showed him off to Mr. Moore each evening.

Louis had a new game with Martha and Tom that made them furious. He would take a favorite toy of theirs and hide it behind a sofa or under a pillow. When they found it, he laughed aloud. Since it was a game they had taught him with his own toys, he connected it with them. He was surprised when they were not amused.

He experimented with sounds he could make using objects around the house. Dropping one object after another in a cup, he seemed to hear the difference in the ring that a block or a metal ball produced. He played with differences. He used a glass for the same play and seemed interested in the new sounds he produced. When

he wanted to retrieve the objects at the bottom of the glass, he first tried to reach through its sides to pick them out. Then he reached down in the open end and attempted to extract them. Although he had been pouring out objects from a cup, he treated the glass as if it bore no similarity to the cup. He seemed to have to learn to deal with this container as if it were entirely different—and as if the visual cues he received through its transparent sides confused him.

Visual cues from glass are confusing. A child must relearn to sort out their meaning and act on them in a thoroughly familiar situation. This is somewhat comparable to the relearning we must do to perform a familiar act in the dark, or from behind a screen.

Louis tried to imitate his mother when she was working. As if to justify his desire to stay close to her, he began to mop the counter when she did, to stir clumsily with a spoon when she stirred, and to hang on heavily to the vacuum cleaner when she was trying to clean. When she sat down to read a book, he pulled out one of his and opened it. If she tried to write a letter, he scribbled with his finger on the paper next to her. He could "go and get" simple objects for her and seemed delighted when he returned with something she had asked for (see Chapter XI). He learned to turn on the television, but was frightened when it came on with a blast—scurrying off to another room on his hands and knees. From the door, he peered around to look at the result of his experiment, not daring to return until someone came to turn down the volume. He learned rapidly that this would bring someone and soon had to be reprimanded to leave it alone.

QUIET BABY

Laura was following her own cautious path. Although she still would not allow her parents to put her in a standing position, she was eager to pull herself up slowly and laboriously onto furniture or at their knees. When they attempted to stand her, she pushed her legs straight out ahead in a firm negative (see Chapter VIII, same resistance to being stood). In contrast to Daniel and Louis, she never

toppled backward. When she understood the technique, she let herself down gradually to sitting. Finding the way to get down freed her to play more on her feet, and she gingerly took a step to each side from time to time, still holding cautiously to furniture.

This is called "cruising," as an infant pulls herself sideways along furniture. Laura is not as late as she looks in comparison with Louis and Daniel. Many babies, particularly heavy ones, do not "cruise" any earlier than this, and some never experiment with standing or cruising. They seem to wait until they can walk, then get up and walk in a matter of days. In this country, the average age for walking alone has been standardized at twelve to fourteen months, so Laura's motor progress is really more "average" than the boys' is. Since these three infants are in stimulating environments and are equipped with above-average endowment, it would be unrealistic to portray them along an average mean. Laura's progress, in other than motor parameters, is advanced for any overall average. But the averages are based on many babies with less fortunate combinations of inborn equipment and environment.

Laura's feet were so flat as she cruised along that she walked on the inner edges of the feet and ankles, rather than on the soles of her feet.

Most infants start standing on what appear to be "pronated" or rolled-in feet. As they balance with their legs apart, the feet splay outward, and they start walking on their ankles like a tired char-woman. A toddler gains balance as she learns to walk and no longer needs the wide base. Then her feet begin to strengthen and to toe in more. As her walk improves, her feet and arches strengthen also. Laura is a "flop-jointed" infant. Many infants have rubbery, overextensible joints that can easily be bent beyond a natural extended position. Since they are so limber, the joints seem hard to anchor in any single position of extension. A child like this needs more developed musculature to provide firmness for her joints when she stands. Before such a child can control her legs and feet to stand and walk, she must practice longer than others to gain more muscular strength. A soft, flexible body, plus collapsible joints, make it more difficult to manage locomotion—even when a child has the urge. I have often felt that the quiet temperament and the flop-jointed body type go together appropriately in these children—they provide a circular deterrent to gathering motor activity. Which is the chicken and which the egg in the development of this less active type of baby?

Laura was more openly attached to her mother now. She followed her around, crawling as fast as she could. She stayed between her legs, leaning on them whenever her mother stopped long enough. Mrs. King had to step over her many times in a day. Occasionally she stepped on her.

Since she was able to say, "bye-bye," "mama," and "dada," she mumbled "mama, mama" all day long. Any fears Mrs. King might have had about losing Laura with the weaning process were long since forgotten.

Of course this is the same increase in dependency that we saw in Louis just before he walked. An only child's dependency will be less diluted because she has no siblings with whom she can play. Nor does a Mrs. King have the reasons to spread herself out that a Mrs. Moore does. A small apartment can reinforce this clinging relationship, and I wonder that mothers like Mrs. King do not go berserk. Many do find their nerves taut and ready to snap at the end of a day (compare Mrs. Moore's reactions). Working mothers who come home exhausted at the end of a long day have a difficult time with this. They must find ways to let off steam without taking it out directly on the child.

When Mrs. King picked up a friend's baby to hold, Laura stood up quickly by her lap. She began pushing at the other baby to shove her out. She tried to climb up into her mother's lap in order to shove more effectively. Mrs. King teased her by continuing to hold the baby and by talking to him. Laura became frantic, whimpering and pulling on the baby's clothes and extremities to dislodge him. After he was put down, Laura sat huddled in her mother's lap, sucking her finger, as if she did not dare leave her lap again. Mrs. King's thoughts turned to getting out of the house on her own—perhaps a job.

This teasing springs from the desperation that a parent feels (compare Mrs. Moore and Louis) when a baby at this stage is so demanding and dependent. A parent feels trapped and tries to push the baby off in various ways. As was the case with Mrs. Moore, these constant bids make the parent feel drained. A mother like Mrs. King, who still hasn't an easy relationship with her child, has to struggle even harder to find her way.

Feedings were fun for them both. Laura was a good eater and enjoyed every mouthful. She also liked to have her mother involved in the feeding situation. She could feed and drink by herself, but (unlike Louis or Daniel) she wanted the give and take that her mother's presence provided. She allowed Mrs. King to fill her spoon, then she could manipulate it to her own mouth. She spilled very little and was eager to wipe it off her mouth or the tray when she did (compare her cleanliness in Chapter X). She used both hands in feeding, using her right hand for complex maneuvers with the spoon, both hands for the cup, and picked up bits of food to stuff them in with her left thumb and forefinger while she waited for a full spoon with the right.

This is agile manipulatory behavior. An ability to use both hands for picking up bits is unusually advanced, particularly while she is concentrating on another maneuver. Her neatness and emphasis on not spilling from a spoon are unusual. This preciseness is almost too compulsive for this age, although I hear this about many babies. She has shown compulsive behavior all along (Chapter X), and her delicacy and preciseness play in with this.

She often smacked her lips with pleasure after a bite of a favorite food. She occasionally took a spoonful of her food to feed to her mother. This was usually the food she liked most herself (compare Louis feeding finger food to his mother in Chapter XII). Her appeals to her mother were touching—even cloying. It was almost as if she must please her mother in order to hold on to her. Babies do this when they sense a parent is remote for some reason. Did Laura sense that Mrs. King was already thinking about returning to work?

Laura watched her mother rocking in a chair as if she noticed it for the first time. She crawled up, pushed on her mother to get out, climbed up in the chair, and began to rock herself. She closed her eyes and hummed as she rocked, completely happy. Mrs. King had rocked Laura a lot as a smaller baby, and it is interesting that when it became something she could do for herself, it became something new.

One day, she crawled up to the full-length mirror where she loved to play—watched herself, talked to herself, watched her mother behind her. Suddenly she spotted a favorite toy reflected in the mirror. As if she had forgotten, she reached for it in the mirror. When she banged her hand on the mirror, she laughed out loud— suddenly brought to the realization that she had made a mistake.

In the middle of the night, Laura's parents heard her whimpering in her bed. They went in to her and found her hot and uncomfortable. She was lying in bed looking up at them with a pitifully helpless look. Her heart was pounding, her breathing rapid, and when they took her temperature (rectally), she had 105 degrees Fahrenheit. Mr. King was so unnerved that he could not get to the phone fast enough to call Laura's doctor. Mrs. King held her hot baby, frantic lest she die before they reached the doctor. While she was rocking her, Laura began to perk up. She smiled and talked to her mother (as if reassuring her). After an interminable fifteen minutes, the doctor returned the call, listened while Mr. King fumbled for words. He attempted to reassure the young man that this was not desperate in all likelihood, and he advised Mr. King to give her aspirin and extra fluids to drink and to sit her in a lukewarm tub of water to bring her temperature down. He advised Mr. King to look for symptoms that might indicate more than a febrile reaction to a simple infection —for example, had she any difficult breathing, did she pull on her ears, had she pain in urination, any severe diarrhea—and he asked that they check her for a stiff neck (one that she could not bend forward on her chest). He suggested that the Kings wait for an hour or two after giving her the aspirin to let it take hold and act on her fever, then to evaluate her with these symptoms in mind. If none of the symptoms was present, and if Laura revived with the aspirin and liquids, he did not feel it necessary to see her that night. In fact, he explained that a physician rarely finds anything to help him localize an infection beyond these obvious symptoms when he examines the baby right away. He asked the Kings to call him again in the morning unless they found one of these symptoms. If they did, they needed him. He assured them that the signs of severe illness can be observed by the parents—a limp, toxic-looking child who will not revive with aspirin and fluids. Mr. King returned to his distraught wife with this information. Angry and deserted by a doctor whom she thought just did not want to get out of bed to come, she set to work on Laura. She gave her the appropriate aspirin and clear fluids (not milk). By that time, Laura had become so playful and cheerful that the Kings decided not to put her in the bathtub. Still fuming at the doctor's off-handedness, they urged Laura to take more and more liquids.

Keeping a hot baby hydrated is the major job of parents. If she were nauseated or tended to vomit, carbonated sugary liquids would stay down best—only spoonfuls at a time and given every few minutes. Many infants refuse to drink when they are ill, but it is so important to keep them hydrated that a parent must virtually force a baby to accept them. As the infant sees that her parents mean business, she will begin to drink. As soon as she drinks, her resistance to drinking again will usually wane. A lollypop or ice or a cracker will often break through this initial negativism.

At the end of the two hours, Laura seemed to be her old self, her temperature was down, and she was ready to play. The Kings stayed up with her the rest of the night, watching and testing her over and over for the symptoms the doctor had outlined. None appeared. Her temperature bounced up again at the end of four hours (when the aspirin wore off), but came down after the next dose. By morning her temperature was normal and she was none the worse for wear. The Kings, however, were exhausted from lack of sleep. Laura took several naps, but her parents staggered sleepily through their day. When she was examined by her doctor, he found nothing, but he warned them that her temperature might rise again in the evening. It did not, and, mystified, the parents felt uneasy and cheated at not knowing why Laura had spiked such a fever with no explanation for it available from her doctor.

Although a reason cannot be found on examination, this is a healthy response to a mild infection. Babies often produce this total body response which "handles" the infection and undoubtedly profit by building up specific immunity to the germ and, perhaps, some general immunity to others. Each of these successful jousts with infections does pile up "money in the bank" for the future. For this reason, pediatricians prefer to give the child a chance to fight infections herself, and to reserve antibiotics, big guns of therapy, for more overwhelming illnesses that the child cannot handle alone. If the doctor joins young parents in their hysteria and starts antibiotic treatment before he knows what he is treating the baby for, he can cloud the diagnostic issue and do the baby a disservice. A high temperature is only one symptom of infection in an infant and need not be treated for itself alone. Many babies run extremely high temperatures (104 to 105 degrees) whenever they have any fever at all. More rarely do their immature temperature-regulating mechanisms allow for a middle-of-the-road fever of 101 to 102 degrees Fahrenheit. Hence, it is important to look at the other symptoms that the child shows before taking the high temperature as seriously as did the Kings. Certainly parents need not and should not assume responsibility for a febrile child over any period without medical advice, but unless she looks and acts acutely depleted, or unless there is evidence of the complications described above, most parents can trust their own judgment for a short period and can work to bring the temperature down first in order to evaluate the child better before calling the physician. The real danger of a high fever is that of a convulsion, and for most children the measures Laura's doctor prescribed would be effective in preventing this. If the child has a tendency to get seizures with high temperatures, a physician must be consulted. Fortunately, not many children have seizures with fever. Laura's body type lends itself to the storage of body heat. Many well-padded babies who do not sweat easily tend to run higher temperatures and more easily than do lean, wiry ones such as Daniel. In these high-temperature-runners, the degree of temperature may be an even poorer index of the degree of illness to which it is a response. Rectal temperatures are 1 degree higher than their oral equivalents. A degree must be added to an underarm temperature to equal that of an oral temperature.

ACTIVE BABY

Daniel preferred walking to crawling now. He could navigate across an entire room, arms high and cycling, legs stiff as he rocked his body sideways to swing one leg after another, his face wreathed in grins.

Slippery little rugs were his downfall, but he was cheerful about them. He was quickly put into hard-soled shoes by Mrs. Corcoran, who felt they were "necessary for foot support."

Actually, when a baby is first learning to walk, he needs his toes to grip the ground. He is better off barefoot or in soft, flexible shoes. Slick, hard soles make it harder for him to learn, since, of course, shoes slip. The fact that the shoes did not hold Daniel back is a testimony to his determination to walk.

He clumped across the room, losing footing constantly on the hardwood floors, as well as the rugs. When he lost his balance, he gathered himself together, pushed back up to standing, and, unless he slipped as he rose in the same place, he was off again. He learned to navigate around furniture, to turn corners, and last of all, to stop himself in the middle of the floor. At first, his body seemed to propel itself onward, and he could stop only by falling or by grabbing onto a passing piece of furniture. Stopping became a new exploit, and he practiced it over and over.

He followed his parents to the door when they left in the morning, waving and saying "bye-bye." He learned to wave his right hand as he walked, the hand flapping forward and backward as he walked.

This is Daniel's first complement to the absorbing act of walking, and it is done in rhythm so that it can be incorporated more easily into the total body action. As walking is assimilated and becomes more automatic, other bits of behavior can be added on.

Mrs. Corcoran had a constant attendant in Daniel. He followed her all day. She wore a dustcap as she worked, and Daniel found an old hat which he put on as he followed her. When he could not find the hat, he was content with any cloth to cover his head.

He now pulled on his socks and started his foot into a shoe. He pulled out shoelaces and untied his own on command. He untied his father's shoes every night at the dinner table, laughing as his father shifted his feet to dodge his approaches. He loved playing with his father and kept after him constantly at the end of a day, wanting to be bounced on the foot of his crossed leg, to be thrown up in the air. The more violent the play, the more excited Daniel became. His father was exhausted after a period of this, but not Daniel. When

Mr. Kay stopped, or tried to leave the room, Daniel protested violently and followed him.

Is this equivalent to Laura's and Louis' clinging to their mothers? Not entirely. It seems to me to be a developing attraction to the active male parent. A father provides both an extension of the kind of active development that is going on, plus an opportunity for a boy to identify with another male. Mothers see this turning to father as "being tired" of having been isolated with a female all day and wanting the novelty of a different kind of person. Certainly, all children put on a revived, new face for their fathers at the end of a rugged day, but a working mother is equally novel. I think a baby like Daniel begins to realize some of his masculine identity as he feels the independence and self-realization of walking.

Negativism began for Daniel. He shook his head, saying "No" to everything—even when he meant "Yes" by it. He loved the head movement and found a way of timing the "No" so that it fitted each swing back and forth. He was so taken up with it that he could spend a whole meal period shaking his head and refusing to be fed or to feed himself. He refused to cooperate with his bath in the same way, and catching his face to wash it as it swung was a real trick. He shook his head through diaper changes, waggling his whole body as he shook. When he was stuck with a pin, or spanked by Mrs. Corcoran, he slowed down so that she could pin on his diaper.

The success he mustered from this "No" seemed to spur him on in another area. He found he could manipulate his mother by dropping to the floor and screaming and kicking in protest against something he did not like. When he wanted a cookie and it was not forthcoming, he fell to the floor crying. Mrs. Kay was both surprised and a bit overcome by this new temper. She gave in because she found it easier than watching him scream. He found little response from Mrs. Corcoran, and it became a maneuver he saved for his mother.

Such a conscious use of tantrum behavior is early in Daniel—and is perhaps not equivalent to real "temper tantrums" (which will be discussed in the next chapter). It is certainly negative behavior, and a kind of realization of his power to control his mother by such a violent outburst.

Mrs. Kay reinforced this behavior with the same ambivalence about adequately fulfilling her role as his mother that she has shown in meeting other new crises. How quickly Daniel sorted this from Mrs. Corcoran's lack of involvement! Mrs. Kay finally sensed the distinction he made in his maneuvers, and she began to pull out on Daniel. She let him collapse and scream on the floor without responding. He kicked louder, rolled his head, but finally quieted, as if he were surprised. Without a word, he got up and started playing.

The lack of deficit at the end of such an episode is evidence of the low investment in them. When a child has real tantrums, he is not able to turn them off so easily and cheaply.

In bed at night, Daniel roused to dreaming and rocking that was accompanied by "No-No-No." Hearing him from another room, the Kays felt a bit sad, and they wondered whether they were doing badly by him.

They need not be doing anything wrong. This is a natural part of a child's development. He must experiment with his own "No" and establish its meaning for himself. Like standing, he must practice it day and night.

He seemed to become more aware of the difference between being good and being naughty. When he was being good, he constantly sought his parents' or Mrs. Corcoran's approval; for example, after he pulled on his sock, or made a block tower of two blocks, he called out "see" with a grin and a request for a comment. After he dutifully ate some of his lunch, he held up the dish to be admired. When he finished his bottle, he held it out—shaking it to show how empty it was. When his mother fed him his night bottle in the dark, he wanted her to turn on the light and admire the empty bottle before he would allow her to put him in his crib.

When he was naughty, he was also conscious of its implications. Caught at the open drawer of his mother's chest, he looked very guilty and scurried away, crawling. Before he turned the faucet of the bathtub, he stopped, looked around guiltily, then turned it on anyway. When his father came in to turn off the water, Daniel was seated in a corner, hands covering his ears, looking very abashed (see

Average Baby, Chapter XIII). Daniel had never been punished
severely, but the concept of being naughty and of deserving punishment was developing along with the surge in his own negativism.

Along with a baby's ability to say "No" to others comes the realization of what his parents' "No" means. This is an important part of his ego's developing boundaries—against outside inroads and the inroads of his own inclinations (see Average Baby, Chapter X, and Quiet Baby, Chapter XII).

Daniel pulled at his ears a great deal. He dug at them, scratched them so often that his mother was afraid they were infected. She had difficulty attracting his attention at times, and she wondered whether he heard well. However, he was able to hear his father's watch tick with real interest and prolonged concentration. He could hear her whisper, "Do you want a cookie?" from across the room. She realized that his poor hearing was geared to the things he did not want to hear, and that he had excellent hearing when motivation accompanied the stimulus. When she had his ears examined, she was told that they were normal in appearance. Since he never ran a temperature and never seemed in the real pain that a child demonstrates when he has infected ears, her doctor assured her that earpulling is normal at this age, when molars begin to bother the baby (see Average Baby, Chapter VI, and Quiet Baby, Chapter IX, teething and earpulling).

A mother can watch for the signs of ear infection: a temperature, tenderness to manipulation of the earlobe, acute pain that does not subside with aspirin, or a discharge from the ear (wax is orange or bright yellow, pus is white and smells foul). A red external ear means very little, as this is a result of rubbing.

CHAPTER XIV

The Twelfth Month

AVERAGE BABY

With every muscle taut, Louis was ready to take steps from one parent to the other. He fixed his eyes on his goal, his face intent, as he teetered unsteadily forward. Martha and Tom held out their hands during the day to walk him. He walked on his toes and fell forward the last few steps into waiting arms. He squealed with pleasure as he fell. Tom was not so reliable at catching him, and Louis learned this quickly. Thanks to Tom, he had to learn how to catch himself, to slow up and turn back. Tom would become diverted by a toy at his feet after Louis had launched himself from Martha. When he arrived, Tom was no longer interested. Louis realized this as he advanced, tottering forward step by step. He slowed himself up, began to describe an arc, and maneuvered back to Martha's arms, where he collapsed. Soon he refused to play the game with Tom.

Walking was still the icing on the cake. He walked for pleasure, but crawling was his business approach to the world. He crawled when he really wanted to get anywhere efficiently. In strange places, he was freer to explore when he was on his hands and knees. All his focus was turned inward when he was walking, and he refused to walk when he was visiting in a new house. After he had explored a new room sufficiently, had tried out all the new toys, had got his bearings with the new people, he was ready to walk. His was not so much a performance for others as a self-fulfilling activity that was saved for last. When he stumbled or fell, he looked ready to weep. Mrs. Moore realized that this was in response to disappointment in himself and a momentary shaking of self-confidence. She bolstered him with her accustomed pat on the back, and, righting him on his feet, she shoved him off again. As soon as he was on his feet, he was confident again.

As he gathered self-assurance and, with it, more and more pleasure in walking, he began to be as difficult to lie down as was Daniel. Diapering and bathing were done standing (compare Active Baby, Chapter XII). He was examined by his doctor in a standing position. As long as he was standing by his mother, he was able to be approached and examined. His doctor remarked that Louis was an inch shorter at this examination than he had been the month before. When he was measured standing, he lost an inch, and he appeared to have shrunk.

Even an adult who has been ill in bed will measure an inch taller than his usual height. As he maintains an upright position again, his vertebrae settle and he loses the inch. An infant measures an inch longer in a flat position than he does in a standing one. A small price for being upright!

His weight gain slowed up, too, as he walked.

The curve in weight gain, which is rapid in small infants, begins to flatten by seven months. This is coincident with crawling, decreasing interest in food, and less intake. By twelve months, the curve is flattening even more, since most of a baby's waking time is spent in active motion. More calories are used for this constant activity. Finger foods and lumpy foods are not thoroughly chewed and digested, so what is taken in is not completely absorbed. All this contributes to a slower weight gain. I am relieved when a baby begins to slow up on the weight curve. Fat is not healthy for anyone, and, at this stage, he lays down muscle instead of fat tissue.

Parents worry about undigested food in a baby's stool at this age. It may even be accompanied by small amounts of mucus, as if the particles were irritating to the infant's intestinal tract. I assure parents that I have not seen pathology as a result of these undigested foods in normal children. A healthy child can absorb what he needs from a lumpy diet. None of these drawbacks outweighs the importance of letting a baby feed himself lumpy food at this time.

He would take only one nap after he learned to walk. Mrs. Moore found that he would rather sleep in the morning than in the afternoon. But when he did, he was fussy from three o'clock on and was too tired to eat his supper. She began to put off his morning nap until

11 A.M. At that time she fed him a small lunch and put him down for his two-hour nap. When he got up, she fed him a second lunch. This tided him over to an early supper. When he could last, she stretched out his morning, feeding him later and later until she had pushed him to a noon lunch and an early afternoon nap, which fitted into the schedule of the other children.

Toddlers are ready for one nap. Slow-but-sure pressure, as we see with Mrs. Moore, to conform to the schedules of the rest of the family is an excellent way to adjust a toddler's day. If a mother allows the baby to decide his own nap period, he may continue choosing the morning. The short collapse at 5 P.M. refuels him for a long evening, and bedtime gets pushed later and later. In a household as busy as the Moores' is, the evening is a sacred and necessary relief from children.

An infant's readiness to go back down for a nap in the morning soon after the night's long sleep has always interested me. Why is he not ready to keep going in the morning? Why must he be pushed to choose an afternoon nap? It looks as if the energy regulator of the body takes a while to fire up the engine that we see perking so heatedly by the end of the day. Different children have different cycles in this respect.

Louis could push himself slowly around the yard on his kiddy car. He tried to follow the older children as they tricycled, inching his way along. First he pushed with both feet, occasionally with one at a time, then with both again, clumsily, slowly learning how to alternate feet to push. The process was a long one and took many months. He learned to toddle much more quickly than he learned the process of pushing himself efficiently while sitting on the small car.

A sitting position is not a natural one in which to learn how to alternate the feet in motion. Pushing is very different from the use of the legs in walking. Is this an example of the rigidity of purpose with which an infant learns a new piece of behavior such as walking? Legs can be used in their proper framework, to walk, but this skill cannot be translated into another use with any ease.

Clinging to his mother was now confined to the end of the day. The rest of the day, he propelled himself around, torturing Martha and

Tom by his constant presence. By evening, they were exhausted with him and he with them, and he retreated to his mother's skirts.

I wonder how many children used to be found under their mother's hoopskirts at the end of the day. In extended families, the old grandmother who sits in one place all day takes up much of this slack. The small children climb in and out of her lap, refueling, at various times of day, completely filling her lap by the end of the day. How much is missed on each side by families in which the parents are "out" or "too busy" to serve this refueling purpose at the end of the day.

Louis was a giddy part of the whirlwind that met Mr. Moore at the door when he came home. Louis was picked up and whirled with the other two. He climbed into his father's lap while he read the children their good-night story. He pointed to all the familiar objects on the pages as they passed. He practiced the few words he knew. One night he repeated the word "damn" over and over, expectantly. When his father finally caught it and expressed the expected surprise, Martha and Tom ran off giggling. Louis loved to perform and was a willing mouthpiece.

The Moores wanted to go away for a week's vacation and leave the children with Mrs. Moore's parents. They discussed the relative merits of displacing the grandparents versus moving the children to their house. Because of Louis they decided to ask the grandparents to come to their house.

This is wise if all things are equal for the grandparents. It is surely easier to take care of children—especially small ones—in their own house and with their own routine. It is always easier for the children to leave them in a familiar setting. At Louis' age, being left by his parents is hard enough—the increase in dependency that has been described, and that we have seen in all three children just as they are ready for walking, makes it especially hard to shift to other parental figures at this time. Older children can be a cushion for a baby when his parents leave. In his own home, and with familiar grandparents, he can do well. But this is not an optimal time in a child's life for a big move, a separation, a hospitalization, or such. When it must be, the child's increased needs should be taken into account. Afterward a reaction should be expected. Parents return after a vacation

*to clinging, often cranky children who need to "pay them back."
When they are able to take the child's retribution, it is healthier for
the child.*

Louis was almost too good for his grandparents, never giving them
any trouble. He stopped walking and his spurt in progress slowed
while his parents were away. He was sober when they returned. Not
until they had been back for a week did he resume his gay activity,
then with a wary eye for his mother's whereabouts.

*Regression to an earlier stage of behavior is a common economy of
the child. He seems to "pull in his horns" in order to conserve energy
needed to make the emotional adjustment. Shaken, he may have the
reaction after the crisis is past and the old secure balance is reached
again. One of our children, who had been cooperative with the nurse
while her mother was in the hospital with a new baby, walked by to
kick the nurse after her mother returned. She was safe then and could
afford to express herself.*

Like Daniel, Louis was becoming self-conscious about "good" and
"bad." When he was about to get into trouble, he looked at his
mother as if to say, "Don't follow me when I go into the next room."
Amused, she accepted his cue and watched him from around the
corner. He crawled over to Tom's toy chest, which was off bounds
for him. Louis looked back to check before he opened the lid, pushed
it up, grabbed a toy that was one of Tom's favorites, and let it slam.
He hid the toy under his arm as well as he could and crawled away
to another corner to play with it. When his mother came into the
room, he started and grinned sheepishly. When she laughed, he
looked surprised.

*Is this the early beginning of the mechanism of guilt? We have seen
Laura acting sheepish about being caught crawling by her father at
a much earlier age (seven months). Daniel shows awareness of levels
of meaning in his behavior (tantrums, testing his parents).*

Had it been Tom who caught him, he might have been more directly
provocative. The sure punishment from Tom would have expiated
him. Since it was his mother, he had to cope with his own feelings

a bit more. His mother reminded him of the mischief he perpe-
trated, and her acceptance of it left him conscience-stricken. Although his act was hardly worth all the aforementioned guilt, one
can see in it the foundation of more testing and provoking in the
future.

QUIET BABY

Cautiously, Laura tried to balance with her legs spread wide apart,
taking her hands off the couch for short experimental trials. She
lifted her arms and fell forward against the couch, making a game
of it. Gradually she gained courage and balance, and by her first
birthday, she stood alone, arms poised several inches above the
couch, ready to grab it.

She was willing to take steps with her father holding firmly to each
hand, but not with Mrs. King. As soon as she attempted to take
Laura's hands to walk her, Laura's legs became rubber, her arms
limp, and she collapsed on the floor. When she tried to pull Laura
up, out went her legs in front of her. This infuriated Mrs. King, and
she whacked Laura on the rump. Laura looked soberly at her mother,
cold determination showing in her eyes. Mrs. King felt guilty to be
daunted by Laura, but she was. She and Laura had a more complicated relationship than Louis had with Mrs. Moore. Laura sensed

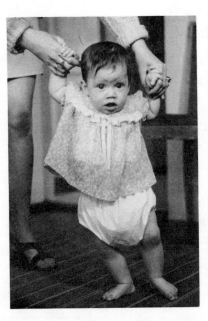 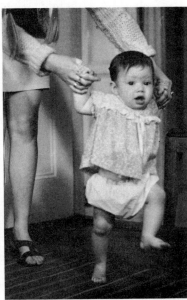 

when Mrs. King was putting on the pressure, and she was completely capable of passive resistance. No wonder her mother flew apart. Perhaps more reactions like that from Mrs. King would eventually force them into a more honest, comfortable relationship. Hiding such tension beneath the surface certainly did not help. She had never really punished Laura, and she was frightened by her angry feelings when she did. She had always believed in the adage, "Never punish a child in anger."

It seems to me that unless a parent punishes while he or she is angry, punishment takes on too cold-blooded a meaning. A good healthy outburst of anger followed by remorse and picking the child up to apologize but say that the anger was justified is so much more credible and understandable for the child. A parent's slow, burning anger, covered with a cold, patient front, is harder to tolerate. Young parents tell me that they remember this from their childhood (in the "permissive era") as the most devastating, frightening experience they had with their own parents. Laura's stubborn, passive resistance is reinforced by her mother's inability to meet her on more earthy common ground.

Their relationship was not all tension. Laura continued to imitate her mother. She loved to put on her clothes and preen. She wanted to wear her hats and had one particular favorite, which she flattened on her head whenever she could reach it. She could be stopped from crying by putting that hat on her head. Showing her her image in a mirror made her laugh. When her mother put on lipstick, Laura begged for it. When it was not given to her, she used crayons and pencils on her lips, imitating her mother. One day she found her mother's eyebrow pencil and had drawn on her lips and all over her face with it by the time she was stopped. She watched her mother wash her own face, and, taking a washcloth, she dabbed at her face in imitation.

This is imitation that will flourish in the second year. Toothbrushing, face- and hand-washing, and toilet training can be instituted via the child's interest in imitation in the latter part of the second year. If this is pushed too hard by parents right now, it will quickly disappear—it is still too fragile and too early.

Laura could be a help in the bathtub, putting up her feet to be washed (even washing them herself) and spreading her legs to have her genital area washed (she took great interest in this procedure). She hated having her hair washed and screamed when she was laid back for the rinsing.

Soap in a child's eyes stings, but it is not as frightening as being held back for the rinsing. The soaps that do not sting cannot get around this part of the hair-washing trauma. A portable hairwasher that allows a child to sit up through it all (to match the portable hairdryer) would be ideal. A shower may serve this purpose, but toddlers are frightened by them and by water running down over their faces—with or without soap in it.

She used her doll in her play—putting her in a rocking chair to be rocked, crooning to her, saying "No" to her (see Average Baby, Chapter XI).

This is symbolic thinking, crystallizing what has happened to her. Putting it onto a doll means she can conceptualize it as an "experience."

The Kings gave Laura a birthday party at the end of her first year. They asked three other babies her age to come. Mrs. King was more excited and made more preparations for it than she did for her own parties. When the others arrived, Laura greeted each one with "hi babee"—as if she were living up to the occasion. Her mother had never heard her put these sounds together before. Having exhausted her repertoire, she sat lumpily in the middle of the floor, while the other babies milled around. Each one opened the present she had brought to Laura, as she was too stunned to open them herself. She was content to rattle the paper wrappings, while the other children played with her toys. Her mother tried to push her into activity, but Laura became stonier and more immobilized. At the birthday table, the other children dived into the cake and ice cream, smearing hands, faces, and hair with icing and ice cream. Laura sat, silent and miserable. Mrs. King was too, in her embarrassment for her stolid baby. The other mothers tried to justify Laura's behavior to her, but as they talked, Mrs. King sensed their condescension, and she was relieved when they left. Laura was too, and waved her good-byes gaily. As soon as they were gone, she went into action and was all over the house, crawling, dragging her new toys after her. When her father came home, Mrs. King greeted him with mystifying tears, while Laura pulled each toy out to show him and babbled away as if she were telling him all about the party.

Had Mrs. King ever thoroughly appreciated Laura's need to take in her universe slowly, largely by watching, she would not have been surprised at Laura's reaction, and Laura might have enjoyed her party. Laura's active participation could have been done visually. Three active little girls her own age, in her own house, all at the same time, present about as big a slice of life as Laura has ever been asked to cope with before. Of course she does it in her characteristic way. Does every child have to grow to be an all-American athlete or a water-skier? Surely there is room for sensitivity, and a contribution to be made by a Laura who participates with her eyes and ears instead of the muscles of her body.

Mrs. King was pregnant. As predicted in Chapter XI, when she weaned Laura, she began to be "ready" for the next baby. Although she talked of the pregnancy as if it were unplanned, she knew she had subconsciously wanted it. She had thought of going back to work. Instead she got pregnant. She felt trapped. She hoped sincerely for an active boy.

This pregnancy was not an "accident." Mrs. King's unconscious readiness was a good seeding ground for the implantation of an egg. She was "ready" to get away. Laura had not been easy for her, and she wanted a way out.

Although she felt she was no different toward Laura, the baby may well have sensed a difference. She began to be more clinging to her mother, often trying to draw her mother out of the dreamy state she withdrew into as she rested off and on during the day.

Mothers say that their babies cannot "know" when they are pregnant with the next one. Symptoms such as the dreamy states that pregnant women withdraw into without being conscious of it; the grumpy, nauseated feelings that make them different in the morning and at the end of the day; the change in shape that children take note of in their mothers—all of these are enough to tip off a baby as sensitive as Laura that something is different. I am sure that they do not have an adult's concept of what is different, but they do "know."

Unless some of the tension in Mrs. King's relationship with Laura is worked out before the new baby comes, Laura will have a difficult time adjusting to it. Two babies to adjust to rarely dilute a mother's problems with one. Suppose Mrs. King had gone back to work, or had gone to school to put these feelings of escape to work? She would certainly have had an easier time than she will with a new baby. However, even if she'd left home (and Laura) to achieve something on her own, she'd need to work out her feelings about Laura. She and Laura are having an easier time than they did in the beginning of the year, but Mrs. King still feels Laura is "not right" and that it is due to some fault in her. This will certainly shape their future together.

ACTIVE BABY

Daniel added play to walking. He pulled a pull toy, walking backward so that he could watch it as it followed him. He backed into furniture, turned, and went on.

Backing always seems easier for children than one might think. Crawling starts backward, and walking backward is usually easy for a child who can take steps forward. I have heard that it is easier because he can fix his eyes on one spot as he backs up, not put off by all of the possibilities for distraction he sees as he goes forward.

He carried toys in each hand, held high in the air, balancing them like a tightrope walker. As balance improved, he gradually learned to drop his arms.

This is quite a big step, for it means that he has learned to balance himself within his body—by manipulating musculature of the trunk. Freeing his hands allows him to make big advances—putting other actions in as he walks.

After he had been walking for a month, it was time to evaluate his feet and legs. Although most infants pronate in the beginning (compare Quiet Baby, Chapter XIII), Daniel tended to toe in, and so badly that he stumbled over his own feet at times. In his new shoes, stumbling was worse.

When shoes are too long, a baby will accentuate the way he usually walks—throwing his feet in or out to avoid the extra toe space. Tripping is worse in shoes that are too big. Shoe stores tend to sell shoes that are too large for the child, saying, "Now his feet will have room to grow." But most active infants wear out their shoes before they can grow into them, so it is no saving. A parent is certainly wise to be sure a toddler's shoes fit properly. If a baby toes in like Daniel does so that he trips over his own feet, one simple remedy (until a mother can consult her doctor) is to simply reverse his shoes—that is, put each shoe on the wrong foot. This works well and is no less comfortable for him. But every dear old lady his parents meet on the street will remind them that thay have put their baby's shoes on the wrong feet!

Daniel could undress himself. One morning his mother went in to find him stark naked in bed, his clothes off and tossed overboard. The bed was a shambles, as he had had a bowel movement in his diapers. Since her reaction was rewarding, Daniel continued to pull off as many clothes as he could at each nap and nighttime. Finally,

Mrs. Corcoran suggested buying sleepers that had snappers in the back that he could not reach and also pinning them securely in back. At night, in his sleeping bag, the zipper at the back stopped him. He could untie and slip off his shoes and socks, and he preferred running around barefoot. (Better for his feet—and he toed in less.) He found he was able to strip off his overalls and diapers. Mrs. Corcoran wearied of dressing him again, so she reversed his overalls, the zipper in back.

Ordinarily Daniel was more interested in his own activity than in playing with toys. To play with Mark, however, was always a goal in itself. Mark was driven now to keeping his construction sets and small trucks on tabletops to protect them from the marauding Daniel. He could get to them and save them before Daniel could sweep them all off. The afternoon arrived, however, when Mrs. Corcoran found each little boy, head cupped in hand, leaning on his left elbow, the right hand maneuvering a truck. A delightful picture, rare in its tranquillity and sharing of play. Daniel learned to rest his chin on his hand and the arm on the table by imitating Mark.

This is an extension of earlier "place-holding" with the left hand while the right is active (Average Baby, Chapters IX and XII, and Quiet Baby, Chapter XII).

Because of Mark, Daniel was becoming interested in toys and in playing with things with his hands. Mark's influence opened a whole new field for Daniel that would have been long in coming with a child as busy as he was. Now that locomotion and most large motor activity was getting under control, he was ready for new fields to conquer. Mark offered them.

Daniel came with Mark at night to their father, bringing a book of his own to be read to. He could not allow his father to finish a page of reading before he turned the page. What he liked better than reading was to turn the pages, rapidly, pointing to one object on each page. His father named them, and he tried to imitate. A few words were coming; more were attempted.

Speech is a second-year task. Many children like Daniel are not willing to try words at all in the first year and a half (after all, it is a kind of small motor activity, and it demands patience for repetition

*that a Daniel may not have available—this boy does because he is
motivated to imitate and compete with an older sibling). With some
children, at the end of the second year, words suddenly come forth
without the preceding experimentation in jargon that is necessary for
most children. A Daniel rushes headlong into speech. A mother
should not be discouraged about her baby's lack of speech—as long
as she is sure he can hear and can make imitative sounds. The deaf
children I have seen made characteristically hollow sounds at this age
and, even when spoken to about something they wanted to hear, could
not be coaxed to respond unless they were watching the speaker's face.
Deafness in an infant can be more difficult to diagnose than one
would expect, but a hearing loss is such a deficit that it affects a child's
total development—the two I have seen at a year behaved like "autistic" children, out of contact with their environments in ways other
than auditory, with a faraway look in their eyes and many repetitive,
rocking, self-stimulating habits to fill the deficit made by the lack of
stimulation from the outside world.*

Daniel could climb out of his playpen. His parents bought him one
with mesh sides that he used as a climbing net. He clambered up
a side, then he bent over to fall down head first on the other side.
Occasionally, he was able to straddle the side and drop, feet first, to
the floor. He attempted to climb up the sides of his crib and on one
occasion had dropped successfully to the floor. On another, he
thudded to the floor on his head. His parents were faced with the
choice of: (1) leaving the cribsides down or putting him in a big bed;
(2) tying him in with a harness; (3) tacking a net over the top; or
(4) getting extensions that added more height to the sides.

*Since I dislike the "cage" idea of #3 and the tying of #2 (I once
had a baby get a "safe" harness caught round his neck), I prefer #4.
This may work only temporarily also, and #1 may become the necessary step. If #1 is necessary, it means that his room will have to be
baby-proofed, as there will be no way of keeping him in his bed. If
#4 is used, Daniel will probably give up easily at this age. By two
years, however, the extensions will no longer stop him, and it will be
necessary to expect his room to set the limits on his nighttime wandering rather than his crib. A firm, disciplinary, and unrewarding approach to his antics will help to cut down on their "secondary gains."*

Perhaps now his tiger should be pushed as a comfort in bed. He needs a "lovey" or a rewarding toy as company in bed with him, if he has not got it already.

Testing his parents increased and so did his tantrums. At night, when they were tired, tension built to a breaking point. He would call them to him as many times as they would come, after he had been put to bed. One of them had to become openly firm or angry, or he built up with more and more demands. Tantrums were more severe, and they were no longer easy to ignore (see Chapter XII). When he was tired, Daniel would lie down on the floor, kick his feet, bang his head, and scream inconsolably over a simple decision, such as whether he should go out of a room or not. They were often situations that involved no one but him. When they did involve his parents, their role seemed to be that of triggering off the tantrums with mild reprimands or refusals. Daniel's demonstration was way out of proportion. They wondered what they were doing that was wrong.

This kind of violent "negativism" comes from within the child and is based on the child's inner turmoil. The environment may add the final straw. The turmoil is based on his developing attempt to sort out "Yes" from "No," "out" from "in," "his" from "not his." These are struggles that must be mastered by the child himself. Since this reflects the kind of torture that all of us feel when we cannot decide which way we want to go, tantrums are painful for us to watch and call up our own memories of such ambivalence. Few parents can really help in the midst of one of these, and most of the time any attempt to reach him may add fuel to the fire of a child's misery. Screaming at him, dashing him with cold water, spanking him, etc., are adults' ways of dealing with feelings that the out-of-control quality of tantrums call up in them. An adult feels that control must be regained immediately. It seems far more appropriate for the parent to wait until the child has run out of steam, and then to be available to comfort the tortured little creature with an understanding: "It's terrible to be your age and unable to sort things out yet—but you will, and, meanwhile, I'm sorry it's so hard for you." He must figure out these decisions for himself, and he will. As I have said earlier, this is no time to throw discipline or important limits to the wind, because of the risk of setting off a tantrum. There is no time when he needs firmness and boundaries as much as he does in this negative period.

These will help him find his own limits, and decisiveness eventually cuts down on the very indecision that throws him into these tumultuous situations. This may not be apparent to a parent at first, when every decision tends to push the child into a tantrum, but it pays off eventually. Daniel's temper and the strength of his tantrums are more characteristic of the second year than of the first. When they occur this early, they may dissolve sooner, too.

His father found that Daniel could swim when he supported the boy's chest in the water. His arms rotated naturally at his sides, and his legs kicked alternatingly as his body undulated along, with very little support necessary from his father. Daniel was excited by the water and he loved to swim. He walked right into it and would stagger in over his head if he were not stopped.

Fear of the water and an anticipation of what it means to get one's head under water comes later—the second or third year. A baby this age will toddle right over his head and must be watched. The swimming movements of the body have already been discussed (Chapter II) and are inherited from our amphibious ancestors.

Another period of concern about strangers and strange situations began to show up in Daniel (see Chapter XII). Although he was eminently self-sufficient at home, he clung to his parents, cried easily, and refused to join other children when he was taken to visit. If they were brought to his house, he was fine. He showed them his toys, allowed them to play with them, and showed his interest in them by hugging them unmercifully and pushing them down when they stood. But this was true at home only, and Mrs. Corcoran gave up taking him to the park, where he would only sit on the bench with her.

This is the third period of awareness of strangers, of strange situations —the first is usually present at four and five months, the second at eight (see Average Baby, Chapter X), and the third is around a year. Each comes at a time when a new layer of sensitivity is being added. Daniel's is coincident with all his negativism and the tantrums, as well as his rapidly increasing dexterity in navigating.

Food idiosyncrasies began to show up. Daniel was willing to eat one good meal, one not-so-good, and refused his lunch or supper. He had very definite likes and dislikes, and it was foolish to try to change him. His mother lamented the fact that he would never try new foods. He would never let her feed him anything, and he was willing to eat only three or four types of food.

This is typical feeding behavior at his age. One good meal and four foods that he will eat is par for the course. I have rarely seen a baby who is willing to eat a "well-rounded diet" in the first half of the second year. As we have discussed in Chapter IX, it is not necessary, and parents do well to stick to the basic requirements and forget their image of a three-meal, well-balanced diet. It is surely time for them and Mrs. Corcoran to be out of his feedings entirely. Any participation is likely to be misinterpreted as pressure and used as a stimulus for a negative response to the entire meal. Since most babies can feed themselves finger foods by now (handling a spoon is a sixteen-month-old's achievement usually), a parent does well to set meals up with finger foods and leave choices to the child. Dr. Clara Davis' famous experiment with children this age who were given a free choice proved that they will eat what they require and round out their own diets over a month's period—as long as there is no environmental pressure to confound the child's free choice.

Since he was so difficult with foods, his mother decided not to wean him from the bottle. Mrs. Kay felt this bottle was an important source of pleasure for Daniel, and one in which she could still participate. She also realized that this was a way of providing him with a known quantity of milk to meet his milk requirement of a pint a day. He was still unpredictable about the cup, and she thought it was an asset to have two ways of providing him with milk—the cup and the bottle—as he was not likely to refuse the latter. She added an egg to his bottle when he refused meat, and in this way she covered some of his iron and most of his protein requirements for the day. The strain on her was considerably reduced by continuing with his bottle, and she found that she pushed him less to eat, knowing his needs were covered.

This is excellent reasoning on her part. We have seen that she worries about his eating, so a crutch that eases her mind is also beneficial for him. Without pressure from the parents I would expect a baby like

Daniel to "conform" eventually and not to be a feeding problem by the age of three. He might be as unreliable as most children are through their second and third years. Perhaps a bottle does interfere with a baby's appetite at this time, and he might even "wait" for it, knowing it will come at the end of the meal. If this worries parents, they can (and perhaps should) cut him down to two bottles (which covers the sixteen-ounce requirement). The bottles can be separated from meals and given at a later time so that they are not associated with or part of the meal. But a baby like Daniel is not that easily diverted from the testing, refusing, and other whims that are at the root of his idiosyncrasies about food. This use of food against his mother is parallel to and part of the differentiation of himself from his environment that underlies his negativism and tantrums. Daniel, as we have learned to expect, is early in his timing and strong in his demonstration of all of these symptoms.

Epilogue

The first crucial year has been navigated by all three teams, with exciting and varying success. The joy and excitement felt by all those who participate in a child's successful development have affected me as I wrote. I should like to convey this to parents as they meet vicissitudes with their own child. The spurt in development that follows a slump can far outweigh any temporary regression that accompanies that slump—a regression shared by both parent and child.

Louis is not necessarily an average child. As became obvious in his motor development when he walked alone at twelve months, he is quicker than the established average for our culture. But he reached each step in development in an average way, with the typical quantity of exhilaration from within as he realized he had made it at last. Laura, in turn, has developed a sensitive, introspective approach to her environment that shows her to be above average in intelligence. She is quiet in one parameter only: motor activity. Her sensitivity balances this in a way that is often typical of nonmotor children.

Since I do not believe that any child fits an average, I have been unable to confine my analysis of the dynamics of child development to a strict model observed in laboratory settings and based on structured, inflexible test situations that cut across and through the vital individuality of the child. Parents who participate in such tests tell me that their own anxiety about the infant's testing was matched by the infant's poor response to the tests. (One might expect as much when, as we have seen, an infant is so sensitive to his parents' moods.) One mother expressed a common complaint about such sampling: "When I tried to tell the tester that my baby had been vomiting all night and might not be herself today, he said, 'Don't add any new variables. I don't want to hear about them. There are enough variables in testing infants already.' So from now on, I'll just keep my reservations about her performance to myself."

Louis' environment is rich and rewarding, and his mother is easy in her experienced attitudes toward his "stages" of development. She does not "coach" him toward each step, but allows his readiness to show her the times for the reinforcement of teaching. She sees him as an individual different from her two other children. She is cushioned from overreacting to his digressions by her experience of deviations with the other two. One of the values of having had two children already is that a mother has had an opportunity to achieve some degree of objectivity in her mothering. By now, she has had to sort out some of her reasons for overreacting to a child's behavior. She is able to look at Louis' demands with more detachment and an awareness of his requirements as opposed to her own. The danger of insensitivity to his particular needs that some overwhelmed mothers of large families do demonstrate is not apparent in Mrs. Moore. She takes delight in each new achievement of Louis' and fosters this appreciation of him in Martha and Tom. Even more importantly, she reinforces Louis' delight in his own achievements. Inherent in such constant positive reinforcement is a kind of refueling that speeds up any baby's desire to develop. No baby can maintain an "average" development with such an unaverage environment.

Mr. Moore is not in evidence in my narrative as much as I would have liked, for he is certainly a strong support for his family. I have been guilty of understating the roles of the fathers—a thing that I deplore in the present literature on childrearing, but I have found it difficult to bring in too many players without creating confusion.

Then too, fathers are important behind the scenes as well as in them. I feel that the classical masculine role of firm decisiveness may have been a major lack in the diets of the last generation. I hope I have indicated why I favor a return to an environment that contains this. Louis' environment does, and he is already demonstrating the rudiments of developing masculinity (e.g., his quick recovery after a fall, his play with father at the end of the day). Soon the force behind imitating his mother will be turned on his father.

Laura's environment has a more complex influence on her development. As a newborn, she demonstrated a degree of sensitivity to stimuli around her that was costly in time and effort for her motor development and was of secondary interest to her mother. Since she is especially attuned to the attitudes of those around her, she senses the ambivalent feelings she creates. Mrs. King is perhaps too much like Laura. She would have had an easier time with a Louis than with a sensitive, quiet, contemplative girl who reawakens her own problems with herself. She compensates for her early anxiety and depression in several ways. She breast-feeds Laura successfully and allows herself to grow very close to her; she develops a sensitivity to Laura's needs (as exemplified by her response to Laura's feeding herself) and is flexible enough to recognize some of her own weaknesses so that she can free Laura to a certain extent. Mrs. King needs to understand her own overreaction to Laura's quiet watchfulness and sensitivity. Perhaps she would have benefited herself, and indirectly would have gained perspective to help Laura, if she had gotten out of the house sooner and had fulfilled some of her own yearnings. She is a sensitive, thoughtful person and will be a wonderful model for Laura in the end. But she needs to free their relationship of some of its ambivalence. Certainly before the new baby comes it would be well for her to understand Laura's characteristics better and to see the real strengths in this child. She undoubtedly wishes for a more active baby who might be freer from her and her overconcern with her firstborn. But she plays in subtly with Laura's contemplative assets, both fostering them and drawing them out into active systems for communication. (A Laura might become withdrawn, even autistic, in a more disturbed environment.)

Mr. King plays a major role—for his wife and for Laura. He supports and accepts his wife in her postpartum "blues." He, more easily than she, understands Laura's quiet complexities as assets. He is a warm, not-too-overwhelming father to whom she can relate with her very feminine assets. He values her for what she is and helps to balance her relationship with her mother.

In addition to her sensitivity, Laura soon developed excellent defenses, paving the way for growth in future years. Her stubborn determination to go her own way at her own speed will give her ample opportunity to listen, to receive, to digest the cues from her world before she must put them into action. Perhaps she will find artistic outlets for this sensitivity in the future.

Daniel is, in many ways, the most rewarding child to write about and to observe as he develops. But this type of newborn, who shows a driving dissatisfaction with himself while he still cannot master the steps he seems to be able to foresee, who seems constantly hungry for stimuli, who achieves a better balance inside himself with each new motor milestone, is not an easy infant to assimilate into a home. A mother feels impotent, unable to fulfill her own fantasy of what the mothering role should be. She feels immediately that such a baby is stronger than she. Faced with his driving strength, the mother of a Daniel must also realize that he could easily be pushed into disintegration; with too much stimulation he could be left without the ability to reach an equilibrium. This kind of infant needs constantly to search for inner balance.

Mrs. Kay responds to this baby as to a challenge. When she was shaken in the delivery room by his choking episode, she might have allowed herself to think of him as a damaged baby. (How much less reality Laura's mother had to go on.) Instead, she sees his disequilibrium as needing a forceful kind of mothering—and sets to work to give it to him and to enjoy it. She becomes an ally in his driving conquest of the world. He probably satisfies many of her own wishes for a more aggressive kind of life. I would like to see mothers postpone their return to work for five months, as she did. Each month of mothering (without too much discontent) is money in the bank for both mother and child in the first months of the baby's infancy. Daniel does well with Mrs. Corcoran's solid mothering, but it is a real strength for both Mrs. Kay and Daniel that they had the first months together. A mother and her baby each pass through many stages of development in the first five months in which they are learning about each other. If these must be shared with another care-giver, one wonders whether it isn't more difficult to feel the same responsibility and closeness.

I would certainly like to see working mothers freed to stay home for at least four months. The first three months with any new infant are bound to be a major adjustment. If the colicky period can be lived through, and the parents can enjoy at least a month of delightful reciprocity—smiling, cooing, increasing delight in the world—the cement of an intense parent-infant relationship is likely to be laid down. From then on, a mother is likely to feel it is "her" baby who is learning new steps.

I would like to see fathers freed as well to be at home and share the responsibility of the early months. But it will be necessary to institutionalize this at a national level. Sweden, Russia, and now Japan have done this already. Otherwise, young parents who take leaves of absence are penalized in the career market. If we believe in families as a nation, we should back them up with just such sanctions. Mr. Kay was certainly a major help to his wife and a strong figure for his son, but had he been home more, he could have been an even more vital force. The new trend in young families is toward more and more sharing of roles. Families are bound to profit from this kind of shared involvement around a new baby. Mr. Kay would probably have delighted in more responsiblity. He is a strong, but gentle male figure (not unlike Mark). The male-female identities are to a certain degree shared in this family.

Daniel is a baby who is strongly motivated to learn. Since large motor activity seems a more quickly achieved goal for such a child, the progress in this area is inevitably precocious and exciting. Small motor achievements, such as using his hands, are strengthened by the presence of Mark—because of Daniel's desire to play with and to imitate him. Mr. and Mrs. Kay (and Mrs. Corcoran, no less) help Daniel achieve a balance of his many drives, and free some of them for more moderate kinds of exploration, with time to be aware, to assimilate, and to enjoy the motor steps he makes so easily.

In each of these infants, I have attempted to demonstrate the strong, inborn differences that predetermine their particular styles of development. In each case, certain reactions from the environment are more "appropriate" than others—that is, each infant can respond more easily to parenting that fits into his capacity to receive and respond. Each of the mothers I have portrayed is motivated by a desire to "understand" her infant and thus is able to find his particular style and fit herself into it. In this way, an infant influences his environment as much as it influences him. These babies show a resistance to being pushed into habits that are not sympathetic to their style, a resistance backed up by all the strength inherent in any well-organized personality, infant or adult.

Since our culture's emphasis on the development of each individual's potential is now pressing us into more and earlier stimulation of this potential, I should like to stress again the balance between personality and cognitive development that may be crucial to the ultimate formation of healthy adults. When a child is "ready" to learn a new step, he needs little help to achieve it. When he must learn it via mechanisms that are not yet ready, he will spend energies that may be expensively drained from more important areas of his total development. Perhaps we have an example of this in many of our adolescents, who have been forced intellectually but drained emotionally, and who cannot cope with the increased demands of our complicated society.

I should like to think that this book will give young, inexperienced parents a feeling for the infant and his world that will help them to experience it with him, to enjoy it with him, to structure it for him in healthy, nonobstructive ways. At the same time, I should like to help them feel less hesitant, more sure of themselves as mothers and fathers than was our generation. Parents who give of themselves, who respect the individuality of their particular child, who are able to say "No" as well as "Yes" when the child needs it, are also able to let go, when the right time comes, confident that this child will find his or her own unique and characteristic way in the world.

Bibliography

AINSWORTH, M. *Infancy in Uganda.* Baltimore: Johns Hopkins Press, 1967.

BOWLBY, J. *Attachment,* Attachment and Loss Series, Vol. I. New York: Basic Books, 1969.

BOWLBY, J. *Separation: Anger and Anxiety,* Attachment and Loss Series, Vol II. New York: Basic Books, 1973.

BOWLBY, J. *Loss: Sadness and Depression,* Attachment and Loss Series, Vol. III. New York: Basic Books, 1980

BRAZELTON, T. B. *On Becoming a Family.* New York: Delacorte Press-/Lawrence, 1981.

BRODY, S. *Patterns of Mothering.* New York: International Universities Press, 1956.

BRUNER, J., OLIVER, R. R., and GREENFIELD, P. *Studies in Cognitive Growth.* New York: Wiley, 1956.

CALDWELL, B. "The Effects of Infant Care," *Review of Child Development Research, I* (New York: Russell Sage Foundation, 1964).

CARMICHAEL, L. (ed.) *Manual of Child Psychology.* New York: Wiley, 1946.

CHILDREN'S HOSPITAL MEDICAL CENTER, DEPARTMENT OF HEALTH EDUCATION. *How To Prevent Childhood Poisoning.* New York: Dell Publishing, 1967.

DEUTSCH, H. *Psychology of Women.* Vols. I and II. New York: Grune & Stratton, 1945.

DEVORE, I. *Primate Behavior.* New York: Holt, Rinehart and Winston, 1965.

EMDE, R. N., GAENSBAUER, J. J., and HARMON, R. N. *Emotional Expression in Infancy: A Biobehavioral Study.* New York: International Universities Press, 1976.

ERIKSON, E. *Childhood and Society.* New York: Norton, 1963.

FLANAGAN, G. L. *The First Nine Months of Life.* New York: Simon & Schuster, 1962.

FLAVELL, J. H. *The Developmental Psychology of Jean Piaget.* Princeton: Van Nostrand, 1963.

FRAIBERG, S. *The Magic Years.* New York: Scribners, 1959.

FRANK, L. K. *On the Importance of Infancy.* New York: Random House, 1966.

FREUD, A. *Normality and Pathology in Childhood.* New York: International Universities Press, 1965.

GESELL, A. *The Embryology of Behavior.* New York: Harper and Row, 1943.

GESELL, A. *Infant and Child in the Culture of Today.* New York: Harper and Row, 1943.

HOOKER, D. *Prenatal Origin of Behavior.* Lawrence: University of Kansas Press, 1952.

HUNT, J. McV. *Intelligence and Experience.* New York: The Ronald Press, 1961.

ILLINGWORTH, R. S. *The Development of the Infant and Young Child, Normal and Abnormal.* London: E. & S. Livingstone, 1960.

KLAUS, M. H., and KENNELL, J. H. *Maternal-Infant Bonding.* St. Louis: The C. V. Mosby Co., 1976.

LEBOYER, F. *Birth Without Violence.* New York: Alfred Knopf, 1975.

LORENZ, K. *Instinctive Behavior.* Part II. Edited by C. Schiller. New York: International Universities Press, 1957.

McGRAW, M. B. *Neuromuscular Maturation of the Human Infant.* New York: Columbia University Press, 1943.

MEAD, M., and MACGREGOR, F. C. *Growth and Culture.* New York: Putnam, 1951.

MEAD, M., and WOLFENSTEIN, M. *Childhood in Contemporary Cultures.* Chicago: University of Chicago Press, 1955.

NEWTON, N. *Family Book of Child Care.* New York: Harper and Row, 1957.

PEIPER, A. *Cerebral Function in Infancy and Childhood.* New York: Consultants Bureau, 1963.

PIAGET, J. *The Construction of Reality in the Child.* New York: Basic Books, 1954.

PIAGET, J. *The Origins of Intelligence in Children.* New York: International Universities Press, 1952.

PIAGET, J. *Play, Dreams and Imitation in Childhood.* New York: Norton, 1962.

PROVENCE, S., and LIPTON, R. C. *Infants in Institutions.* New York: International Universities Press, 1962.

SPITZ, R. A. *The First Year of Life.* New York: International Universities Press, 1965.

SPOCK, B. *Common Sense Book of Baby and Child Care.* New York: Duell, Sloan and Pearce, 1945.

STONE, L. S., and CHURCH, J. *Childhood and Adolescence.* New York: Random House, 1957.

THOMAS, A., CHESS, S., BIRCH, H., HERTZIG, M. E., and KORN, S. *Behavioral Individuality in Early Childhood.* New York: New York University Press, 1963.

WHITING, B. B. (ed.) *Six Cultures: Studies of Child Rearing.* New York: Wiley, 1963.

WOLFF, P. *The Causes, Controls and Organization of Behavior in the Neonate.* New York: International Universities Press, 1965.

Index

A

Accidents
  burns, 156, 206–207
  choking, 7–8, 89
  closing self in, 209
  concussion, 101
  electric, 181
  falls, 100–101, 193–94
  head injuries, 100–101
  poisons, 198
  prevention, 157
  See also Safety measures
  stairs, 225–26
  swallowed objects, 163
Activity
  at birth, 3
  of fetus, 23
Air bubble, *see* Gas
Airing, 93
Airplaning, 135
Airway, clearing, 7–8
Allergies, 109, 125–26, 144
Amphibian reflex, 41, 128, 279
Anesthetic effect on baby after delivery,
    2–3, 4, 14, 16–17, 25
Aspirin
  for high fever, 257–59
  poisoning, 198
  use during teething, 126–27
Associations in learning, *see* Learning
Autistic child, 130, 277, 285
"Average" child, what is it, 283–84

B

Babinski reflex, 37
Balance, development of, 169–70, 275
Banging, 193
Bath, 62–66, 76, 101, 120, 131, 137
  fear of, 216, 272
  newborn, 10, 15

problems, 70, 101, 137, 266, 272
  time for, 101, 131
Bedtime, *see* Sleep
Bedwetting, *see* Toilet training
Birthday party, 272–73
Birthmarks, 53–54, 133
Birthweight, 2, 14, 24
Bladder training, 247–48
Bleeding in infants, 15
  See also Blood
Blindness, 87
Blisters on lips, 64
Blood in bowel movements, 68, 146
Blues, postpartum, 18, 63, 69
Bonding at delivery, 3
Books, 208
Bottle feeding, *see* Feeding, bottle
Bottles, sterilizing, 49
Bounce chair, 139, 158–59, 162
Bouncing for locomotion, 186
Bowel movements
  blood in, 68, 146
  in bottle feeding, 75
  in breast feeding, 60, 67–68, 94
  color of, 60, 67–68
  diarrhea, 68
  fussing and, 67, 74, 92
  green stools, 67
  in infections, 257
  infrequency in breast feeding, 68
  looseness of, 67–68, 72
  mucus in, 75, 266
  straining in breast feeding, 67
  undigested food in, 266
  See also Constipation
Bowel training, 247
Bowlegs, 8, 104
Brain damage, 5, 8, 19, 87
Breast feeding, *see* Feeding, breast
Breasts, swelling in infancy, 54–55
Breathing, 6, 8, 15, 24
  after delivery, 7–8
  breath-holding, 102

W